D1737135

JUST LIKE US

Just Like Us

THE AMERICAN STRUGGLE TO UNDERSTAND FOREIGNERS

Thomas Borstelmann

Columbia University Press
New York

Columbia University Press
Publishers Since 1893
New York   Chichester, West Sussex
cup.columbia.edu

Library of Congress Cataloging-in-Publication Data
Names: Borstelmann, Thomas, author.
Title: Just like us : the American struggle to understand foreigners / Thomas Borstelmann.
Other titles: American struggle to understand foreigners
Description: New York : Columbia University Press, [2020] | Includes bibliographical
references and index.
Identifiers: LCCN 2019043058 (print) | LCCN 2019043059 (ebook) |
ISBN 9780231193528 (hardback) | ISBN 9780231550352 (ebook)
Subjects: LCSH: National characteristics, American—History. | Cultural awareness—
United States. | Race awareness—United States—History. | United States—Race relations—
History. | Cultural pluralism—United States—History. | Globalization—Social aspects—
United States—History. | Exceptionalism—United States—History. | Americanization. |
Cold War—Social aspects—United States.
Classification: LCC E169.1 .B759 2020 (print) | LCC E169.1 (ebook) |
DDC 305.800973—dc23
LC record available at https://lccn.loc.gov/2019043058
LC ebook record available at https://lccn.loc.gov/2019043059

Columbia University Press books are printed on permanent and durable acid-free paper.
Printed in the United States of America

Cover design: Milenda Nan Ok Lee

Cover image: Courtesy of the Statue of Liberty–Ellis Island Foundation, Inc.,
and the American Flag of Faces, Ellis Island National Museum of Immigration

For Dan and John and their generation

Contents

Preface

I n August 1966, I sailed out of New York Harbor on the Dutch ocean
liner SS *Maasdam* with my family, bound for Ireland. I was eight years
old, the youngest of four children. My father, a professor of psychology at Duke University, had won a Fulbright fellowship to teach at Trin-
ity College in Dublin. Five days later, we docked in the middle of the night
in Galway Bay. I had never been out of the United States, and I had never
been awake and outdoors at 2:30 a.m. As we drove our beige 1964 Plymouth station wagon up the ramp from the ship's hold, I was amazed to see
hundreds of adult faces crammed up against the chain-link fence in the
dead of night. These Irish yearned to see their loved ones, returning for a
visit from America, the greatest destination of the Emerald Isle's emigrants
for more than a century.

Living in Dublin for a year in the mid-1960s taught me for the first time
about foreigners. I had met some international kids around Duke, but
immersion abroad was different. I was now the foreigner. People in Ireland were a lot like us, it turned out, and my family made lasting friends
there. But the Irish did things somewhat differently: how they spoke English, playing soccer and rugby rather than football and basketball, driving
exotic double-decker city buses, eating distinctive sausages and smoked fish
for breakfast, snacking on mysterious kinds of licorice and toffee candies—
everyday matters central to a child's life. I was busy enough not to think
too much about American things I might have missed. At the end of the

year, after a summer camping tour of Europe, we boarded the Italian ocean liner SS *Michelangelo* in Naples for the trip home. In the ship's dining room the next morning, the waiter, to my amazement, served us Welch's grape juice from its then-iconic glass quart bottle with a narrow neck and a small white metal cap. I hadn't seen Welch's in a year, and my nine-year-old heart leapt. Home!

Fifty years later, products flow much more freely across the Atlantic and across most bodies of water and national boundaries. In the current era of global integration, the world feels much smaller. As citizens of the most powerful and influential country over the past seventy-five years, Americans come into greater contact with other peoples than ever before, both around the globe and within the United States. The resulting interactions require them more than ever to try to understand foreigners, a challenge since the nation's earliest days. Americans have long believed themselves a special people, and they considered anew whether other peoples were fundamentally similar to or different from them. How Americans thought about and think about non-Americans is the question this book seeks to answer.

The "Americans" at the center of this story occupy the mainstream of U.S. culture and society. This tale aims to capture the evolving "common sense" of the large majority of residents of the United States, as evident in laws, declarations by elected officials, common public behavior, popular publications, widely viewed films and television shows, and other similar sources. This is not a book about dissidents, though several of them will make appearances, nor is it a definitive, weighty tome that seeks to include the voices of all members of U.S. society. Capturing the mainstream of American political culture as it developed over time is the purpose, which cuts somewhat against the grain of the past two generations of American historiography, with their focus (for good reason) on peoples long omitted from earlier histories, such as women, racial and ethnic and religious minorities, gays and lesbians, and immigrants. I am a product of and contributor to that historiographical development, and my previous books as well as the sensibility and tone of this one reflect that development and those interests. But the purpose of this current book is different; it explores the story of a contested but widening acceptance of foreigners within mainstream American life.

A comprehensive history of this topic would be a gargantuan task. What is offered here instead is an extended exploratory essay, one that aims to discern key themes and trends. In one sense, it brings together the long-separated histories of immigration to the United States (traditionally a domestic story) and U.S. foreign relations (primarily an overseas tale), meshing these with the histories of American political culture and popular culture. The book shares the cosmopolitan sensibility of recent scholarship in transnational history, with an emphasis on the movements of people and ideas across borders, even as it focuses primarily on Americans and their views of others. A related but different series of books might concentrate on other peoples in other countries and how they viewed outsiders; yet another series might highlight how the rest of the world viewed the United States and its people. Such worthy projects, however, lie beyond this book's reach. The attention here to the thinking of Americans implies no greater valuing of residents of the United States than those of other nations. Rather, this tracking of mainstream attitudes within the most important and influential nation across the past century merely offers one path toward a greater understanding of the history of the United States and its relationship to the rest of the modern world.[1] The United States deserves attention for its power and influence, regardless of judgments about its virtue. Readers will make their own assessments of the latter.

The United States may not be exceptional, but it is distinctive. An exception requires a rule to stand outside of. But there is no single rule or pattern of development that all other nations have followed and that the United States has not. All nations have similarities and differences compared to others. The United States can be usefully compared to other affluent industrialized countries, such as Germany and Japan; to other white settler states, such as Canada and Australia; to other revolutionary republics, such as France and Haiti; to other modern great powers, such as China and Russia; or to other hegemonic empires, such as those of ancient Rome and Great Britain. Every land is unique in its history. It makes little sense to view the United States as somehow more uniquely unique than other countries. The United States is, however, distinctive in a deeply significant way in the modern world: it is both the most powerful state and the most demographically diverse of all the great powers, a result of its reception of the greatest number of immigrants. So how Americans have thought about foreigners has mattered a great deal for the shaping of the world today.

Anyone examining American views of outsiders and newcomers at the end of the 2010s risked experiencing something close to whiplash. On the one hand, in an era of gay marriage, a two-term black president, surging female empowerment, and a populace headed toward a nonwhite majority, the United States seemed to operate as a mecca of tolerance and egalitarian spirit. On the other hand, the subsequent election to the presidency of a crude and mendacious stoker of xenophobic and racist resentments suggested a very different set of exclusionary values. Such ambivalence no doubt reflected a perpetual uncertainty about those perceived as outsiders in all human communities across time. But U.S. history had also been elementally shaped by a particular project of human equality and cultural openness. "From the beginning, America has been of two minds about the Other," the noted author George Saunders writes. "One mind says, Be suspicious of it, dominate it, deport it, exploit it, enslave it, kill it as needed. The other mind denies that there can be any such thing as the Other, in the face of the claim that all are created equal."[2] This contest clearly continues in American politics and society.

Just Like Us tracks this ambivalence and its outcomes from the earliest European colonial settlements in North America to contemporary U.S. cultural and political life, with a primary focus on the post–World War II era. It will pay particular attention to concerns about race and religion, the so-called American way of life, the exclusion and incorporation of immigrants, competition with communism, Americans abroad, and U.S. expansion into Asia. I will also explore the subversive power of individualistic American culture in the world. The six main chapters examine, in order, the historical problem of foreignness; the development of a "freedom culture" that Americans considered uniquely their own; three primary perceived threats (from immigrants, communists, and peoples encountered abroad); and the arc of the United States as a subversive force in the world, rather than as a target of subversion by others.

The argument here will be neither Whiggish nor Pollyannaish, but simply this: that across the twentieth century, and particularly over the Cold War years, the United States engaged increasingly with foreign peoples in and from every part of the globe, and those interactions significantly spurred the expanding definition, in mainstream American society, of who could be considered fully American, in legal terms and also in terms of politics and popular culture—that is, in the common sense of mainstream American life. The radically more inclusive public society in which Americans lived by the early twenty-first century, compared to the early twentieth century, stemmed in large part from the imperatives of the nation's foreign relations. And the absorptive, acquisitive individualism of American culture had at least as subversive an effect on other nations and other peoples as any outsiders or newcomers had on the United States.[3]

Both individuals and societies curate some kind of narrative, either explicit or implicit, that helps them make sense of the world and their place in it. Best-selling historical works tend to be highly narrative in a biographical sense: they trace the lives of unusual individuals or important battles. The narrative offered here is neither individual nor military but instead tracks the remarkable development of one of humanity's most inclusive, egalitarian public cultures in a land of great diversity. There have been many periods of "one step forward, two steps back" along the way, and there has always been struggle. The future, too, has yet to be written. This book was conceived and mostly researched at the tail end of the Barack Obama presidency, an era that seemed quite different from what followed the 2016 election. But the long-term historical pattern to date did not disappear after that election. It remains traceable, and it may offer more encouragement than is sometimes appreciated in the backwash of any particular recrudescence of nativism.

For their assistance in helping me craft my personal narrative, I thank my family of origin, particularly my brother John ("JB") Borstelmann; my sons, Dan Borstelmann and John Borstelmann; inspiring teachers along the way at Exeter, Stanford, and Duke, above all Peter Wood; and my long-term supporters Daniel Nelson, Elizabeth Nelson, Tim Beaton, Barb Beaton, Suzanne Mettler, and Wayne Grove. I am grateful for the solidarity of colleagues in the History Department at the University of Nebraska–Lincoln, particularly department chairs Will Thomas and James Le Sueur. Lisa Adams of the Garamond Agency remains a fount of wisdom, support, and professionalism. Thanks to Caelyn Cobb, Robert Fellman, and Columbia University Press for producing the book. The Society for Historians of American Foreign Relations (SHAFR) kindly created the opportunity to test an early version of some of the arguments here in a 2015 presidential address. Andy Graybill, Brooke Blower, and David Cahan graciously provided suggestions on that brief draft, and Elaine Tyler May and Daniel Immerwahr generously offered encouraging but penetrating critiques of the entire manuscript. Their wisdom remains visible in the strongest parts of what follows here, while responsibility for the rest is mine alone. My wife, Lynn Borstelmann, has left the largest mark on the book and the author, to my continuing great good fortune.

CHAPTER I

The Challenge of Contact with Foreigners

"Foreign": it's a very familiar term. So, too, is "foreigner," a person who lives elsewhere or has come from elsewhere. But what do they mean? The English word "foreign" derives from the Latin for "door" and "outside": what is outside the door and, thus, not part of us and our household, whoever we are, here on the inside of the door. It is close to the Italian adverb "*fuori*"—outside—and opposite of the Spanish adjective "*familiar*," meaning "family." Foreigners do not belong to the family.

Or do they—or could they? A door, after all, is not a wall. It is designed to swing open. People pass through from inside to outside and from outside to inside. The foreign can and does become familiar. It can lose its foreignness. Much of human history is the story of people moving, bringing them into contact with unfamiliar others, and perhaps nowhere in the modern world has there been more movement and more contact than in the lands of the United States and in this most powerful state's ventures abroad. So how Americans have understood the nature of other peoples underpins a great deal of U.S. and recent world history. Are they essentially similar to Americans, or are they, in their cultural or even biological essence, different? On the answer to this question has hung great significance for how the United States has interacted with the rest of the world.

Perhaps the most compelling answer to the question of how Americans imagine foreigners may have been crystallized in a scene from *Full Metal*

Jacket, Stanley Kubrick's 1987 film about a group of American GIs serving in Vietnam. A U.S. colonel is instructing a skeptical young army journalist in his unit about the purpose of the American war in Southeast Asia. "We are here to help the Vietnamese, because inside every" foreigner "there is an American trying to get out." Sometimes close to the surface, sometimes buried under layers of miseducation by other cultures, a core of every human being was assumed to be fundamentally American—that is, yearning for American-style individual freedom and opportunity. Human nature, in this view, was best and most fully expressed in American culture and society. This universalist assumption arises not merely in fiction or art. John Prior, a U.S. Army sergeant serving in Iraq two decades later, explained the same view to the journalist George Packer: "In my heart," declared Sergeant Prior, "I believe everybody's American." This way of thinking was, simultaneously, both blindly ethnocentric and warmly inclusive of all peoples. Such a combination helped produce both the most devastating and the most impressive developments of the American story, from genocide and war crimes, on the one hand, to the most multicultural, diverse, affluent great power in world history, on the other.[1]

From early English settlers establishing commonwealths in Virginia and Massachusetts to the authors of the Constitution gathered in the Philadelphia convention hall in 1787, from Woodrow Wilson in the White House deciding to go to war in Europe in 1917 to the American soldiers pouring across the Kuwaiti border into southern Iraq in 2003, there has been an abiding assumption that American culture—American principles and practices—are not only the best ever created by human beings but also closely aligned with the very essence of human nature. The ultimate logic of American exceptionalism, on most prominent display during the Cold War, held that U.S. history and American institutions had facilitated the full liberation of the human spirit and the fulfillment of the highest human aspirations. This was, it seemed to many of its people, the nation that had finally embodied liberty and happiness for its residents. American democratic culture was thus seen as truly "natural," in common American thinking, giving citizens self-rule, individual freedom, and a market economy that sold them what they wanted and needed.[2]

Such assumptions about the essential character of American society and the inner yearnings of non-Americans reached unprecedented influence in the mid-twentieth century. But they were not entirely new in the Cold War. The revolutionaries of 1776 had expected other peoples in the hemisphere to emulate their actions and, in fact, had watched as most of Latin America in the following generation also threw off the European imperial yoke. The subsequent story of U.S. expansion awkwardly balanced conquest with attempts at conversion, from Powhatan and Pequot Indians along the Atlantic shore in the 1600s to Afghanis and Iraqis in the greater Middle East in the early 2000s. A letter sent by the Continental Congress to the inhabitants of Québec in 1774 perfectly squared the circle of an expanding empire imagining itself as a center of freedom. The letter invited the Québécois to join the anti-British union of colonial troops marching north with these words: "You [will] have been conquered into liberty, if you act as you ought." While Québec and the rest of Canada managed to avoid being "conquered into liberty," many others did not. They were more likely to experience conquest as taking away their freedom. Through the nineteenth century, widening U.S. dominion ranged from Liberia in the east to Hawai'i and the Philippines in the west and from Alaska in the north to Nicaragua in the south.[3]

But certain constraints had to be shed to enable the full flowering of American universalism. One such constraint was hierarchical racial thinking. Persistent racial and ethnic prejudice cramped the ability of white Americans to fully imagine non-Europeans—and even many Europeans from south and east of the Alps—as being like themselves. Another constraint was a certain lingering cultural insecurity among American elites. While intensely proud of U.S. economic success, they still looked to Europe for the highest standards in such arenas as art, literature, drama, fashion, and cuisine. And a third constraint was the tradition of hemispheric, if not isolationist, resistance to global engagement and militarism. The political and military position of the United States in international affairs before World War II remained modest in comparison to the nation's economic might.[4]

These constraints began to fade rapidly in the 1940s as the distinctive circumstances of the mid-twentieth century ratcheted up the stakes for how Americans understood non-Americans. The outcome of World War II left millions of U.S. military personnel on duty on every continent and on every ocean, the startling resurgence of the U.S. economy expanded American trade interests everywhere, the retreat of European colonial rule reshaped global politics, and the Cold War drew the American presence outward around the world. "There is no longer any real distinction between 'domestic' and 'foreign' affairs," the State Department announced in the opening sentence of its 1950 summary of "Our Foreign Policy." Given their newly extensive and intensive contact with foreigners everywhere, Americans had to figure them out.[5]

What a majority of Americans did in the decades following World War II was to shed some older hierarchical notions of humankind, grounded particularly in ideas about race, ethnicity, and religion, and to confirm instead a growing sense of foreigners as potential Americans. Despite some ongoing dissent and despite persistent racial discrimination, the broad middle ground of "common sense" in mainstream American society came to agree eventually with the colonel in *Full Metal Jacket* and with Sergeant John Prior in Iraq that other peoples, despite often growing up and living under repressive political and religious regimes, still, in their hearts, if they were truly allowed to, would reveal themselves by preference to be American. They wanted, in other words, U.S.-style freedom, opportunity, and affluence. This view of foreigners was both profoundly ethnocentric and inward-looking, on the one hand, and also universalistic and inclusive, on the other, and it came to be shared across the U.S. political spectrum, from liberal proponents of immigration reform to conservative advocates of preemptive war in Iraq, and by most moderate Americans in between. Very few modern Americans believed in cultural relativism.[6]

If American culture was natural and allowed for the fullest expression of human freedom, and if other peoples aspired to live like Americans or even to *be* Americans, then what Americans most feared was the loss of their natural freedom to unnatural subversion. Captivity was the threat, and supposed communist brainwashing—mental captivity—emerged as the quintessential challenge of the Cold War era. While the shrinking sphere of what was foreign to Americans is the primary theme of the story pursued here, Americans' concomitant anxieties about possibly losing their freedoms to subversion and captivity provide a second, closely related theme. And a third theme is the potent magnetism of relatively democratic American capitalist culture, whose individualistic pursuit of material comforts and personal freedoms may have operated as the greatest subversive force in late-twentieth-century international history.

The Meaning of Foreignness

A great deal of human history has been the story of people of one culture coming into contact with people of different cultures. How have they resolved the inherent tensions and conflicts in such engagements? Often war and slavery predominated. But at other times alliances, intermarriage, and shared meals—the beginnings of "ethnic food"—worked better. From early nomadic tribes to contemporary global migrants, the relationships resulting from human cultural encounters have been wildly complicated and diverse. They have provided the basis for a large fraction of the best and wittiest novels, plays, movies, and television shows, from romances to tragedies.

The American version of intercultural contact has been particularly intensive and continuous. The largest-scale human-contact story unfolded in the Americas after the voyages of Christopher Columbus, where the depopulation of indigenous peoples by disease and warfare gave way to a swift repopulation by new peoples from the other hemisphere. "Colonial conditions produced an unprecedented mixing of African, European, and Indian cultures," notes Alan Taylor, a leading colonial historian. "The world had never known such a rapid and intense intermingling of peoples—and of microbes, plants, and animals from different continents." This process continued with large numbers of migrants from the nineteenth century from Asia and from the late twentieth century from the Middle East.[7]

The unprecedented cultural mixing of the so-called New World reached its apex in the United States. The demographic churn of the colonial era only accelerated during the nineteenth century, when tens of millions of newcomers from the "Old World" of the Europe-Asia-Africa supercontinent flowed into the new nation. For all the press of migrants into places such as Argentina, Canada, and Australia, no country received close to the numbers pouring into the United States as it expanded westward to the Pacific Ocean. Divinely guided destiny offered a persuasive explanation to many white Americans at the time, but available land, industrial employment, a temperate climate, and relative proximity to Europe's large and multicultural emigrant pool underpinned the preference for U.S. shores. Disease had devastated indigenous populations throughout the Americas since the original Columbian voyages. Relentless settler violence and U.S. military aggression further depleted Native American numbers, creating still more space for newcomers from the Old World.[8]

The still-young nation of unusual human diversity did not just stick to its own recently acquired territory. Rather, the United States in the twentieth century surged outward in influence around the globe, in literally every direction. Through trade, investment, tourism, missionary work, and two world wars plus several other armed conflicts, Americans engaged with peoples in every land. With the world's most powerful economy and military and its third-largest population, the United States pressed its goods, culture, and values on other countries. American citizens encountered new peoples abroad even as they interacted with immigrants and visitors at home. The continued flow of newcomers into the United States and the rush of American influence outward beyond U.S. territory reached a peak together in the decades after 1945. By the end of the twentieth century, observers talked of "globalization" and the distinctly American flavor that it had.[9]

All cultures imagine themselves to be natural and normal. They offer the best response, their members assume, that has evolved over time to match the circumstances they face. Few cultures, however, received the powerful external validations of success that the United States did in the second half of the twentieth century: a booming economy with the largest middle class ever seen, a smorgasbord of affordable consumer goods, a military force and popular culture that dominated much of the world, steady demand from people elsewhere to move to the United States, and widespread admiration for American political ideals. Such success encouraged pride and parochialism among many Americans, who were tempted to equate national status with national virtue and superiority. The historian Thomas Bender notes that U.S. expansion and power encouraged "a passive, consistent failure of empathy" with others, who were expected to act more like Americans. Many citizens felt confirmed in their assumptions of American exceptionalism, a term that obscured more than it clarified. All nations, after all, are exceptional in the sense that each is distinctive. And there is no rule for other nations from which the United States stood out as an exception. What may actually be exceptional about the United States is its citizens' widespread *belief* in American exceptionalism.[10]

Like European explorers who rode the wave of late-nineteenth-century imperial expansion out into the far reaches of the globe and sought to understand the peoples and places they encountered there, Americans in the 1940s launched into an intense engagement with the myriad cultures with which World War II and the Cold War brought them into contact. This reached far beyond the usual neighboring exotics of Canada and Mexico. Like pith-helmeted imperialists finding Machu Picchu, Troy, Great Zimbabwe, and Angkor Wat, American Cold Warriors carried their promises of development and democracy to the newly independent nations of the so-called Third World—India, Egypt, Kenya, and the like—and struggled to understand the cultures they encountered there. Were these peoples like Americans, or were they something completely different? The same question concerned Eastern Europe, newly controlled by communists and deemed "captive nations" by the U.S. Congress, and the Soviet Union, the original "captive nation." American missionaries had long labored to reveal the Chinese to be much like Americans, but by 1949 the people of the Middle Kingdom had instead turned to communism—were they still at heart like Americans, or no? Western Europeans were casting off their overseas empires, surely a positive sign of becoming more like Americans, yet they seemed tempted by democratic socialism, or at least social democracy. Most immediate were the challenges of West Germany and Japan, recently loathed and defeated enemies, now occupied by American GIs and potentially the closest U.S. allies of all.[11]

The unprecedented worldwide challenges facing the United States from the 1940s onward hinged on how the newly powerful Americans understood the peoples they encountered abroad. The United States had replaced Great Britain as the most influential nation and the leading Western model of constitutional government. Educated Americans believed, with one of their leading novelists, F. Scott Fitzgerald, that "we will be the Romans in the next generations." The ancient world's conquerors had been known, like the modern United States, for assimilating newcomers and becoming the great multiethnic state of their time. At the height of their own trajectory in the early Cold War, Americans were already three times as numerous as the peoples of the Roman Empire at its peak, and American influence ranged far beyond Rome's known world of the Mediterranean basin to the entire globe. How and whether Americans imagined their own version of assimilation would help determine much of the history to come.[12]

Figuring out to whom one belongs may be the deepest human concern. From the earliest communities of *Homo sapiens* in east-central Africa, people have striven to define clearly who was inside and who was outside any community. It was often a matter of life or death. Killing or fending off outsiders in order to protect insiders is an ancient story. In the lands of what became the United States, the first inhabitants typically referred to their communities as some version of "the human beings" or "the People." In the Kawuneeche ("Coyote") Valley at the headwaters of the Colorado

River, high up in the snowy Rocky Mountains, for example, the original residents were called "Yutas" by the invading Spanish but knew themselves as the "Nuche," which translates to "the People."[13]

Psychologists make a similar point. "A key social factor that we human beings track is who is 'us' and who is 'them,'" note the psychologists Jonathan Haidt and Lee Jussim. The distinction between "in-groups" and "out-groups" provides the most elemental social and emotional connections and community. Modern high-schoolers know this in their bones, and so have all cultures throughout human history. As social creatures, people feel a powerful need to belong to a community that provides them comfort, purpose, and identity. Hermits are, by definition, peculiar. People are designed to fit in.[14]

What feels natural or familiar to people derives from their earliest experiences as infants and young children. Their tactile sense of the world is not yet mediated by self-awareness and rational analysis. An infant's world with its sights and smells is not yet compared with and weighed against other worlds—it simply is what it is. Children then grow up to discern which of all the external stimuli they encounter—all of which is initially foreign to them—are actually comfortable and safe. They figure out where they fit through the communities they encounter, from their families outward through their neighborhoods, villages, cities, regions, and nations.

In the early twenty-first century Americans talk a lot about identity. Who they imagine themselves to be hinges on several variables. Age distinguishes millennials from baby boomers. Politics separates Republicans and Democrats. Geography carves up urban and rural. Religion sorts unbelievers and believers, in their various stripes. Gender, once a given, now opens questions about identity. The kind of work people do defines much of who they are, particularly in a culture as obsessed with work as this one.[15] Family responsibilities shape those who are parents and siblings. But no identifier in the modern public realm is as powerful as the nation. Americans, like others, derive enormous personal meaning from the country to which they belong. And it is the nation that most clearly defines who is a foreigner.

It was not always this way. National borders and identities seem commonsensical today, along with passports for travelers. But nations are a relatively recent product of modern history, mostly arising in the past two hundred years. Previously, for the vast majority of human history, political and social identities were both smaller and larger. In the much less mobile past before industrialization, most people lived and died within a few dozen miles of where they were born. This gave them a more local identity, in a village or region. At the same time, political life tended to be organized at a much higher level by kingdoms, empires, and religious authorities. An English peasant might be a resident of Kent and a subject of the Crown, just as a Chinese peasant might live outside Guangzhou and under the authority of the emperor.[16]

Nations, in other words, are not natural, though they may seem that way to modern Americans, citizens of a country whose very birth coincided with the rise of nation-states. National borders are also not natural or given but have changed over time. Nations are not permanent in the long run. Cullen Murphy observes that "half the world's national boundaries are less than a century old." Nations are instead, as the distinguished political scientist Benedict Anderson first argued more than a generation ago, "imagined communities." This hardly means they are not real. They are, however, constructed rather than natural. They were imagined as political projects and then brought into being in particular forms with enormous real-world effects. They raised armies and fought wars, the most powerful way to separate their citizens from foreigners. The memory of sacrifices made on behalf of the nation then fertilized future generations of national loyalty. Nations became real in the modern era, and no nation became more powerful than the United States.[17]

That nation might have been much larger and more powerful still. In the summer of 1776, the Continental Congress created three committees, one to draft a Declaration of Independence, another to write up the Articles of Confederation, and a third to create a Model Treaty as a template for the new nation's future foreign relations. In drafting the Model Treaty, John Adams "demanded that Europe's governments recognize the United States as the rightful successor to all of Britain's North American empire," in the words of the historian Eliga Gould, including Nova Scotia, Newfoundland, the rest of Canada, East and West Florida, and Bermuda. This vision did not fully prevail. But it could have—it was a serious twinkle in the eyes of the Founders. There was nothing preordained about the eventual borders of the United States. For the next century European Americans pressed this truth westward, seizing territory from indigenous peoples whom they viewed as nomadic and lacking in legitimate claims to the land. Adams's son John Quincy Adams, another future president, later wrote in his diary that "the United States and North America are identical." One can only imagine the might and impact of a modern single meganation unified from the Rio Grande to the Arctic Ocean.[18]

The definition of what is foreign tends to change. It is a moving target. What may seem an absolute difference between groups at one point in time can disappear with remarkable swiftness. Probably no shift in mainstream American public sentiment about foreignness has been as dramatic as recent thinking about sexual orientation and, increasingly, gender identity. There is no historical precedent for the speed of change in the legal status and public views of homosexuality in the early twenty-first century. Indeed, it was the conservative Republican George W. Bush who first welcomed an openly transgender person to the White House. At a 2003 reunion of his Yale class of 1968, a woman in an evening gown made her way through the president's receiving line and extended her hand. "Hello, George," said Petra Leilani Akwai, "I guess the last time we spoke, I was still living as a man." Bush smiled and responded graciously, "And now you're you."[19]

Not only imagined boundaries of difference but also physical borders and their meanings change over time. A quintessential American example is the Ohio River. In the earliest days of the republic, this mighty waterway divided the original Northwest Territory from the new state of Kentucky, established in 1792. It thus demarcated the slaveholding lands on its southern bank from the free states that developed on its northern shore: Ohio, Indiana, and Illinois. To cross this water was to pass from slavery to freedom—or the opposite. Thousands of American lives were shaped in the most elemental ways by the river, as Toni Morrison illuminated so brilliantly and painfully in her Pulitzer Prize–winning novel *Beloved*. Yet today commuters and others zip daily across the Interstate 64 and 65 bridges in Louisville with nary a thought of the human trauma and life-and-death drama that played out a hundred feet below them for so long. For many locals, the Ohio River seems mostly to separate fans of rival college basketball teams in Indiana and Kentucky.[20]

One other example can illustrate the lack of wisdom in imagining definitions of foreignness and borders as permanent or ultimately meaningful in the American past. In 1917 the United States enacted a new immigration law that banned people coming from within a so-called Asiatic Barred Zone. U.S. law had already previously excluded most Chinese migrants,

Japan had agreed to restrict emigration to American shores, and the Philippines were managed separately as U.S. territory. The new act aimed to keep out all other Asians. The Barred Zone it created began at the Red Sea and stretched eastward, incorporating residents of the Arabian Peninsula, the Levant, today's Turkey, southern and central Asia, and the Asian part of the Russian empire. But were Syrians really "Asians" and Egyptians not? Were Turks on one side of the half-mile-wide Bosporus strait "Asians" and Turks on the other shore not? Most telling of all was the border drawn from eastern Turkey to Russia, to get from the Black Sea to the Caspian Sea. Here the line ran through the middle of the Caucasus region. As a result, northern Caucasians were, well, Caucasian, while southern Caucasians were Asian. Evidently, if Caucasians could be Asians, the meaning of such boundary distinctions between supposed races was opaque to the point of absurdity. The line between familiar and foreign for Americans, never clear, would become only harder to trace over the next century.

People Move

To the consternation of authoritarian rulers and census takers everywhere, many human beings do not stay put in one place. They tend to move around. People literally move all day long in their daily routines—walking, riding, driving, flying—and an awful lot of them change their place of residence. In the second half of the twentieth century, for example, roughly 20 percent of Americans shifted their address each year. Cartographers and historians, like most policy makers and regular folks, may know this at some level but too often act as though people remain in one place. They emphasize stability and the bright lines of map borders. Yet moving from one place to another changes who one is, at least in some ways, and as identity shifts, so too does one's sense of what is familiar and what is foreign.

Like most peoples, Americans have tended to cherish a firm sense of who they are and to imagine other nations having similarly clear, timeless national essences—thus the stereotypes of Germans as orderly, Japanese as self-effacing, Italians as emotional, and British as stoic. Indeed, the very idea of an entity called Germany or Japan or Italy or Britain seemed inherently logical, with the nation-state, if not liberal democracy, assumed as a kind of "end of history." It is as though all of the past has been aiming just to get here to the present, and history's churn will now stop, leaving all just as it is. Americans have paid much less attention to the implications of the continual process of human movement and migration across history. This was the largest story of all, a two-step process. First, the earliest modern humans walked out of east-central Africa and spread around the globe, creating the rich diversity of cultures, phenotypes, and languages (including at least 375 distinct languages in North America alone by 1492), making Africans the greatest imperialists, in a genetic sense. Second, globalization reconnected the world's far-flung peoples ever since Columbus's voyages initiated permanent links between the hemispheres, and industrialization accelerated this integrating process.[21]

In other words, people move. If every person ever to walk the earth had been equipped with a pedometer, the collated results would reveal a tale of extraordinary motion. Human history is the story of continuous movement, with perpetual cultural evolution and political change as a result. Even Britain, the model for Americans of a contained nation-state with the natural borders of an island, had of course derived from multiple waves of invasion and settlement from the European continent and fierce wars with the Highland Scots. In geological terms, the ancient British peninsula was only sundered from the European mainland by two enormous floods roughly 430,000 and 160,000 years ago that created the English Channel—the original Brexit. Today's Channel Tunnel, in this sense, replicates a past connection rather than undoing some permanent British separateness.[22]

Anglophilia pervaded American culture in the decades after World War II. Historians focused on English Puritans in New England. Novelists retold the tale of King Arthur and the Knights of the Round Table, and John Kennedy's admirers compared his presidency to Camelot. Hollywood produced films about King Henry V exhorting his "band of brothers" to battle at Agincourt, and American movie stars such as Katherine Hepburn spoke in quasi-British tones. The highest-achieving young Americans won Rhodes Scholarships to study at Oxford University. Until the 1960s the Anglican-affiliated Episcopal Church was known, only partly in jest, as the Republican Party at prayer. Particularly for educated Americans, England appeared the source and inspiration for the best in American constitutional government and high culture.[23]

Americans seemed almost to imagine a primordial English essence— they sometimes called it national character—that arose from the land. It may even have had a geographical center, near or in London, perhaps in Greenwich as the epicenter of longitude and latitude or at Buckingham Palace as the symbol of unified British power. Here was a nation, it seemed, that knew who and where it was. No one personified British cohesion and determination to modern Americans like Prime Minister Winston Churchill, the embodiment of supposed Englishness for Americans during and after World War II. Yet Churchill was actually only half-English, thanks to his American mother. His lineage represented the not-uncommon marriages of wealthy American women in the Victorian era to titled European aristocratic men. What was national tended often to blur upon closer inspection.[24]

The churn of human movement that shaped England and all other parts of the globe has been nowhere more visible than in the development of the United States. The global diasporas of various peoples—African, Irish, Jewish, Italian, Indian, Chinese—found U.S. shores often the most attractive landing place (for slave traders, in the case of the involuntary African migration). A tiny new nation of a few million residents in 1800 clinging to the Atlantic coastline morphed into a sprawling, transcontinental behemoth of 75 million citizens by 1900. What Alexander Hamilton called "an empire in many respects the most interesting in the world" came to rival the largest landed empires, such as Russia, as well as the largest overseas empires, such as Britain. It did so largely on the backs of the vast army of some 50 million Europeans, mostly southern and eastern, who left their continent of origin in the nineteenth century and crossed oceans to pursue greater opportunities, most of them winding up in the United States. At the same time that European imperial power spread farthest abroad, so too did European emigrants fan out across the water in unprecedented numbers. The United States was the greatest beneficiary of all this movement.[25]

Despite their history of repeated territorial expansion amid dramatic demographic growth, most Americans by the mid-twentieth century imagined their own national borders as solid, permanent, and sanctioned by some degree of divine approval. Some of this was visual. On a map, the oceans provided anchors on the left and right, and the relatively straight east-west lines just seemed right or at least geometrically logical. Admittedly, there were a few imperial complications around the edges. Hawai'i and Alaska muddied the picture with their noncontiguousness, just as their real geography continued to confuse both schoolchildren and adult citizens.

The Philippines slipped off to at least formal independence in 1946. Puerto Rico and the U.S. Virgin Islands seemed mostly just obscure, tiny destinations for tourists in the winter. The Panama Canal Zone and Guantánamo Bay remained beyond most Americans' consciousness. And those straight lines west from El Paso and west from Lake of the Woods had, of course, little to do with natural dividing features such as rivers or mountains. Nonetheless, few U.S. citizens had any doubts about the geographical identity of their newly powerful nation.[26]

The long story of human movement did not slow down after World War II. All wars displace people, and the largest war in human history displaced more than any other. Beyond the 60 million who died during the conflict, tens of millions more survived but were left homeless and transient, particularly in such places as Germany, Poland, and China. The new United Nations spoke for their interests in the 1948 Declaration of Human Rights, stating that "everyone has the right to leave any country, including his own, and to return to his country." Within the United States, the Depression-era search for work and the wartime mobilization gave way to unprecedented migration to the blossoming new suburbs. The flood of migrants out of the old industrial Northeast to the new Sunbelt could be measured in the movement of professional sports teams, including baseball's Dodgers and Giants from New York to California in 1958 and basketball's Lakers from Minnesota to Los Angeles two years later. The pattern continued with large new numbers of immigrants arriving on American shores after the 1970s. Americans went the other way, too: by 2014, 7.6 million U.S. citizens were living abroad. They were enough, combined, to constitute the thirteenth most populous state. For all the apparent permanence of boundaries on maps, millions continued to move, altering the familiar and the foreign.[27]

Racial Identity

Gallons of ink have been spilled on the subject of race, a tiny echo of the oceans of blood shed for the same subject. Race is crucial to this story, too. Usually, the quickest approach to identifying foreignness is by phenotype, by surface physical appearance. Categorizing individuals as members of a "race" offers a way to situate them in a fixed status based supposedly on the genes that manifest themselves in that appearance. Racial categorization requires racial categories: discrete and recognizable boxes like "white" and "black." Americans also used "yellow" or increasingly "Oriental" and then "Asian." But they recognized that there were people in any one box who often looked quite different from one another, and a lot of people did not seem to fit in any box. There was also the "red" or Native American box, with the same problems. And there was "brown," or Hispanic, perhaps the murkiest and most plainly diverse of all. By 1977 the U.S. government, after two centuries of shifting understandings of race, formalized the five-category system of racial-ethnic classification that has remained official policy ever since.

The problem is that any system of racial categorization involves artifice or fakery. White people are not actually white, as a blank piece of paper held next to a "white" arm will demonstrate. Nor are people with varying shades of brown skin actually black. "Yellow" and "red" are even more obviously inaccurate terms, as any child with a coloring set can tell. Children do not naturally see people in these boxes; they must be trained to do so. Perhaps no one studies skin colors more carefully than those in the cosmetics industry, where the Pantone Corporation's standard Color Matching System uses more than a thousand tones. Certainly, race thinkers have long combined skin color with other particular criteria—hair color and texture, nose shape, eye shape—to produce certain desired categories. But these are not races. They are "races."[28]

Biologists use the term "population" rather than race. Populations with enough stability and isolation over long enough periods can develop certain shared genetic characteristics, such as predispositions to sickle-cell anemia or Tay-Sachs disease. But as populations move and mingle their genes with other populations, such tendencies alter over time. The general American public may have understood that racial categories are slippery, as they have long been unsure what to do with such peoples as Arabs and Iranians, not to mention Finns or Jews, whose racial status in the United States has changed at the whim of Congress or federal judges. Yet the common American use of racial categories has long implied that, whatever slippages there may be in ambiguous intermediary zones, there are pretty clear racial heartlands—white from the Atlantic to the Ural Mountains, "yellow" from the Ural Mountains to the Pacific, black from the Sahara to Cape Town—and perhaps even, by implication, core racial essences of whiteness (probably around London), of Asianness (likely around Beijing), and of blackness (perhaps around Kinshasa).[29]

Race, as is often suggested in college classrooms, is ultimately a social construction. The crest of the Ural Mountains in Russia has no sign saying "Europeans" to one side and "Asians" to the other, with people to the west all looking English and those to the east all appearing Chinese. Human phenotypes are a continuum rather than a small set of boxes. Race has been understood in different ways at different times, with different conventions underlying different legal systems of enforcement. Conventions are, by the root definition of the word, *convenient*—at least for the dominant populations in a society. Common sense in the United States by the twentieth century operated on the so-called one-drop rule: the surface appearance of even a fraction of non-European descent—"one drop of blood"—rendered one not white. A society of primarily European and African heritage used this system to exclude those Americans with any visible evidence of African descent from the privileges of being considered white.[30]

Even before World War II, Americans knew that heritage and racial identity were not carried in the blood. Blood comes in types A, B, AB, and O, shared among all peoples—though, in fitting with the logic of genetically isolated populations, some human communities have had more of certain types than others. But there is no such thing as "black blood" or "white blood." Americans nonetheless used such terms in more than metaphorical fashion, obscuring the continuum of genetic diversity behind a language of distinct racial boxes. Such habits may have indicated ignorance or laziness, but they helped reproduce, generation after generation, a false way of understanding real human diversity.[31]

For all its artifice, racial categorization has had enormous real power in the lives of Americans. From the tip of the slaveholder's lash to the muzzle of the cavalryman's rifle, race has been enforced with extreme ferocity to divide some Americans from others. It has been made real, the results handed down, the sins of the fathers and mothers to the daughters and sons. Since the 1960s, even the effort to undo the damaging effects of racial categorizing through affirmative-action policies has required, ironically but logically, the collection of racial data. The alternative would be the French way: refusing to distinguish officially among French citizens on the basis of race or religion, emphasizing instead their common French identity. This leaves open the question of whether racial discrimination grows or shrinks in the light of official public attention. While conservative Americans might prefer a more French path in this regard, U.S. law has tended to pay attention to race, rather than ignore it, in order to try to overcome its legacies.[32]

The implications of racial categories for foreignness in the American past are not clear-cut. At one level, race has obviously been the great dividing line. It underpinned the greatest original sources of American wealth: the seizure of land previously inhabited by Native Americans and the subordination and extraction of African labor. But with the devastation of the indigenous population and the subjugation of African Americans, the foreign over time either disappeared or became familiar. After slavery's destruction in the 1860s, black men gained at least legal status as citizens, and the subsequent violence of Jim Crow aimed to define African Americans not as foreign but as subordinate. They were clearly American, despite earlier efforts at colonization to Liberia, even if they were not to be treated equally to white citizens.[33]

The same might be said about sex, gender, and foreignness. Female and male identities have been elemental for the vast majority of Americans throughout the past. There may have been nothing more foreign, at a tangible, intimate level, for most women and men than the idea of being a member of the other sex. The recent visibility and partial liberation of transgender people, for all its helpfulness in reimagining gender, does not change this historical reality. Like all peoples, however, Americans have always understood themselves, as a *people*, to include both women and men. No nation can be a nunnery or monastery, a fraternity or sorority. Simple reproduction precludes this, but so too does the development of any society's gender roles and assumptions. Women and men, like African Americans and European Americans, may not be seen by some as fully equal, but neither are they seen as foreign.[34]

An entire shelf in some libraries now testifies to the intriguing story of what happened when the rise to global influence of a segregated United States intersected after World War II and the Holocaust with a world turning rapidly the other way—away from the racially coded hierarchies of empire and into a new era of national self-determination under the aegis of the United Nations. In order to lead a multiracial "Free World" in the anticommunist struggle against the Soviet Union, the United States embraced, however haltingly, what the historian Mary Dudziak has called "desegregation as a Cold War imperative." The geostrategic imperative of getting on the right side of history was obvious to the great Southern writer William Faulkner when he famously told a meeting of the Southern

Historical Association: "To live anywhere in the world of A.D. 1955 and be against equality because of race or color, is like living in Alaska and being against snow."[35]

The dramatic shift in white public attitudes about racial equality and integration across the past seventy-five years can be measured in many ways. Perhaps the most revealing are the polling numbers regarding interracial marriage, the inner sanctum of racist fear. In 1958, 91 percent of Southern whites and 79 percent of Northern whites affirmed that black-white marriages would "hurt in solving the Negro-white problem." In 1967 the U.S. Supreme Court overturned the last state laws restricting interracial marriages. By 1999, 65 percent of all Americans agreed that "interracial marriages are good because they help break down racial barriers." Resistant older generations have been replaced by younger generations with different racial sensibilities. Gay marriage overtook interracial marriage as a public issue, and in 2015 that, too, became legal. By 2015, 17 percent of all new marriages were interracial, a pattern likely to continue growing in a diverse nation bound within a few decades for majority-minority status. While personal animus against such couples has hardly disappeared, the historian Peggy Pascoe was correct to observe that "in what must be regarded as one of the most dramatic shifts in public opinion in American history, the overwhelming majority of Whites had come to believe that laws against interracial marriage were clearly, irrevocably wrong." Racism, like race, is socially constructed and can be deconstructed.[36]

Doing so, however, will not be easy. The campaign to end formal racial discrimination required a quarter of a century after 1945, and the weeding out of private prejudice and institutional racism endures as an ongoing task. A cursory look through the pages of any major newspaper reveals just how persistent the weeds of racism remained, even before the lacerating 2016 presidential campaign of Donald Trump. Symbolic victories have been won, most notably the two elections of a black U.S. president early in the twenty-first century. The era of public lynching and white riots mostly fades into memory, but public and private violence against people of color endures. Official discrimination in public life has largely disappeared, but segregation in the private sphere remains widespread in American society. The professional basketball superstar LeBron James observed this in an amiable conversation with reporters where he laughingly described the private Roman Catholic high school he attended in Akron as "99 percent white American" and his nearby neighborhood as "110 percent African American." The distinguished Harvard sociologist Orlando Patterson estimates that among white Americans "there's a hard core of about twenty per cent which still remains thoroughly racist." Any doubts about the persistence of white racism vanished with the racially divisive Trump campaign of 2016.[37]

What is the relationship, finally, between race and foreignness in the American past? The color line has powerfully shaped the contours of inequality and the distribution of power and opportunity. Race and ethnicity have also been used, as we shall see in greater detail, to try to define certain peoples as outsiders and exclude them from citizenship and even residence. Native Americans were the first to receive such treatment. Asians were the next, along with Europeans from the wrong parts of Europe, the south and east. Latinos were officially white but frequently excluded. And most recently Middle Easterners, if seen as Muslims, continue to struggle against such discrimination.

But the idea of nonwhiteness as foreignness was undercut from the beginning of colonial settlement by the crucial and abundant presence of people of African descent. America was never simply white. All the phenotypically discriminatory immigration laws could not change this essential fact. If African slavery was the nation's original sin, as some observers have suggested, it is equally true that the nation's multiracial origins meant that race would not ultimately work as a criterion for determining who was foreign and who was not. The arc of history pointed, eventually, the other way, toward a definition of Americanness that included people of different colors. And the contemporary United States is, plainly, the most multiracial and multiethnic of the great powers of the earth.

Freedom and Captivity

Americans forged a sense of who they were in large part out of their contacts with others. While national identity evolves over time and remains contested, particularly in a large and diverse society, Americans early on took on a mantle of individual liberty and a rejection of tyranny. From the start, they were sojourners from elsewhere, primarily England at first, come to a new land for opportunity. Whether in the Virginia model of entrepreneurial priorities or the Massachusetts model of building a godly community, the early colonists took great personal risks to pursue a freer, better life on American shores. A century and a half later, the revolutionaries of 1776 launched themselves fully free from the old monarchical relationship with Great Britain. No longer subjects of a king, they stood as autonomous citizens of a republic. The first overseas colonies of a European empire to win their independence, the United States had pulled itself out of the orbit of feudalism and kingdoms. Americans were modern and free, they believed: the people ruling themselves. The Constitution and the Bill of Rights sought to institutionalize the rights of "life, liberty, and the pursuit of happiness" promised in the Declaration of Independence.

Not every American was free, of course, and the prospect of captivity had troubled the American culture of individual freedom since the earliest days of colonial settlement. Losing one's liberty could happen in different ways. The most obvious was physical capture. From 1619, when slave traders deposited the first stolen Africans in Jamestown, to 1865, when the Thirteenth Amendment abolished slavery, Americans built and sustained the most successful slave society in the modern world. The coerced labor of Africans and African Americans underpinned the burgeoning U.S. economy, outlasting even the end of the slave trade by more than fifty years. One in five residents of the colonies labored in bondage. American historians in recent decades have feasted on the contradiction of a land of freedom built on unfreedom. The British observer Samuel Johnson noted dryly about American revolutionaries that "we hear the loudest yelps for liberty among the drivers of negroes."[38]

Indeed, the persistence and growth of plantation slavery in the American South, when slavery was declining in the North, raised questions about whether the region really was fully part of the United States. Or was it, instead, a fundamentally different society, more like a vast Caribbean sugar island? Defenders of slavery had no doubt. Edwin C. Holland, editor of the *Charleston Times*, warned in the early 1820s: "Let it never be forgotten that our NEGROES are truly the *Jacobins* of the country; that they are the *Anarchists* and the *Domestic* enemy." Holland's language suggested slaveholders' intense fears that black people, too, might someday claim their own natural right to liberty, just as they had done in Haiti. Slavery in the land of individual freedom sowed mistrust in every direction: abolitionists toward white Southerners, slaveholders toward the enslaved, and the enslaved toward other slaves who might betray secrets to their owners.[39]

Black people bore the overwhelming bulk of the burden of slavery but were not the only ones to lack freedom. Indigent English workers came to the new American colonies by the thousands, contracting themselves for years of unfree labor in order to win eventual liberty in a land with greater opportunities than the poverty from which they came. Indeed, the system of race slavery that emerged in the British North American colonies reflected precisely a determination to keep these European unfree laborers from finding common cause with African unfree laborers. Such alliance directly threatened the existing order in Virginia in the case of Bacon's Rebellion of 1676.[40]

From the earliest days of settlement, European Americans near the frontier lived in steady fear of capture by Native Americans. Life in tiny communities and rural settings closest to the frontier led to frequent white-Indian interactions, some of them involving trade, diplomacy, and inter-marriage, particularly at times and places where each side shared roughly equal numbers and power. But other interactions provoked extreme violence. In the raids and wars that unfolded across the colonial backcountry, captives were seized on both sides and often brutally executed. White women and children were more likely to be kept alive and assimilated into Indian tribes as indigenous numbers thinned over time.[41]

Even after white settlement thickened beyond the Appalachian Mountains and after independence had been won from Great Britain, white Americans continued to face the threat of being taken captive by Europeans. After defeat at Yorktown in 1781, the British did not depart from North America. Instead, they doubled down on those colonies they still controlled, from the Caribbean to Canada. The U.S.-Canada border provided abundant opportunities for conflict between British and American forces, and British commanders did not hesitate to let the upstart Yankees know how substantial British military might remained. Above all, the young republic, with its eagerness for transatlantic trade, could not completely avoid the central roiling imperial conflict of the era, that between France and Great Britain. Americans barely dodged an armed clash with France in the 1790s, and by 1812 they were back at war with the British. A primary cause was the British navy's persistence for years in "impressing" American sailors: taking them captive and putting them to work, claiming they were British subjects. Henry Clay, Speaker of the U.S. House of Representatives, denounced these "piratical depredations," and Representative Richard M. Johnson called on Great Britain to "liberate our captured seamen on board her ships of war." It took two years of warfare and a burned capital city of Washington before the United States emerged from this second American war of independence, finally free from the threat of imperial captivity.[42]

More subtle means could also deprive Americans of the individual freedom they cherished and believed to be the natural expression of the human spirit. It was not just a matter of seizing bodies and placing them in chains. Psychological and spiritual captivity could be just as threatening and perhaps tougher to identify and overcome. Such captivity of the soul could happen at the hands of British colonialism. Some twenty thousand Loyalists served as soldiers in the royal forces during the American Revolution, as did a similar number of enslaved black workers. Roughly 20 percent of the colonies' population remained sympathetic to the Crown, many of them leaving after independence to settle in British territories in the Caribbean islands or in Canada, where they provided the demographic core of the new English-speaking province of Ontario along the northern shore of the Great Lakes. From the perspective of the new United States, such Loyalists had failed to grasp their chance at liberty. They had clung to the rule of others over them, both tyrannical king and distant Parliament.[43]

Early Americans feared another avenue to spiritual captivity: Roman Catholicism. Despite the relative tolerance of religious dissenters in Rhode Island and Pennsylvania and the explicit welcome that Maryland provided to Catholics, the vast majority of American colonists and citizens of the early republic were Protestants who feared what they saw as the corrupting influence of Rome. For devout Protestants, the entire structure of the Roman Catholic Church demanded enslaving obedience—to superstition, to priests, and to the tyranny of the pope. All that hierarchy came between the free individual and God, corrupting the most important relationship of all. Not until the late twentieth century would anti-Catholicism finally lose its persistent power in American life.

The threat of Catholicism rode into American society not on the shoulders of an invading Vatican army but instead in the hearts and minds of working-class Catholic immigrants from places such as Ireland and Germany. Thomas Jefferson and others warned of the danger of new arrivals from monarchical societies, where values and behaviors of hierarchical obedience might not have prepared them for responsible citizenship in a republic. The worst such places were those where the Catholic faith bolstered kings and queens in their despotism. To America's "freest principles,"

Jefferson feared, "nothing can be more opposed than the maxims of absolute monarchies." Such migrants would "bring with them the principles of the governments they leave, imbibed in their early youth." Even "if able to throw them off, it will be in exchange for an unbounded licentiousness" rather than settling "at the point of temperate liberty." The pendulum would swing too far. Jefferson worried that responsible "republican Americans" would be unmoored by too many such immigrants. Before 1763, the presence in Québec of the Catholic French empire right on the American colonies' northern border only amplified the danger.[44]

The threat of having white Americans' personal freedom taken away can be traced back ultimately to Indian-captivity narratives. The real horror in these stories of the frontier, first in the New England backcountry, came not from the visceral details of confinement and torture, grim as those often were. The worst terror of all was the real danger of "going native." Accommodating to one's captors and choosing to assimilate into Native American society happened often enough to raise the most profound challenge to Americans' sense of who they were. Why would anyone voluntarily convert *away* from American life, even to the point of not wanting to be liberated and redeemed? For American settlers and citizens who viewed their culture as embodying human nature's essential yearning for individual liberty, shedding that culture like a snake sheds its skin and taking on an entirely different culture represented dehumanization. It was unnatural. The historian Alan Taylor tells of settlers at Jamestown in Virginia in the early 1600s who raided an Indian village and "captured some fellow colonists who had run away to the Indians to escape the hunger, hardships, and brutality of their domineering leaders." The colony's governor "made examples of them by burning them at the stake or breaking their backs slowly on the wheel." Going native would persist as a fundamental threat to Americans' sense of who they were, from the U.S. occupation of the Philippines at the end of the nineteenth century, to the Korean War and the struggle against communism in the twentieth, to Afghanistan and the conflict with Islamist jihad in the twenty-first.[45]

White Slaves in Africa

Nothing in the early republic brought home to white Americans the awful prospect of losing their individual freedom like the Barbary captivity narratives. After the 1783 Treaty of Paris formally acknowledged the independence of the United States, American ships lost the protection of the mighty British navy. Eager Yankee traders plying the waters of the Mediterranean and the adjacent Atlantic shores of Spain and Portugal quickly grasped their new vulnerability to pirates. In the summer of 1785 Algerian privateers seized two American merchant ships, the *Maria* of Boston and the *Dauphin* of Philadelphia, and held twenty-one Americans hostage. The dey (ruler) of Algiers expected a large ransom for their freedom. The proud new U.S. republic refused to pay, however, and most of the captives died of the plague or languished in bondage for more than a decade.[46]

While the plight of the crews of the *Maria* and the *Dauphin* garnered considerable attention in the United States, the story of white Americans seized by North African privateers actually stretched back to the earliest days of British colonists in the Western Hemisphere. The Muslim rulers of the Barbary Coast states—Morocco, Algiers, Tunis, and Tripoli (today's Libya)—had been engaged for many centuries in complicated trade and conflict with their Christian neighbors just across the waters of the Mediterranean Sea. The Muslim Ottoman Empire had done the same, at one point holding captive Captain John Smith, famous later as a leader of the Jamestown settlement in Virginia. As Europeans established overseas empires, their sailing routes brought them into regular and contentious contact with oceangoing North African raiders.[47]

Both sides took captives. Algiers alone held more than twenty thousand Christian hostages in the 1620s. In 1625, just five years after the Pilgrims first landed at Plymouth in what was soon called Massachusetts, North African pirates seized two ships carrying other North American colonists and escorted them into the Moroccan harbor of Salé, adjacent to Rabat. The Boston shipwright Joshua Gee wrote the first American captivity narrative about his seven years enslaved by Algerians in the 1680s, including rowing on one of the notorious Algerian slave galleys. Just a few years earlier, Native Americans had raided Lancaster, Massachusetts, taking hostage Mary Rowlandson, who would eventually author the most widely known American captivity story. The famed Puritan minister Cotton Mather, more commonly known for his condemnations of Indian seizures of fellow colonists, referred to Barbary servitude as "the most horrible *Captivity* in the world" and declared the "Hellish *Moors*" to be "worse than the "*Egyptian task masters*" who tormented the Jewish Chosen People of the Old Testament.[48]

U.S. independence revived this older history of white Americans enslaved in Africa. In the thirty years from 1785 to 1815, beginning with the *Maria* and the *Dauphin*, the Barbary states seized thirty-five American ships and more than seven hundred U.S. sailors. Such evidence of American national weakness figured prominently in discussions of whether to ratify the new, more robust Constitution to replace the initial Articles of Confederation. "Despicable shall we appear in the eyes of other nations," a Virginian wrote to the *Alexandria Times*, "if the idea is to go forth that an American may be robbed of liberty and held in vile bondage." The United States developed its first permanent navy in part to respond to Barbary demands for ransom, overcoming republican distrust of permanent military establishments. Only U.S. wars with Tripoli and then Algiers finally eliminated in 1815 the North African threat to Americans on the open waters. North Africa subsequently slipped into the European sphere of influence with the French conquest and colonization of Algeria in 1830.[49]

Anxieties about freedom and captivity remained high in the new American republic for its first thirty years. Americans wanted to read about captive fellow citizens. U.S. publishers issued more than a hundred American Barbary-captivity editions between 1798 and 1817, along with reprints of earlier popular Indian-captivity narratives. Continuing captures on Indian frontiers blended with those at sea at the hands of Muslim North Africans. Newspapers wrote of the depredations of "savage" Indians and "savage" Algerians and noted the captors' similar complexions. Letters to the editor indicated considerable public engagement with the issue of U.S. hostages. At the same time, enslavement of black workers in the American South had defied predictions and continued to grow. Even as the African slave trade ended in 1808, a resurgent plantation economy rode technological innovations to new productive heights and expanded to the west. Captivity or its shadow seemed omnipresent for Americans.[50]

While those seven hundred U.S. citizens languished in bondage on African shores, some one million Africans labored in bondage on American shores. But only a very few American captives linked these two facts, at least explicitly. They managed to write letters home—at least ninety, many published in newspapers and other widely read publications. They begged to be ransomed, and they later published memoirs tinged with outrage at their treatment along the southern shores of the Mediterranean Sea. Out of these writings emerged a sense of particular horror at what they most often called "turning Turk," "Turk" then being a common term for Muslim.

They loathed their few fellow captives who converted to Islam and made a new life in North Africa. Just as Americans recoiled at news of Indian captives "going native" on the nearby frontier, they despised and feared the loss of freedom and autonomy overseas that they saw as the birthright of U.S. citizens.[51]

Conversion to Islam, for early Americans, represented a peculiarly degrading form of captivity. This was true regardless of evidence that converts were often treated well in the Barbary states. Like Europeans, Americans in the nineteenth century tended to view Islamic societies as a wicked combination of political tyranny and moral debauchery. Even sympathetic Western intellectuals who acknowledged Islam's former civilizational greatness, associated with science, libraries, and universities, considered contemporary Muslim societies barren and desolate. Such lands were seen not as wounded by the West but as having poisoned themselves and now exporting terror in the form of piratical depredations. Going native by turning Turk seemed self-evidently depraved.

Early Americans disliked despotism of all stripes, including that of autocratic Muslim states. Citizens of the U.S. republic believed Islam, in the words of the historian Robert Allison, "not only stifled religious and intellectual freedom, it killed the spirit of enterprise by which societies could flourish." It was against the better nature of people, in contrast to American society. In addition, lurid tales of large harems kept by some Muslim rulers both titillated and repelled Protestant Americans. The idea of abundant enslaved women available for an owner's sexual gratification might not have seemed completely foreign to antebellum elite white Southerners, of course. But this was not a model embraced openly by any Americans. Readers of one Philadelphia newspaper in 1798, for example, learned of the Ottoman sultan reportedly purchasing virgin female Circassian and Georgian slaves—that is, truly Caucasian women—thereby debasing international commerce into a white-slavery prostitution ring. White Americans were determined, by contrast, to preserve the individual liberty they considered central to their culture.[52]

Who Americans believed they were provided a foundation for how they understood the many other peoples they encountered. So what makes humans, both Americans and others, think and behave as they do? Much of modern social science and the humanities—two of the three traditional divisions within universities—works to answer these questions.

Economists, political scientists, philosophers, novelists, and others all labor in this vineyard. They even get help from the third division, the sciences, particularly biologists. Of all of them, historians may take the broadest view, examining human behavior across the full sweep of the recorded past and across the wide global array of human cultures. Historical explanations of people's choices tend to come down to some combination of interests and ideas. Material interests count: the pursuit of food, safety, sex, wealth, family protection, and the like. So, too, do ideas, which are never fully separable from material circumstances—we cannot know how our ideas might have turned out had we grown up in a different situation—but which take on a power of their own: ideas about what is just or godly or practical.

A particularly vivid demonstration of the power of ideas in contemporary American life is the much-observed fact that many white working-class Americans vote for Republican Party political candidates. Republican policies have tended to favor the economic interests of more affluent citizens, at least on measurable matters such as taxation. So critics have noted, often with dismay, this inclination of many workers to vote "against their own interests." Instead, they note, these voters seem to prioritize such cultural issues as opposition to abortion or expanding gun rights. Their ideas or values, that is, trump their economic interests. Much less noted is the same behavior on the other end of the political spectrum. Affluent liberals tend to vote for Democratic Party candidates whose policies do not favor their economic interests. Instead, they also cast ballots on the basis of other values or principles, such as greater equality or opposition to discrimination. Careful calculation of narrow economic self-interest, in other words, does not usually suffice to explain human behavior.[53]

Ideas matter, and ideas about identity are among the most powerful conceptions that people hold. Over the past generation, it has become almost a cliché to talk about "the Other" and how individuals and societies separate themselves from those they see as outsiders. The use of "otherizing" and "otherness" has become common phrasing. An older generation used the phrase "beyond the pale," a reference dating to the stakes ("pales," sharing the root meaning of "impale") that marked the boundary of English settlement in early-modern Ireland. Beyond the pale were the wild Catholic Irish, outside of Protestant English control—true foreigners. In the twentieth century, from the worldwide turmoil of the 1940s arose one nation more powerful than any other, a new colossus of economic, military, and cultural might, thrust forward into unprecedented global prominence. Its newly worldwide strategic interests favored a renewed openness to engaging with peoples from every land. How the citizens of the United States understood all the outsiders with whom they now interacted would help determine a great deal of subsequent world history. How they viewed others hinged, in turn, on their assumptions about themselves, their own national character, and their own national trajectory. To this topic we now turn.

CHAPTER II

Freedom

American Culture as Human Nature

" It's just human nature!" Anyone who spends enough time in a history classroom will likely encounter this claim at some point. Historians work at figuring out not just what happened in the past but why people did what they did. This can be a frustrating task. Human motivations tend to resist ready explanation. They are complicated, overlapping, changeable, and sometimes conflicting. There is "no such thing as an unmixed motive," the writer Katherine Anne Porter observed. Some motivations are conscious; others are not. Internal psychological factors jostle against social pressures. So why did person X choose to do what she did? A student will eventually metaphorically throw up his hands and assert that "it's just human nature" to want power or to seek wealth or to pursue security or to desire to know the truth.[1]

Like all peoples, Americans carry usually unspoken assumptions about what makes humans tick. Cultures develop over time as language, behaviors, and values become settled enough among members of a community to seem like common sense. The very term "commonsensical" implies that something is obvious. Anyone questioning it reveals a lack of common sense, a damning judgment. And the most important common sense in any society regards its highest values, those its members most cherish. For Americans, that common sense has pointed to two values: individual liberty and the pursuit of greater material wealth. From its earliest days of independence, the United States was a culture focused on commerce and freedom. Even the contradictory persistence of race slavery did not negate the fierce aspiration for liberty shared by most Americans of all colors.

"Our people have a decided taste for navigation and commerce," Thomas Jefferson once observed. From the colonial era forward, "Yankees" were known to other peoples as ambitious traders, entrepreneurial and skilled at profit making. They also enjoyed material comforts. In the afterglow of independence from Britain, Jefferson felt obliged to defend his abiding taste for British goods. "It is not from a love of the English but a love of myself that I sometimes find myself obliged to buy their manufactures," he wrote to Gilbert du Motier, Marquis de Lafayette in 1786. His fellow citizens evidently felt the same, as British manufactured items flooded back into the United States immediately after the wartime interruptions of the Revolution and the War of 1812. A similar story unfolded across the Pacific Ocean a few decades later. Like Japan before 1853, Korea shunned U.S. efforts to open trade with that peninsula, resulting in a brief armed conflict in 1871 as the U.S. military sought to force it open. "Korean resistance to the American pursuit of wealth through global trade was considered unnatural, not just an erroneous policy," the historian Thomas Bender observed. For Americans, the desire for business and material acquisitions seemed hardwired into human character.[2]

From the English settlement at Plymouth Colony in 1620 to the forging of the Constitution in Philadelphia in 1787, the development of the eventual American nation had been profoundly intentional. Community members and leaders *intended* to create a certain kind of society. It was neither random nor inevitable, nor was it the result of a long accretion of habits by people whose ancestors had lived on the same land for centuries and millennia. It was done by choice. English Puritans on the shores of Massachusetts Bay aimed to build a godly society, the famed city upon a hill, by starting from scratch. Constitutional framers debating in Independence Hall constructed a founding document to embody the commitment to "life, liberty, and the pursuit of happiness." Grounded in private property and representative government, the new nation cut itself free from the Old World of kings and castles. Americans believed they would thrive in a democratic republic because its arrangements better reflected their true nature as independent human beings, free in minds and free in commerce. Only in a new, intentional society could human nature fully flourish.[3]

It would require struggle. Rather than emerging fully formed like the goddess Athena from the head of Zeus in the ancient Greek myth, this new righteous society did not simply emerge pristine from Independence Hall in the late 1780s. Americans of color, for their part, had to continue to fight against bondage and expropriation, while white women labored mightily to win full citizenship. These struggles and their legacies shaped much of the nineteenth and twentieth centuries and continued in the twenty-first. Like all societies, the new American one also sought to balance the role of individuals with the common good—while other states had traditionally emphasized the latter, Americans leaned toward the former. The American culture of individualism would be worked out in various ways across the first century of the rapidly expanding young republic.[4]

By the early decades of the twentieth century, with the Civil War receding in memory, a process of national homogenization became visible. An increasingly industrial and urban society was carried forward by new technologies of transportation (highways and airplanes) and communication (film and radio). Mobilizations for the two world wars and the interwar Great Depression further stimulated the growing feeling of a unified national culture. The common sense of this newly national culture by the 1940s centered on political liberty and freedom of commerce. Americans considered themselves not only the freest people on the earth but also the wealthiest. It was therefore common sense to most of them that other peoples would want to be like them. Who would freely choose to reject freedom and affluence? That would run, it seemed to them, against human nature. Understanding how Americans thought about foreigners requires first examining how Americans understood their own society as reflecting humanity's essential nature.

Creating a National Identity

"What then is the American, this new man?" J. Hector St. John de Crève-coeur memorably inquired in his 1782 *Letters from an American Farmer*. One answer came a few years later from a careful and trenchant observer of the new United States, Alexis de Tocqueville: "The American is the Englishman left to himself." In other words, if the English were freed from their own feudal history, their limited island landscape, and their complicated relationships with nearby European powers, they would be . . . American. Residents of the American colonies were British subjects and considered themselves as such. Paul Revere on his famous pre-Revolution ride in

Massachusetts would not have said "the British are coming!" since he and his neighbors were themselves British, but rather "the regulars are coming out!" The colonists spoke English, after all—"the King's English," as the saying went—without so much of the distinctive nasal accent that later Americans would develop. This explains some of the ease of Royal Navy captains seizing and impressing American sailors into duty in the years leading up to the War of 1812. They simply *seemed* English.[5]

From the start, however, Americans were never only English. They were also Native, African, and eventually Asian and Middle Eastern, and they came from all over Europe. Most of them had lived in landscapes vastly different from England. Indeed, for many European observers, the British American colonies were most interesting for the exotic presence of large numbers of Native Americans and African Americans. During the Revolution, several thousand American sailors and other personnel were captured and imprisoned in English seaports. One of them, Charles Herbert, described the curious wives of some Royal Navy seamen asking, before they could behold the prisoners, "What sort of people are they? Are they white?" Once the prisoners were pointed out, they exclaimed, "Why! They look like our people, and they talk English!"[6]

So just how British would the newly independent Americans be? For more than a century and a half, British ideas about religion, politics, and culture had served as a polestar for the colonists. A gap had widened in the pre-Revolution decades, allowing the Patriots of 1776 to feel themselves now a separate people, but the swiftness of political change after the Revolution left uncertain the degree of cultural change. Jefferson's anxiety about his continuing taste for British goods illustrates the challenge. The first American diplomats and travelers to Britain—still the most powerful nation on the earth—had to learn how to dress, act, and be republican and middle class in the presence of a monarch and genteel aristocrats. The earliest American representatives typically felt a blend of resentment and admiration toward the English, both rejection and identification. They sometimes preferred Scotland, which they found more fully Protestant and similarly ambivalent about the centralized imperial authority of London.[7]

Distinguishing themselves from the British was an obvious priority for Americans, but it seemed difficult to more distant observers. To the dismay of early American travelers, continental Europeans often failed at the task. Americans still just seemed British to them. Chinese officials in the 1780s proved no better. "From the Asian perspective of vast cultural difference between themselves and all westerners," the historian Kariann Yokota notes, "there was little that separated these two peoples who shared language, blood, and material tastes." Sixty years later, the elite Chinese official responsible for the first U.S.-China treaty still had trouble understanding Americans, who were overshadowed by the more powerful British Empire. The United States "is the most uncivilized and remote of all countries," he reported to his emperor, "an isolated place outside the pale, solitary and ignorant." To communicate with Americans, he concluded, "we must make our words somewhat simple"—an ironic foreshadowing of later U.S. assumptions about certain enemies only understanding the language of force.[8]

The young nation's first leaders recognized from the start that they would have to earn international respect and standing. This would require power. Having just won formal independence from the British, George Washington summarized the challenge for a new American identity. "It is only in our united character as an empire," the new president noted, "that our independence is acknowledged, that our power can be regarded, or our credit supported."[9]

Encountering their fellow countrymen abroad deepened early Americans' sense of national identity. In England or Italy or farther afield, Virginians and Vermonters found each other more familiar than they did at home. Internal divisions paled before the cultural distance created by the Atlantic Ocean. American visitors to Europe in the early 1800s were often troubled by the extremes of poverty and wealth, stark religious and civil hierarchies, and the sharply inferior public status of women. On the other hand, they tended to admire such features as the cleanliness of streets in German-speaking central European lands and the more vigorous policing of public spaces than in the United States. The sheer Roman Catholicism of much of Europe left them ambivalent: Americans disliked the superstition and corruption they associated with Rome but were powerfully drawn to the religious art and cathedral architecture of Catholicism. Most of all, they hoped that Europeans would become more like Americans. They took hope from the wave of revolutions across the continent in 1848, as demonstrated in a sermon title at Washington's First Presbyterian Church: "America, Teacher of Nations."[10]

Conservatives in Europe, for their part, found the new United States mostly a horror. It represented the world turned upside down. The individual liberty so cherished by Americans meant the overturning of traditionalists' sense of human hierarchies as natural and divinely ordained. The common reference to the United States after independence as a "pirate republic" was nearly redundant: a republic, to them, was by definition a kind of piracy of the natural order. Highbrow European disdain for plebeian American manners and culture provided a perpetual fount of criticism. "If I must stay here a year, I shall die," the French foreign minister Charles Maurice de Talleyrand declared during a visit. The diplomat and epicure considered Americans to have "thirty-two religions and only one dish." The British writer Rudyard Kipling rued the absence of leisurely dining rituals. The American, he said, "has no meals. He stuffs for ten minutes thrice a day." The lack of aristocratic tradition dismayed the British art critic and social reformer John Ruskin: "I could not, even for a couple of months, live in a country so miserable as to possess no castles." The prevalence of public spitting, particularly linked to tobacco use, appalled elite visitors, stimulating Oscar Wilde's arch suggestion that "America is one long expectoration."[11]

Other Europeans identified a very different source for an unattractive American national identity. Rather than bemoaning republican culinary manners and architectural style, they were horrified by enduring human bondage. The Marquis de Lafayette, the great French ally of the American revolutionary forces, claimed later that he "would never have drawn my sword in the cause of America, if I could have conceived that thereby I was helping to found a nation of slaves," though it is unclear how he could have missed that likely prospect. Coming from England to the United States after independence, Isaac Candler, an admirer of American egalitarianism, was disturbed by the scale and intensity of white racial prejudice and violence. Racism in the new republic, he feared, was like "gangrene corrupting the whole."[12]

Most Europeans, however, took a more sanguine view, sharing neither elite disdain nor abolitionist fears about the United States. They saw it instead primarily as a land of opportunity. During the nineteenth and early twentieth centuries, roughly 50 million Europeans left their homelands and moved abroad. The tsunami of European departures in this era rolled out in every direction, and its main force washed ashore from Maine to Florida. Economics—work, land—drew them. So did prospects of greater personal liberty. For various Old World admirers, Americans seemed "the hope of the human race" and "the great organizers of modern democracy." A German observer called the United States a "republic without guillotines," surpassing the French version as a democratic model for the future. The French historian Ernest Renan dismissed aristocratic criticisms of American manners, highlighting instead freedom of speech and thought in the new republic. "American vulgarity would not have burned [the freethinking priest] Giordano Bruno," Renan argued, and "would not have persecuted Galileo."[13]

The challenge for both Americans and others in understanding what it meant to be American stemmed from the nation's youth, diversity, and rapid expansion. It was new, its contradictions still raw: a self-governing slaveholding society built on reverence for private property while vigorously seizing lands from Native Americans and Mexicans. It was wildly diverse in its regional cultures, climates, and demography, and it spread west across an entire continent during the course of the nineteenth century, more than quadrupling in size. Could there even be a unified national identity in such a variegated land?

Regional differences continued to complicate the meaning of Americanness well into the twentieth century. The local and regional pride that may sometimes seem nostalgic or kitschy today was grounded in profound earlier variations. The Civil War made vivid the absence of national unity, and the conquered South remained an outlier in American life for generations thereafter. Various parts of the nation claimed to be uniquely emblematic of American identity. Massachusetts boasted the Pilgrims and the bulk of the nation's early Christian missionaries, sailing off to bring the light of the gospel to such distant lands as the Hawai'ian ("Sandwich") Islands and such unchurched regions as Texas. This was not an aspect of history much noted in the Lone Star state, where regional pride long held Texas to embody the very essence of American character, except when the governor was publicly contemplating secession and a return to Lone Star Republic status. The latter prospect gives a particular cast to Texas's modern state tourism slogan, "It's Like a Whole Other Country."[14]

Other Americans promoted their own regional claims to special symbolic status for the nation as a whole. Philadelphians touted the Liberty Bell and the writing of the Constitution—though French revolutionaries in 1793, before beheading King Louis XVI, apparently considered instead simply exiling him to Philadelphia as sufficiently cruel punishment.[15] New York City became the most famous and diverse place in the country, later the symbolic target of the September 11, 2001, attacks. Washingtonians shared that targeting with their status as the nation's capital. Ohio came to serve as the bellwether state in presidential elections. Further west, Utah represented probably the most distinctive homegrown American religious faith, Mormonism, while the northern panhandle of Idaho evolved into a bastion of white supremacist survivalists who cherished a racialized view of what they considered America's real national identity. Westerners in general tended to imagine their landscapes as the most distinctively American of all, with Alaskans promoting the Last Frontier and Montanans proclaiming the Last Best Place. California transformed from the remotest region into the most populous and wealthiest state, the cutting edge of American popular culture and technological innovation.

No region made a firmer claim to embody Americanness than the Midwest. This was the fabled heartland, the space at the nation's center from which its truest self supposedly emanated. Some of this claim stemmed from the large-scale agriculture that fed the nation even as the United States became an urban, industrial society. Some of it derived from being farther from oceans and borders and most large cities, farther from foreigners of every kind and thus more distinctly American. And some of the heartland idea came from Midwesterners' speech patterns, which supposedly lacked an accent. But this "neutral speech" was a fiction, as Edward McClelland showed in his book *How to Speak Midwestern*. "Accents are an important element of regional identity," McClelland noted, "and an important element of Midwestern identity is believing you don't have an accent." Similar thinking underpins the American belief that it is the British who speak English with an accent. Seemingly straightforward mapping of the Midwest was also problematic. The region could theoretically extend all the way from the crest of the Appalachian Mountains to the peaks of the Rocky Mountains, taking in the entire vast watershed of the Mississippi, Missouri, and Ohio Rivers. Alternatively, it could be just part of that landscape. Residents and others did not agree about the borders of the Midwest and whether they included the northern Great Plains, the southern Great Plains, Minnesota, the Great Lakes, or the former slave states of Missouri and Kentucky. Only Illinois seemed to qualify in nearly every version of the Midwest.[16]

All societies are complicated, and dramatic growth made the United States more and more so. The fourth-largest nation in the world in territory, with an immigrant-filled population of 75 million in 1900, 150 million in 1950, and 300 million in 2000, the United States did not lend itself to simple characterization. Americans did, however, generally revere the ideas of personal freedom and freedom of commerce. The expansion of U.S. power in the twentieth century would help spread, for better and for worse, the gospel of individualism and personal consumption around the world.

An American Way of Life

American national identity came into clearer focus in the generation spanning from the 1910s to the 1940s. Rapid industrialization in the last decades of the 1800s laid the foundation for a more tightly unified nation. An integrated national market developed from innovations in transportation and communication. Railroads, highways, and airways enabled the steam engine and then the new internal combustion engine, fired by abundant coal and oil, to move people and goods at a speed and scale previously unimaginable. Telephones, film, and radio allowed citizens to share a common culture that increasingly overshadowed local and regional distinctions. The sending of the first telegraph message in 1844 had pointed to this more homogenous future. Despite Henry David Thoreau's famous skepticism that Maine and Texas—then the opposite ends of the nation—might "have nothing important to communicate" to each other, the inventor Samuel Morse predicted accurately that such instantaneous long-distance communication would make "one neighborhood of the whole country."[17]

Nothing unites a country as much as external enemies and national emergencies. Both of these defined the U.S. experience in the first half of the twentieth century. Entering the two globe-straddling conflicts of World War I and World War II required mass mobilizations of American soldiers and workers and the U.S. economy. By moving millions of citizens around the country and the world, fighting these wars stimulated social and particularly racial tensions in many communities. But these mobilizations also brought people together from across a vast land and gave them a common and patriotic purpose of helping defend the nation. On either side of World War II, the extended national emergency of the Great Depression of the 1930s gave rise to a national government more intimately connected to its citizens in every corner of the country, and the Cold War pointed to a future of open-ended military tension and combat readiness.

The generation from the 1910s to the 1940s marked the final geographical and political consolidation of the nation. In 1912, New Mexico and Arizona entered the Union as the last contiguous mainland states, coming hard on the heels of Oklahoma five years earlier. The Japanese attack on

Pearl Harbor in 1941 drew the United States into war in the Pacific, forever altering American perceptions of Hawai'i and Alaska. No longer an exotic tropical island chain on the periphery of the national consciousness, Hawai'i became the epicenter of a vast U.S. war effort. Americans fought and died to defend the territory, and millions of soldiers and sailors from the mainland spent time there. Alaska also served as a frontline in the Pacific War after the Japanese attack on the Aleutian Islands. The United States built the Alcan (Alaska–Canadian) Highway in 1942 to link its northernmost territory more directly to the lower forty-eight states. The war years made once-distant Alaska and Hawai'i much more concrete and familiar to continental Americans, who granted them statehood in 1959. Commercial aviation expanded rapidly after World War II, further consolidating the new bonds of the far-flung nation and fulfilling *Fortune* magazine's 1945 prediction that air travel would encourage the "great mixing up of peoples, so vastly accelerated by war, [to] be continued into the peace."[18]

How did Americans talk about their identity in these years of national consolidation? One popular and enduring slogan emerged from the depths of the Great Depression: "The American Dream." The Pulitzer Prize–winning historian James Truslow Adams coined the term in his 1931 book *The Epic of America*, to capture the sense of optimism about social mobility long available in the United States through hard work and perseverance, even as it was being tested in the steep economic downturn. Adams contended that the American Dream was not simply a yearning for material wealth. Rather, it meant the chance to overcome barriers and the limits of social class, in order to reach one's fullest potential. The United States, Adams believed, embodied that opportunity more than any other country. The evidence lay in the vast American middle class visible by the 1920s and growing rapidly again after World War II ended the Depression in the United States.[19]

Another popular slogan arising in the 1920s and 1930s was "the American way of life." This term combined the politics of democratic republicanism with the economic opportunity provided under capitalism. Radio entertainment and advertisements, sporting events, and Gallup opinion polls helped Americans understand their country as a unified, distinctive, modern society. The historian Brooke Blower has shown that observers in the 1920s and 1930s began for the first time to "discern the contours of a new and, many thought, utterly distinctive American society populated by distinctively American inhabitants." The interwar years saw "wide-ranging social consolidation in the United States," Blower notes, "when a fractured and far-flung population, drawn into the orbit of emerging national markets and media, increasingly began to imagine themselves as a united people." Tightening bonds of transportation and communication helped reshape Americans' consciousness of who they were and how they lived in "the American way of life."[20]

Under attack with the soaring joblessness of the Depression, the American way of life came roaring back in the 1940s. World War II ended unemployment as war work put money in Americans' pockets, more than most had ever seen. American abundance accompanied GIs overseas, where other peoples were often amazed by the physical size, relative health, and modern equipment of American personnel. U.S. troops gathering in Britain for the eventual D-Day invasion of northern France were famously referred to by grumpy British observers as "overpaid, oversexed, and over here." Japanese civilians during the postwar occupation of their country were struck by the informality and casual confidence of American soldiers, walking the streets with hands in their pockets and flush with chocolate and cigarettes. The "thing that shocked us was seeing adult men chewing gum," one Japanese woman recalled. "Eating on the street was considered very bad manners . . . [and] unthinkable for a well-brought-up person to do so." Yet many Japanese warmed quickly to the Americans, who were "healthy, smiling all the time, very friendly."[21]

The American way of life took vivid form in *Life* magazine's promotion of the allures of American women in the waning days of World War II. Aimed at the more than five million U.S. servicemen abroad who would soon be returning home, *Life* splashed a prominent photograph of seven attractive young women, modestly dressed and smiling warmly at the camera. "What Is the American Look?" asked the May 21, 1945, headline. "A clean ready smile with teeth that show the result of plenty of milk and orange juice and of braces when young, is the badge of the American girl." American women "have somehow acquired an unmistakable American look," and "it appears to roving GIs that quantitatively there are more attractive women on their home shores than anywhere else on earth." Foreign observers in this era often remarked on the straightness and health of American teeth. Orthodontics seemed a natural part of a society known for the Hollywood smiles of its film stars.[22]

Americans during the 1930s and 1940s began to use one other revealing formulation to describe their national identity: "the Judeo-Christian tradition." Like the exceptionalist implications of the American way of life, the Judeo-Christian tradition tapped into a widespread sense among its citizens that the United States served as a unique bastion of religious liberty in an increasingly dark and unfree world. Both phrases placed the United States in explicit opposition to the oppressive forces of communism and now, particularly, fascism. Fascists typically appealed to Christians to split them away fully from Jews, whom they sought to persecute and, in the Nazi case, exterminate. Thus, the Judeo-Christian tradition went far beyond its occasional earlier use as a theological assertion about Jesus fulfilling ancient Jewish prophecies. Now, as the world slid over the precipice into World War II, appealing to an American Judeo-Christian tradition served a specifically antifascist purpose. It implicitly called Protestant Americans, in particular, to shed their traditional anti-Semitism and anti-Catholicism. Only as "one nation under God," in the 1950s language of the Pledge of Allegiance, could the United States lead a free world.[23]

The American dream, the American way of life, and the Judeo-Christian tradition helped Americans articulate their sense of themselves by the 1930s as a special people of unique national virtue. The course of the 1940s then confirmed this sentiment with a sweeping victory of arms against the Axis powers and subsequent leadership of what was often called the "free world" in a new Cold War. With an extraordinary position of relative economic might and a monopoly on nuclear weapons for several years after 1945, Americans understood themselves as a people of power as well as of righteousness. In comparison, their Western European allies in the North Atlantic Treaty Organization (NATO) took rather different lessons from the trauma of World War II. They shifted postwar government spending away from the military and toward health care, education, and social welfare. With the outbreak of war in Korea in 1950, by contrast, the United States military budget quadrupled and hardly declined for the next four decades. "The budget reveals the true nature of the state," the historian James Sheehan observes, "after its deceptive ideology has been ruthlessly stripped away."[24]

The consolidation of a robust American identity in the 1940s only partially succeeded in patching over enduring tensions regarding ethnicity and race. The struggle for a civic rather than ethnoracial identity remained a work in progress. Public appeals to a Judeo-Christian tradition and winning a war against the genocidally antisemitic Nazis could not mask the persistence of anti-Jewish sentiment at home on American soil, where polls revealed it actually peaking during the war years. Restrictive immigration laws enacted between 1917 and 1924 had drastically reduced the number of new European arrivals who were Roman Catholic or Jewish, as native-born Protestants sought to preserve their demographic dominance. A generation with few newcomers then encouraged a shift of Americans previously seen as outsider "ethnics" to be more fully subsumed in the broad category of "white," even as, ironically, scientists and anthropologists in the same years moved away from using race as a meaningful category. The drive for unity showed up in the common scenes of multiethnic platoons in U.S. wartime films, with their members carefully noted to include surnames like the Irish O'Sullivan and the Jewish Cohen.[25]

These platoons often had a single black GI, too. But race remained the fundamental challenge to a cohesive national identity. The whiteness that increasingly included Catholic and Jewish ethnics was defined by its exclusion of Americans of African and of Asian heritage. Thus the United States fought World War II with a racially segregated military while imprisoning Japanese Americans and Japanese nationals in stark internment camps. Adolf Hitler, for one, dismissed what he saw as a society "half Judaized, and the other half Negrified. How can one expect a state like that to hold together?" Repeated outbreaks of racial violence in U.S. cities and on U.S. military bases during the war highlighted the issue. Nonetheless, Chinese Americans were largely shielded by the U.S. alliance with China, and the immediate postwar years saw the rapid desegregation of the U.S. military and the acceleration of the campaign to end legal discrimination on the basis of race.[26]

The 1940s decade of wars, first hot and then cold, and the accompanying sense of crisis encouraged Americans to overcome their differences by emphasizing a common national identity. As in most societies, the vast majority of citizens sought to fit in, even more so in wartime. Minorities of any kind often seized the opportunity to prove their patriotism, including thousands of young Japanese American men recruited straight out of the internment camps into military service. Just as many German Americans in World War I had Anglicized their names to eliminate any signs of foreignness, so many Jewish Americans saw in World War II the chance to reduce their own markers of difference from gentile fellow citizens. In New York City, for example, thousands of name-change petitions were filed in city court during the war years, the large majority seemingly Jewish in origin, along with smaller numbers of apparently Slavic or Italian background. So Laura Ginsberg became Laura Gale, and Saul Jack Kaufman became Jack Kay, British-sounding names still providing the safest seal of American identity. The popular *Captain America* comic debuted in 1941, its Jewish authors using gentile-sounding pen names: Joe Simon (Hymie Simon) and Jack Kirby (Jacob Kurtzberg), soon joined by Stan Lee (Stanley Lieber).[27]

Even as the United States labored toward greater ethnic and racial equality in this era, building on the greater gender equality that had come with women's voting rights in 1920, one group of Americans remained outside the inclusive spirit: convicted felons. This was not unique to the United States. All societies wrestle with whether to exclude any category of people from full citizenship. The revolutionary French National Assembly of 1789, for example, famously included for the first time as French citizens non-Catholics and people in the previously excluded professions of executioner (for killing other human beings for pay) and actor (for pretending to be people they were not)—the latter would have omitted later U.S. president Ronald Reagan. People convicted of a felony lost the right to vote in most American states, a policy aimed originally at African Americans in the South after the end of slavery, who were targeted for arrest and conviction at an extremely high rate. Later in the twentieth century most states moved to reenfranchise felons upon completion of their sentences, a move toward greater inclusiveness though irrelevant to those on the receiving end of the enthusiastic American use of capital punishment, which peaked in 1935 at nearly two hundred executions that year. The centripetal force of a common American identity in the World War II era had not yet shed all of its inequalities and exclusions.[28]

American Culture for All

At the very moment that Americans were consolidating a sense of national unity and purpose in the early 1940s, the United States broke through the clouds of international conflict into the clear air of unprecedented global power and influence. Its enemies Germany, Japan, and Italy—recently so potent—now lay prostrate and militarily occupied. Its Western European allies had been stunned by the costs of the war, both the formally victorious British and the defeated and only lately liberated French, Belgians, and

Dutch. They faced the imminent loss of their global empires. The Soviet Union occupied eastern and much of central Europe, but its economy and population had been devastated by fighting the Germans. At home, by contrast, demands for war goods had reignited the stunningly productive U.S. economy after the 1930s. Director of War Mobilization and Reconversion Fred Vinson observed that "the American people are in the pleasant predicament of having to learn to live 50 percent better than they have ever lived before." With 5.3 million American service personnel abroad in 1945, stationed on every continent and every ocean, the United States was poised for maximum impact on the world.[29]

Confident in the rightness and naturalness of their culture, Americans carried it with them abroad and expected others to embrace it. The appeal of what they thought of as a culture of individual freedom seemed obvious. Who would reject self-government and personal liberty? "It was God Himself who placed in every human heart the love of liberty," William Jennings Bryan's presidential campaign platform had announced in 1900. "He never made a race of people so low in the scale of civilization or intelligence that it would welcome a foreign master." Americans had long rejected authoritarian options, beginning with the British monarchy, whose origins Thomas Paine had famously skewered in his 1776 treatise *Common Sense*. A "French bastard [William the Conqueror in 1066], landing with an armed banditti, and establishing himself king of England against the consent of the natives, is in plain terms a very paltry rascally original" monarch. Inherited dynasties could all be traced back, Paine had argued, ultimately to a "principal ruffian of some restless gang." For Americans in the mid-twentieth century, that principal ruffian was now most likely Vladimir Lenin of the Soviet Union and the restless gang the Bolsheviks.[30]

Americans abroad at the dawn of the Cold War represented a culture of personal fulfillment through individual opportunity. They stood in stark contrast to the collectivist trends visible elsewhere: in the Labour Party's 1945 victory in the United Kingdom, in the Communist Party and Socialist Party electoral gains in France and Italy, and in China's Communist Revolution of 1949. Leftist critics denounced as imperialist such early U.S. Cold War policies as the Marshall Plan and the creation of NATO. Most Americans, however, would have agreed with the formulation used by Senator Charles Sumner to describe Radical Reconstruction in the post–Civil War South: "Call it imperialism, if you please; it is simply the imperialism of the Declaration of Independence, with all its promises fulfilled." Helping others to access life, liberty, and the pursuit of happiness seemed simply commonsensical.[31]

All societies balance the needs of the individual and the community, and American culture stood at the far individualist end of the range. This was a culture of disruption and change. Entrepreneurship and risk taking were widely admired and even revered in the United States. Technological innovation and novel consumer goods abounded. Economic and political liberty depended on each other. "Individual self-reliance and independence of spirit are the greatest sources of strength in this democracy of ours," President Harry Truman explained in 1950. "Our form of society is strong exactly where dictatorships are weak. We believe in self-reliant individuals." Individualism and entrepreneurship encouraged Americans to move in pursuit of new opportunities, often leaving behind extended families and traditions. American society by the mid-twentieth century was the most mobile in human history, powered by ubiquitous automobiles and inexpensive gasoline.[32]

A culture of mobility, change, and disruption was, by definition, not a conservative culture. Many Americans may have imagined themselves as conservatives, but they lived in and celebrated a society, for all its limitations, of remarkable relative individual freedom. True conservatives instead sought to keep things as they were, not to change them. The eighteenth-century Anglo-Irish writer and politician Edmund Burke, modern conservatism's progenitor, emphasized the slow, steady accretion of tradition within any society as the foundation of social order. In this view, societies were distinctive and orderly in their own ways, deriving specifically from their particular histories. They looked not solely forward, as U.S. culture did, but also backward. Even the revolutionary communist regimes of the Cold War, ironically, looked backward to the sacred texts of Marx and Lenin, in order to tease out their meanings as a predicted path forward.[33]

While Burke and a few more recent conservatives highlighted the organic character of differences among societies, most modern Americans tended instead toward a more universalist understanding of human cultures. People were people, for the most part—and surely they wanted to live like Americans. When President Truman in 1947 bisected the globe's enormous diversity into just two "alternative ways of life," echoing the biblical division of goats from sheep, he articulated the commonsensical American assumption that no people would knowingly choose communist enslavement over democratic capitalist freedom. All people desired freedom; only despots kept them in chains. Freedom was the natural state of human beings. So the United States was not opposed to any other *peoples* but only to oppressive regimes. Other *peoples* identified with the United States, with both the American people and the U.S. government, in common American thinking.[34]

President Woodrow Wilson had placed this assumption front and center in the first U.S. engagement in a global war. "We have no quarrel with the German people," Wilson announced in 1917 as he asked Congress for a declaration of war. "We have no feeling towards them but one of sympathy and friendship." The enemy, he said, was solely "the Prussian autocracy," although, in fact, anti-German sentiment abounded in the United States. Twenty years later, most Americans were inclined to see the German people as not really responsible for the Holocaust and another war in Europe but rather as themselves the first victims of "Nazi gangsters." Late in World War II, President Franklin Roosevelt continued to insist that "we bring no charge against the German race" but only against "the Nazi conspirators."[35]

This American view of other peoples carried forward into the Cold War. In the midst of the escalating nuclear missile crisis in Cuba in 1962, Secretary of State Dean Rusk insisted that the United States had "no quarrel with the Cuban people—only with the regime that has fastened itself upon that country." Such parasitical governments operated like leeches, in this view, drawing the lifeblood out of oppressed peoples. The U.S. Congress and President Dwight Eisenhower issued the first annual "Captive Nations Declaration" in 1959 to highlight the injustice of peoples kept unfree in Eastern Europe. Communist rulers were merely the latest in a long, grim history of authoritarian opponents of democratic self-determination.[36]

Foreigners, in other words, could be much more like Americans, if only they were allowed to. This way of thinking about hostile governments and the peoples they ruled continued on after the end of the Cold War. In the most dramatic example, the 2003 U.S. invasion of Iraq and overthrow of its government proceeded on the promise of Vice President Richard Cheney that "we will, in fact, be greeted as liberators." Partially true at first, the assumption quickly broke down as the U.S. occupation lingered and armed resistance spread. But mainstream American thinking and the policies that flowed therefrom had remained consistently optimistic across the twentieth century. This was a liberal, universalist vision of American culture and government as optimal for everyone. This was not a conservative, Edmund Burke–style understanding of societies as organic, coherent, and fundamentally different from one another.[37]

Perceptions followed the unfolding of events. The sweep of global history during the first half of the twentieth century had bolstered American assumptions about the essential importance of individuals and their liberty. The First World War had destroyed the four great empires that ruled from the Alps to the North Pacific (Ottoman, Austro-Hungarian, German, and Russian) and sent shock waves through the remaining Western ones. The Great War, as it was then known, had been "a war of empires, fought primarily by empires and for the survival or expansion of empire," the historians Robert Gerwarth and Erez Manela observed. But it resulted instead in the ascendancy of "the logic of popular rule, which argued that political legitimacy derived not from divine sanction but from the people, [and] had finally, after a long and arduous process, achieved near universal recognition." The 1919 Treaty of Versailles and the other postwar accords emphasized the group rights of minorities in the realms of language, education, and religious autonomy within the new states carved out of the defunct empires.[38]

When World War II delivered another staggering blow to the remaining Western European empires, the international agreements that followed reached beyond minority-group rights this time to a more explicit enunciation of individual human rights. The opening lines of the charter of the new United Nations in 1945 emphasized "fundamental human rights" and "the dignity and worth of the human person." The United Nations' Universal Declaration of Human Rights in 1948 laid out in great detail "the equal and inalienable rights of all members of the human family." Some nervous white Southerners worried about the implications for racial segregation at home. But to most Americans the United Nations' language would have seemed familiar and commonsensical, perhaps even an example of Senator Sumner's "imperialism of the Declaration of Independence."[39]

In the aftermath of the Holocaust and their joint defeat of genocidal fascism, the United States and Soviet Union set forth in a new competition for worldwide leadership. Their capitalist and socialist models offered alternative paths to a fully modern, self-governing society. In the subsequent decades of the Cold War, the competition aimed primarily at the audience of the so-called Third World, newly emerging from European colonial rule, first in Asia and the Middle East and then in Africa. Imperialism receded rapidly in the third quarter of the twentieth century. So, too, did associated biological theories of human difference that came to be known in retrospect as "scientific racism." "No longer were certain groups seen as innately incapable of progress," the historian Sara Fieldston explained. "Instead, all people of the world, given the proper tutelage, might advance along the path to modernity." The historian Susan Carruthers identified "an emergent postwar sensibility of same-under-the-skin cosmopolitanism." Kurt Vonnegut, a novelist and World War II veteran, recalled of his postwar anthropology studies at the University of Chicago, funded by the GI Bill of Rights: "At that time they were teaching that there was absolutely no difference between anybody."[40]

U.S. policy makers and social scientists in the postwar decades used the language of "development" and "modernization" to describe the path forward for poorer, less-industrialized lands. The theory of development asserted that "all nations followed a common historical path and that those in the lead had a moral duty to aid those who followed," the historian Nick Cullather explained. There was no question which nation was furthest out front by economic measurements. President Truman's secretary of state, Dean Acheson, memorably observed that "in the final analysis, the United States was the locomotive at the head of mankind." Modernization theorists, who became particularly influential in the early 1960s, understood the United States as the world's first truly modern state. It was liberal, capitalist, and pluralist, in contrast to traditional societies burdened by older cultural and religious hierarchies. Modernizers aimed to help Third World societies move up the American path to health and success. Communists, from this perspective, were like jackals waiting to pick off weak societies at their moments of vulnerability in the transition to modern democracy and capitalism.[41]

Not every American, of course, saw the world in such universalist terms during the Cold War years. The cultural differences struck plenty of U.S. travelers abroad much harder than the similarities, and American scholarly experts focused on other areas of the world tended to remain cultural relativists. Some of the American public retained older ideas of the hierarchical Right. Many white Southerners and more than a few non–Southerners, for example, resisted the rising force of racial egalitarianism in the 1950s and 1960s, preferring not to think of nonwhite peoples abroad as being similar to Americans, or at least to white Americans. And some of the public resisted the brothers–under–the–skin logic from the other side, that of the multicultural Left. The U.S. debacle in Southeast Asia raised questions about whether Vietnamese really aspired to be like Americans, as did revolutions from Cuba to Nicaragua to Iran. Left-leaning critics feared that U.S. support for undemocratic governments abroad might serve as a new kind of informal imperialism.

At the height of U.S. global influence in the second half of the twentieth century, however, mainstream American thinking retained great optimism about the U.S. model for the rest of the world. "What's wrong with the kind of urge that gives people libraries, hospitals, baseball diamonds, and movies on a Saturday night?" the actor Humphrey Bogart asked in the popular 1954 Hollywood film *Sabrina*. The success—not perfection, but success—of American society seemed simply obvious to his fellow citizens, as did its attractiveness to others. This kind of innocence survived defeat in Vietnam and received a renewed boost from the demise of the Soviet Union in 1991 and the disappearance of a socialist alternative to the U.S. model of liberal democratic capitalism. The September 11, 2001, attacks therefore stunned most Americans. "I'm amazed that there is such misunderstanding of what our country is about, that people would hate us," President George W. Bush ruminated. "I am, I am—like most Americans, I just can't believe it. Because I know how good we are, and we've got to do a better job of making our case."[42]

If support for anticommunist but authoritarian regimes undercut some of what Americans hoped would be the appeal of American culture in the Third World, in Europe it was often Americans' public piety that seemed most jarring. Western European public culture had become deeply secular by the end of the twentieth century, while Americans moved in the other direction. President-elect Dwight Eisenhower in 1952 proclaimed the importance of democratic self-government being "founded in a deeply felt religious faith, and I don't care what it is," and by the late 1970s each new U.S. president felt pressure to speak openly about a personal relationship with God. "There is a kind of American speech that sounds too inflated to Europeans," the prominent British literary theorist Terry Eagleton observed, an official patriotic rhetoric "too pious, elevated, hand-on-heart and histrionic for us jaded Europeans." Political discourse in Europe, Eagleton concluded, "is much more downbeat. You might get away with a reference to freedom, but certainly not to God. Suggesting the Almighty has special affection for your nation"—which Americans do regularly— "would sound as absurd as claiming that he has a special affection for gummy bears." Americans' sense of their own culture as a successful and even divinely sanctioned model for others did not always find receptive audiences abroad, even as it remained common sense to most of them.[43]

The Spread of English

One of the most distinctive features of late-twentieth-century world history was the rising tide of American-accented English. To Americans this seemed normal, another aspect of pervasive U.S. influence abroad and another indicator of the attraction of other peoples to American culture. The expansion of American English was not mere destiny, however. It had a particular history that unfolded over time, that could have happened differently, and that held no guarantees for the future.

People talk. Human history up until about 1500 CE saw the continued diversification of cultures as people spread all over the earth. They wound up with thousands of different languages. In order to communicate with foreigners, they sometimes learned the languages of others. Powerful states drew outsiders to learn their languages, which opened up opportunities for these speakers. Ambitious East Asians learned Mandarin Chinese, just as Cold War Eastern Europeans learned Russian. In the ancient Mediterranean world, Greek emerged as the common tongue of cosmopolitan peoples, replaced later by Latin with the rise of the Roman Empire. In the early modern period, as European states grew powerful and began building overseas empires, the Latin-derived Romance language of the mightiest continental power, the Enlightenment-leading kingdom of France, gradually surfaced as the predominant vehicle for international diplomacy and commerce. Worldly travelers and educated elites across Europe and beyond communicated in French well into the nineteenth century.[44]

But just as British forces defeated French troops across the globe in the Seven Years War a decade before the American Revolution, so too did English steadily come to surpass and supplant French as the dominant means of international communication. By the mid-1800s the British had built the most extensive empire in world history, on which the sun reportedly never set. The very lines of longitude for locating places around the Earth began at 0 degrees in Greenwich, London. The long arm of the British navy and British trade seized attention around the globe, helping win converts to the English tongue. An intellectually curious young Japanese named

Fukuzawa Yukichi, for example, moved to Nagasaki in 1854 at age nineteen in order to learn Dutch—and thus more about the outside world—from the small colony of Dutch traders long allowed to reside there. Within a few years, he realized they were being replaced by other Western traders whose words mystified him until he determined that "as certain as the day, English was to be the most useful language of the future," and he switched to learning this new language of power.[45] British settlers built new states across the globe that evolved into important independent nations, including Canada, Australia, South Africa, and New Zealand, all benefiting from the influence of British cultural reach and expanding the Anglophonic sphere. None carried more weight than the original breakaway bundle of English colonies, the United States, which seized its own overseas empire from Spain in 1898.

The United States thus rose to world power in the twentieth century at the very moment when the economic and military might of the British Empire had moved the English language to the center of international affairs. The great Prussian statesman and German unifier Otto von Bismarck claimed that the decisive factor in world affairs in the late nineteenth century was "the fact that the North Americans speak English." Americans benefited directly from British cultural power, and the results helped shape world history across the twentieth century. "In the history of humanity, there have been many languages, including French, that served as universal languages," notes the Japanese linguist and novelist Minae Mizumura. "Yet none of them ever ruled the world the way English does today. No language has ever been as completely and absolutely dominant."[46]

It was not that English was easier to learn than other languages. In fact, a recent study demonstrated that infants take significantly longer to learn English than Spanish. English has only the third-largest number of native speakers, after Mandarin and Spanish. But over the course of the twentieth century English became, crucially, the language with the greatest number of *non*-native speakers. English served as the lingua franca of modern educated people. Science offered a revealing demonstration of this fact. Since science requires unusual precision as well as new words to describe newly discovered phenomena, it presents a particular challenge for multilingualism. But scientists around the globe wrestle with the same kinds of problems and need to communicate and work together. So as industrialization and globalization accelerated after the late nineteenth century, the need for ready communication intensified. German remained an important scientific language well into the interwar period thanks to German innovations in chemistry, and more than ninety Russian-language scientific journals were translated abroad throughout the Cold War to keep abreast of Soviet technical advances. But English rose steadily to become the dominant language of international science.[47]

The prevalence of English reached across all disciplines in modern universities, to the benefit of Americans and residents of other Anglophone countries. The majority of the highest-rated universities in the world are in the United States, and 70 percent of Nobel laureates have either taught or are teaching in American universities. English proficiency among educated Europeans is extremely high, particularly in the Scandinavian countries and the Netherlands. Since the early twentieth century, American films, radio programs, and television shows have carried their English-language content around the globe, along with American-style popular music from jazz to rock 'n' roll to hip-hop. English even took over in the twenty-first century as the lingua franca for international bicycle-racing teams and media interactions in the most distinctively French of sporting events: the Tour de France. A string of seven victories by the American Lance Armstrong (later voided for the use of banned substances) and seven by other Anglophone riders between 2011 and 2018 reduced the incentive for young professional riders from non-Francophone countries to learn French. "English has become more and more international," the sport director of the recently dominant English Team Sky, Nicolas Portal—himself a Frenchman—admitted in 2013. "It's the language of the world, you know."[48]

Few Americans found this surprising, since they viewed their culture—and therefore the language it came in—as naturally attractive to others. Other peoples were not always so sure. As is typical of people confronting a powerful culture expanding from elsewhere, non-Americans felt ambivalent about American English and the society for which it spoke. While many were drawn to American popular culture, others were not. The French capital after World War I was one of the early places to experience the disruptive force of multitudinous American visitors and residents, stimulating a Danish visitor to exclaim, "If you go to Paris in August, you go to America!" Many French associated the United States with speed, productivity, and efficiency, visible in Americans' demands for faster restaurant and bar service. The French feared the loss of what they saw as their own more graceful and less hurried traditions. If Americans continued culturally colonizing France—itself a great colonial power—one French-man worried, in the pursuit of convenience and efficiency, "like the barbar-ians of America, we will number our streets and our boulevards." Others, both inside and outside the United States, appreciated the idea of a global language for a globalized era but preferred Esperanto, a relatively simple language constructed for that purpose in the late nineteenth century.[49]

French dissenters complained loudly about the linguistic imperialism of English as "franglais": the incursion of some eight thousand English words into common French discourse by the late twentieth century. The very scope of the problem reveals the extent of the influence of English in every-day life in non-Anglophone countries. In 2013, against great resistance, the Paris government began allowing French universities to offer courses taught only in English. Such a concession by the government of France, a nation immensely proud of its own globally influential language and cul-ture, appeared a serious cultural setback.[50]

Even the progenitors of the English language sometimes demonstrated unease with the extent to which American accents had replaced British ones, occasionally framed in nervously witty observations. In his 1887 short story, "The Canterville Ghost," Oscar Wilde suggested that "we have really everything in common with America nowadays, except, of course, lan-guage." George Bernard Shaw has long been credited with the famous but apparently apocryphal description of Americans and British as "two peo-ples divided by a common language." In the twenty-first century, Presi-dent George W. Bush's Texan pronunciation of "terrorism" sounded to many British ears closer to "tourism," causing consternation about his fre-quent warnings against "the evils of tourism." British cultural critiques often carried an element of class disdain as they surveyed certain Ameri-can linguistic imports. For example, Lady Violet, the grandmother and grande dame in the hugely popular British television series *Downton Abbey* and a representative of a leisure class of aristocrats unfamiliar with modern working hours, responded blankly to a question about plans for an upcom-ing weekend: "What is a 'weekend'?" The British critic Terry Eagleton suggests that "every now and then, an American reveals by a casual word or gesture that he or she is more alien than you might imagine. This is rather like those science fiction movies in which the extraterrestrials appear in convincing human guise, but betray by some well-nigh imperceptible blunder—a word slightly mispronounced, a coffee cup held at a bizarre angle, a tiny drop of green blood—that they are not what they seem."[51]

Americans have long been of two minds about learning other languages beside their own. On the one hand, it has been seen as a virtue and a strength. From the colonial period forward, wealthier and more educated citizens have been expected to learn at least one foreign language, most commonly French, a language long associated with high culture from art to food. Earning a PhD degree in the United States traditionally required at least a reading knowledge of a second foreign language, typically German, associated with scientific and scholarly culture. Diplomats, missionaries, and international business people all had strong incentives to learn other languages. Tens of millions of American-born citizens were children of immigrants and learned, to varying extents, the languages spoken by their parents and other older relatives. U.S. soldiers abroad often hoped a little linguistic knowledge might improve their social lives and romantic prospects, though a little occasionally proved worse than none. When the American GI Joe Hodges, serving in France in 1944, met an attractive young local woman and tried to say "How do you do?" in his very limited French, it came out instead as "How do you want to do it?" Rather than a date, he received a quick slap in the face.[52]

In the 1970s, as Latin American immigration into the United States increased and American family ties to Europe thinned, Spanish replaced French as the leading foreign language taught in U.S. schools. This reversal of Spanish and French carried class implications as Americans came to see Spanish as the language of working-class Latinos and French instead as the language of elite Europeans (no doubt to the dismay of elite Spaniards). The popular 2013 Hollywood film *Elysium* layered this linguistic shift on top of the sharpening divide between wealthy and poor. In a grim dystopian future set in the year 2154, the planet is smothered by overpopulation, disease, poverty, and ecological disaster. A tiny elite live high above Earth in the security of a pristine, celestially suburban, wheel-shaped space habitat called Elysium, having left the poor below. Up there the sleekly affluent speak English and French; down below the poor and the rough working class speak English and Spanish. The actor Matt Damon plays Max Da Costa, the good-hearted protagonist Everyman fluent in English and Spanish who lives in a rundown Latino neighborhood. The moral coding of the languages is clear.[53]

On the other hand, knowing another language has been viewed by some Americans at times as a vice. Children of immigrants tend to be highly motivated to learn English perfectly to avoid identification with the often distinctive accents of their parents and grandparents. In wartime, self-described superpatriots condemned and even assaulted residents speaking in the language of the enemy, most notably German in World War I and Japanese in World War II. Nebraska in 1919 went so far as to briefly ban primary-school instruction in foreign languages, with one perhaps apocryphal Cornhusker legislator declaring, "If the English language was good enough for Jesus Christ, it's good enough for us"—an assertion sure to have mystified a first-century Aramaic-speaking Nazarene. The uptick in Latino and Asian immigration stimulated an "English-only" backlash movement in the 1980s and 1990s that demanded rapid assimilation by newcomers. Activists sought local, state, and federal laws to eliminate accommodations to non-English speakers. For such opponents of multiculturalism, language was a portal to a potential corruption of the Republic. To think like Americans, people had to talk like Americans.[54]

The long-term trajectory of Americans learning languages other than English has been clearly downward. Schools and colleges have reduced foreign-language requirements. The only foreign "language" seeing dramatic growth in classroom enrollments is computer coding. Latin, once a central part of a serious education, is now found only occasionally in a U.S. classroom. Its most prominent continuing use may be numerical, in the annual designation of the professional football championship game. This huge television extravaganza came labeled in 2015, for example, as Super Bowl XLIX. The numbering system is a legacy of the origin of the event in 1967, when Roman numerals were still common enough to be understandable to average citizens. But Americans today seem more likely to imagine XLIX as a super-large clothing size rather than merely the number 49.

The continuing spread of global English allowed more people to communicate with one another more rapidly, both Americans and non-Americans, while also encouraging Americans to remain ignorant of other languages and thus of many aspects of other cultures. When Americans traveled abroad, and most particularly when they went to fight wars abroad, in Vietnam and elsewhere, they primarily depended on others to translate for them. So they were drawn to those foreigners who knew English. Very few of the Americans occupying Iraq after 2003 "could speak more than a few words of Arabic," the journalist Dexter Filkins noted, just as very few had spoken any Vietnamese thirty-five years earlier. "A remarkable number of them didn't even have translators. That meant that for many Iraqis, the typical nineteen-year-old army corporal from South Dakota was not a youthful innocent carrying America's goodwill; he was a terrifying combination of firepower and ignorance." It was not a recipe for successful communication.[55]

Filkins described the shooting and killing of almost an entire family of Iraqi civilians fleeing the fighting in Baghdad in a minivan. They had failed to stop soon enough for U.S. Marines manning a roadblock, who were jumpy from recent suicide bombings. As the only survivor, a fifteen-year-old boy covered in his father's blood, sat weeping by the roadside, one of the Marines muttered, "What could we have done?" A corporal explained: "We yelled at them to stop. Everybody knows the word 'stop.' It's universal." Counting on others to communicate for them, Americans abroad far too often fell short of the mark. The global spread of English both empowered and undermined them.[56]

The United States has long been the world's most diverse great power. It was always multicultural, just as it was always multiracial, multiethnic, and multireligious. It has long received the largest number of immigrants of any single nation. At no point in history could American society be understood as simply homogeneous. "I am large, I contain multitudes," the poet Walt Whitman wrote. If some of American diversity resulted from its demographic history, some also derived from geography. Of all the major immigrant-receiving nations of the modern era, such as Canada and Australia, the United States has by far the most diverse geography and climate, ranging from the tropical to the arctic. The resulting diverse regional economies within the country have been peopled with the varied migrants settling in these lands. From its origins to the twenty-first century, American society developed with a greatly variegated economy and culture. It has seemed second nature to Americans to be part of a large, complex nation.[57]

Such diversity has not prevented the evolution, particularly since the late nineteenth century, of a robust shared national identity. Technological innovations and international crises pulled citizens into a more centralized and unified society. It came to be common sense among most Americans by the middle of the twentieth century that they were a uniquely free and entrepreneurial people who lived in a nation of unusual opportunity. This was precisely why so many people had migrated to the United States from every corner of the world. Such an exceptionalist understanding of the nation's history underpinned Americans' confidence in their newly dominant position in the world after 1945.

The common sense about American freedom and opportunity did not hold that the country was perfect. Mark Twain had earlier gibed his fellow citizens in a fashion that would continue to make sense through the Cold War anticommunist political repression of the early 1950s: "It is by the goodness of God that in our country we have those three unspeakably precious things: freedom of speech, freedom of conscience, and the prudence never to practice either of them." Struggles over economic reform and social justice continued from the Progressive era in the early 1900s, through the New Deal order of the 1930s through the 1960s, to the conservative era that followed. It was a work in progress. Along the way, however, the extraordinary events of World War II and the onset of the Cold War thrust the United States into unprecedented global involvement and influence, leaving one out of every twenty-seven Americans stationed overseas in 1945. Americans at home and abroad engaged with non-Americans in larger numbers than they ever had before, and they did so with a common assumption that other peoples were, in their hearts, for the most part similar to Americans and eager to live more like Americans.[58]

CHAPTER III

Inbound

Immigrants from Internal Threat to Incorporation

Migration has shaped all societies. Since the first *Homo sapiens* walked out of Africa some sixty thousand years ago, people have refused to stay put. The reasons have been many and the means of transportation diverse, but people keep moving. In every modern nation, borders have changed, and residents have never shared a fully uniform ethnicity or lineage of descent. This has been true of the lands of the "Old World" Eastern Hemisphere of Europe, Africa, Asia, the Middle East, and Australasia. It has been even truer of the "New World" Western Hemisphere of North and South America, with its post-Columbus indigenous-population decline and vast inflows of transoceanic migrants, both voluntary and enslaved.

All modern nations have received new peoples in one form or another. But the story of the Americas was different. After the original human settlers found their way from Siberia into what is now Alaska, in a colder era when ice provided a land bridge, they spread throughout the Western Hemisphere, all the way to the southern tip of Patagonia. When warmer temperatures some 13,000 years ago melted the ice and rising sea levels cut off Alaska from Siberia—the Americas from Asia, one hemisphere from the other—these first peoples developed thereafter in isolation from the larger Eastern Hemisphere. Just over five hundred years ago, the voyages of Columbus and subsequent European explorers then created a reconnection, bringing new weapons and, worse, new diseases. The existing population plummeted. The result was a tremendous availability of new land and, with Europe's rapid population growth in the nineteenth century, an unprecedented movement of people across the Atlantic Ocean.

As the part of the Americas both closest in geography and most familiarly temperate in climate, the lands of what became the United States attracted the bulk of outbound Europeans. The relative political liberty of the United States, at least for white migrants, added to the appeal, as did the availability of both arable farmland and, later, industrial employment. The United States thus became the greatest immigrant nation, with far and away the largest foreign-born population of any country (more than 44 million in 2017). It also developed as by far the most demographically diverse of the great powers, emerging in the later twentieth century with the largest economy, the most powerful military force, and the third-largest national population. This history did not render the United States "exceptional" in the way that term is typically used to indicate patriotic sentiment, but it did make the country distinctive in its combination of diversity and power.[1]

How Americans *felt* about the diversity brought by immigrants varied dramatically. The Declaration of Independence in 1776 cited a key list of King George III's "repeated injuries and usurpations, all having in direct object the establishment of an absolute Tyranny over these States." Chief among them were his efforts "to prevent the population of these States; for that purpose obstructing the laws for Naturalization of Foreigners; refusing to pass others to encourage their migrations hither." Subsequent encouragement of immigration by the new U.S. government led to nearly one hundred thousand new European arrivals on American shores in the 1790s. The founding generation considered robust immigration essential for national success. As a new republic, the United States also served as a refuge for political dissidents fleeing oppression and retribution from autocratic rulers in Europe.[2]

In his 1849 novel *Redburn*, the great American writer Herman Melville captured the widely held sense of the United States as defined by the inflow of migrants from around the globe. "Settled by the people of all nations, all nations may claim her for their own. You can not spill a drop of American blood without spilling the blood of the whole world." Melville concluded, "We are not a narrow tribe . . . our blood is as the flood of the Amazon, made up of a thousand noble currents all pouring into one. We are not a nation, so much as a world." This was true enough in the mid-nineteenth century with a population almost entirely stemming from Europe and Africa. By the late twentieth century, the American populace had grown into even more of a world nation, with large new streams from Latin America and Asia.[3]

Other Americans, ever since independence, demonstrated less comfort with the ethnic, racial, and cultural diversity accompanying immigration. International crises, in particular, revealed enduring anxiety about people identified as outsiders. The two world wars in the twentieth century provided the largest challenges in this regard. From each of these global conflicts emerged a vast new revolutionary communist state, the Soviet Union out of World War I and the People's Republic of China following World War II. Their appearance exacerbated the hyperpatriotic and xenophobic inclinations of some Americans. Both cases resulted in a postwar backlash of political repression and anti-immigrant sentiment, commonly known by the labels of "100% Americanism" after World War I and "McCarthyism" after World War II—or simply the first and second Red Scares. The immediate postwar years marked high points on the graph of varying but persistent American anxiety about foreigners.

The reception of large numbers of immigrants represented a tradeoff for existing American citizens. Excitement about new workers, new skills, and new energies, along with pride in the nation's attractiveness to others and the provision of refuge to many, jostled against concerns about foreign ideas, different cultural values, public health, and competition for jobs. Ambivalence and contestation about newcomers remained a constant theme in the American past. At its core was the question of how fast and how fully newcomers would fit into American society.

Europeans from Columbus to Ellis Island and Beyond

After the post-Columbus thinning of the first peoples of the Americas, the demographic history of the lands that became the United States developed primarily as a story of Europeans. Russian explorers pushed into the Pacific Northwest, French trappers and priests mapped and settled the St. Lawrence and Mississippi River valleys, and Spanish (later Mexican) citizens dominated the desert Southwest. Adventurous English established the Atlantic coastal colonies that formed the core of the eventual American state and its relatively democratic character. Enslaved laborers from Africa formed the one significant demographic exception, constituting at times a majority in colonies such as South Carolina and some 20 percent of the total American population at independence. But the end of the slave trade in 1808 and accelerating flows of European migration in the nineteenth century reduced the African American share of the U.S. population to roughly 13 percent, where it has more or less remained ever since.[4]

The scale of European emigration to the Americas and particularly the United States should not be exaggerated. What the historian Alfred Crosby called the "Caucasian tsunami" made up of "the greatest wave of humanity ever to cross oceans" may have helped determine North American demography for generations, but it represented a very small slice of Europeans. The vast majority of people from that continent never left home at all. If they did, it was more often for a different destination within Europe. Even in the peak emigration years at the start of the twentieth century, the highest national departure rate was 6.6 out of 1,000 from Norway, while the lowest was France, with a mere 0.2 out of 1,000. Most people simply stayed where they were. Among the many roadblocks to departure, even in times of hunger and hardship, was the fear of losing what one had. In the Czech author Josef Kajetan Tyl's 1850 play *The Forest Nymph, or A Journey to America*, a group of naïve Czech villagers are seduced into leaving by an unscrupulous emigration agent, robbed by gypsies while en route, and assaulted by Native Americans while living in a community of fanatical, hypocritical Quakers. The play ends with them returning at last to their own Bohemian village, delighted to be home, as one of them declares: "I now feel as if my heart has burst its strings! The Bohemian climate—and the beer! America can't measure up to that."[5]

Some of the first people whom early English migrants to the North American colonies mistrusted were not foreign folk but simply one another. Puritan settlers in Massachusetts sought their own freedom of worship but had little patience for dissenters, who they believed went too far. Roger Williams and Anne Hutchinson, for example, were exiled to Rhode Island, where their heresies might do less damage. Their free thinking and tolerance of other dissenters helped lay the cultural foundation in Providence for the later establishment of Brown University, the first college to accept students regardless of religious affiliation. Charges of witchcraft in the 1690s against two hundred people and the execution of twenty of them in Salem, Massachusetts, made clear that English descent provided no guarantee of safety.

England remained the touchstone for American thinking about immigrants and foreigners well into the nineteenth century. Most citizens of the early U.S. republic traced their heritage to the British Isles. They spoke English in a new nation founded on British ideas about government and liberty. They were acutely aware of Britain's world-straddling economic and military might, which continued to grow despite American independence. But resentment of the British monarchy and aristocracy also lingered long after the War of Independence, stimulated anew by essentially refighting the Revolution in the War of 1812 and by lingering border conflicts with British North America, as Canada was then known. U.S. policy toward Great Britain was inevitably contentious, with elements of Anglophobia lingering longest in the Democratic Party.[6]

This ambivalence largely dissolved by 1900. Over the course of the nineteenth century, U.S. continental expansion and reconsolidation after the Civil War eased American anxieties about British influence and allowed memories of earlier military conflicts with Britain to fade. The appearance of large numbers of new immigrants, particularly from Ireland in the 1840s, encouraged many native-born Americans to identify culturally with what they called Anglo-Saxonism. The embrace of Englishness has persisted ever since. This attitude can be measured in U.S. readership of English authors, U.S. tourism in Britain, enduring American fascination with British aristocracy and the royal family, and remarkably close U.S. political and military ties with the British government. In his recent Pulitzer Prize–winning novel *The Sympathizer*, Viet Thanh Nguyen described the impact of a scholarly visitor from the United Kingdom, whose "English accent . . . affected Americans the way a dog whistle stimulates canines" and whose "heritage and accent triggered the latent Anglophilia." The narrator, a Vietnamese refugee in 1970s America, concludes: "I was immune to the accent, not having been colonized by the English"—leaving open the question of how he might have responded to a Parisian voice.[7]

As white Americans in the middle decades of the nineteenth century grew more comfortable with an Anglo-Saxon identity, they regarded other European newcomers more skeptically. The crucial question was how much others might be improved in order to become more like Americans and English. The wave of revolutions rolling across the European continent in 1848 highlighted this issue. Would the revolutionaries in such places as France, Hungary, Italy, and the German states prove to be orderly and freedom loving, as white Americans imagined themselves to be, or would they turn out to be too radical to fit the U.S. model? Americans debated such questions as events in Europe helped shape the ebb and flow of emigration across the Atlantic. Later, by the middle of the twentieth century, European immigrants in the United States would come to be categorized together as simply "white" and seen as readily assimilable. But such a clear identity remained elusive in the second half of the 1800s, as first Irish and then southern and eastern Europeans journeyed by the tens of millions to American shores. What today is considered an ethnic and therefore cultural and changeable identity—Hungarian, Italian—was then more often framed as a racial and thus biological and permanent identity, such as the Teutonic (German) race or the Irish race.

The Europeans who perhaps most baffled Americans were the French. The French-speaking *habitants* of Québec fought fiercely against American colonists in the French and Indian War, but fifteen years later French forces under Marquis de Lafayette provided crucial assistance to the American War for Independence from Britain. The French Revolution unfolded just a few years after the American one, and the two became twin beacons of liberty but also competing models. There were far fewer French immigrants to the United States than from other parts of northwestern Europe. Place names demonstrate this marginal presence, with most Francophone geographical designations on American soil the result merely of early French exploration along the Great Lakes and the Mississippi River. The only small exception was the French refugees from Acadia—in today's eastern Canadian Maritime Provinces—dispatched to southwestern Louisiana in the 1750s by the British, there to become known eventually as Cajuns. But there was no equivalent south of the Great Lakes of the predominantly French-settled Québec to the north.[8]

The absence of a large French presence in the United States reflected the particularities of French history, with relatively greater economic opportunities stimulating less emigration. Their lack of need for a foothold in the boisterous new American nation seemed to fit with France's reputation as the land of cosmopolitan high culture: art, literature, philosophy, food, wine, music, and even romance. Thomas Jefferson and other Francophiles greatly admired Paris and the lifestyle of its educated classes, and France remained a primary destination for American tourists (and later students) abroad.

Elite French culture contrasted starkly with a decidedly practical and entrepreneurial American society. The realms of art, literature, and philosophy seemed quite different from Americans' emphasis on business and profit. The brief boom in Americans living in Paris after World War I, particularly writers and artists, reflected precisely their appreciation of France's differences from the United States. The U.S.-French alliances in both world wars brought the nations and peoples together but also highlighted American military power and French dependence, which encouraged elements of U.S. condescension and French resentment, leading to what the historian Frank Costigliola has called "the cold alliance."[9]

Ambivalent feelings toward France have persisted across the American past. "Oh, the French! The unspeakables!" Mark Twain satirized his countrymen's sentiments. "I don't think they have improved a jot since they were turned out of hell." Others were less amused. French resistance to U.S. hegemony during and after the Cold War stimulated particular American annoyance on the Right. France's refusal to support the U.S. invasion of Iraq in 2003 led Republicans on Capitol Hill to rename French fries "freedom fries" and French toast "freedom toast" in the congressional dining room. President George W. Bush, who was proud of his ability to speak some Spanish, belittled an American reporter for asking a question in French to Jacques Chirac, France's president. Bush's staff mocked Democratic presidential candidate John Kerry in the 2004 campaign for being "too French" and even for "looking French," since Kerry spoke French fluently. House Majority Leader Tom DeLay (R-Texas) liked to greet supportive crowds by saying, "Hi. Or, as John Kerry would say, 'Bonjour.'"[10]

Americans did not always distinguish between the character of immigrants and the fortunes of the places from which they came. Newcomers from a powerful state such as Britain carried some hint of that authority, while those from a weaker nation such as nineteenth-century China, as we shall see, had no such reflected glory—nor possible appeal for assistance. Migrants from German-speaking areas of Europe provide a particularly useful example because their homeland's status changed dramatically in the modern era. The first German came to the British American colonies in 1607, at Jamestown, Virginia, but large numbers began arriving only after the founding of Germantown in what is now a neighborhood of northwestern Philadelphia in 1683. Some one hundred thousand Germans migrated to the colonies, particularly Pennsylvania, by the time of U.S. independence, making them the single largest non-British immigrant group of the 1700s.[11]

Their new neighbors were not quite sure what to make of the Germans. One colonial official in New York called them "a laborious and honest but a headstrong and ignorant people." They seemed to work hard, with a practical bent, but they also struck some observers as clannish and perhaps a little simpleminded. Their numbers moved Benjamin Franklin to warn in 1751 that Pennsylvania was becoming "a Colony of Aliens, who will shortly be so numerous as to Germanize us instead of our Anglifying them and will never adopt our Language or Customs any more than they can acquire our Complexion." Franklin was giving voice to a common concern about newcomers' cultural differences. But he also revealed the impermanence of ideas about color and race, as German complexions would come to be seen as identical to those of English descent—thus the term "Anglo-Saxon," since Saxons were early Germans.[12]

Five and a half million Germans moved to the United States in the 1800s. By 1860 one-third of foreign-born residents were German. The presence of so many mostly Roman Catholic newcomers, along with their fellow congregants from Ireland, stimulated the first large-scale nativist reaction: the creation of the American or Know-Nothing Party, an 1850s precursor to the rise of the Republican Party. Since the unified nation of Germany was not established until 1871, people coming from those lands tended to identify themselves more narrowly as "Palatines," "Prussians," or "Bavarians." Only upon arrival in the United States were they identified by others primarily as Germans. The same process of discovering their new national identity only by sojourning abroad happened with migrants from the Italian peninsula as well, where local and regional identities superseded the newer national one. Sicilians and Napolitanos discovered in Boston and New York that they were actually Italian.[13]

The creation of a unified German empire in 1871 out of the dozens of smaller German-speaking states marked a turning point for how Americans understood Germanness. In modern Germany's first fifteen years of existence, another 1.5 million of its residents emigrated, 95 percent of them to the United States. Americans alternatively admired and worried about the rising Central European power. A bipolar stereotype emerged. On the one hand, Germans were seen as educated and cultured people from the land of Beethoven, Bach, and the great new research universities making dramatic advances in technology, science, and industry. On the other hand, the imperial German government under Kaiser Wilhelm II after 1888 behaved in an increasingly autocratic and militaristic fashion. German construction of a modern oceangoing navy threatened Britain and France, and Americans feared growing German investments in Latin America. This bifurcated view showed up in education as well. Over a thousand young Americans were studying in German universities in 1880, but a dislike for German politics helped reduce that number by two-thirds by 1912. Yet in the early twentieth century fully one-quarter of American public high school students were still enrolled in German language courses.[14]

Fighting two world wars against Germany failed to resolve American ambivalence toward people from that country. German immigrants by the twentieth century had for the most part become well integrated into middle-class American life. Few worried much anymore, as Benjamin Franklin had, about their complexion. Racial Anglo-Saxonism had folded them fully into the top tier of white-American status. This was part of the reason for American hesitancy about entering World War I, including the first three years of neutrality. Once Americans and Germans were actually killing each other on the battlefield, anti-German sentiment erupted across parts of the United States, with harassment, occasional violence, and a crackdown on German language instruction and cultural organizations. But even in his declaration of war in 1917, President Woodrow Wilson carefully distinguished between the regime in Berlin and the character of the German people. "We have no quarrel with the German people," he declared. The menace to the peace and freedom of the world "lies in the existence of autocratic governments backed by organized force which is controlled wholly by their will, not by the will of their people." Indeed, Wilson concluded, Americans were "the sincere friends of the German people."[15]

Positive views of their German-descended fellow citizens helped Americans retain sympathetic feelings toward Germans in the Nazi era, even as they fought against them in World War II. Once again, ambivalence reigned. Popular support in Germany for Adolf Hitler, German responsibility for the war, and early reports of the horrific genocide of the Holocaust might have been expected to eliminate such sympathy. But Americans in the years after World War I had felt betrayed by the mixed outcome of that struggle and skeptical about reports of German war crimes. They supported the Second World War against Germany after 1941, but their most visceral hatred targeted the Japanese in the Pacific theater instead. The historian Michaela Hönicke Moore notes that "many Americans thought they knew and understood Germans" and were disinclined to see them all as Nazis. A study on the eve of the war revealed U.S. citizens ranking Germany third, not far behind Britain and France, in the psychological distance that they felt from other peoples.[16]

President Franklin Roosevelt, who generally took a darker view of the essential Germanness of the Nazi regime, remained ambivalent, wielding images of disease and gangsters to portray the Nazis as hijacking the German nation. This interpretation, widely held in the United States, positioned the German people as the first victims of Hitler. "During World War II, the United States never achieved a politically coherent consensus on whether the enemy was the Nazi regime or the German nation as a whole," Hönicke Moore concludes. "Only in retrospect did the war effort against the Third Reich take on clear purpose." Only at the very end of the fighting, as evidence of German atrocities became widely known, did U.S. public assumptions about Germans begin to waver, but they hardly collapsed. The U.S. government felt compelled to begin its widely distributed *The Soldier's Pocket Guide to Germany* with this reminder: "You are in *enemy* country! These people are not our allies or our friends." No such warning seemed necessary for U.S. troops fighting Japan.[17]

The American public's disinclination to vilify the German people eased the postwar rehabilitation of western Germany. Officers and soldiers of the American occupation forces often felt greater affinity for German civilians than for Jewish survivors of the Nazi concentration camps, who tended to be poorer, sicker, and more traumatized. The historian Susan Carruthers has demonstrated that "the surprise—sequentially repeated in Italy, Germany, and Japan—was that defeated populations behaved much better than expected." U.S. soldiers did not like to think of themselves as occupiers and did not relish the task of long-term guard service in Germany or elsewhere. But with their power, health, and relative wealth, they did often enjoy "easy access to women's bodies," by consensus the greatest common interest of these young men. The resulting sexual relationships ranged from the brutal and coercive to the fond and even permanent, and thousands of GIs eventually returned home with German wives. Here was the most powerful rejection of the idea of foreigners as ultimately different, and the pattern was repeated in other areas of U.S. military engagement during the Cold War, from England, France, and Italy to Japan, South Korea, and Vietnam.[18]

U.S. troops liberated and occupied Italy in World War II, with similar results for American understandings of Italianness. Italian migrants had been coming to the United States for sixty years by that point. They were part of a large emigration from the Italian peninsula and Sicily in pursuit of better employment opportunities within Europe and around the world.

In 1900, Italians were one of the largest immigrant groups arriving in the United States. They were parallel in many ways to Mexicans as the largest such group in 2000: primarily rural and Roman Catholic, with slightly darker complexions on average, speaking a different European language, and bringing with them a cuisine that at first smelled and tasted odd to other Americans but soon became folded into core American comfort food. Exotic at first, Italians lost their strangeness. Rhode Islanders elected John Pastore the first Italian-American U.S. senator in 1950. A year later, a huge "Italy-in-Macy's" display of merchandise directly from Italy, combined with the annual celebration of the Feast of San Gennaro in the Little Italy neighborhood of Manhattan, stimulated the *New York Times* to declare that the "rich culture and gay spirit of Italy . . . serve to remind Americans that one of our greatest sources of strength as a freedom-loving nation is the extraordinary diversity of our national origins."[19]

Immigration Policy

U.S. government policy regarding immigrants began in a radically different era from twentieth- and twenty-first-century concerns about controlling the flow of new Americans. In the early years of the American republic, policy makers simply wanted more workers. With an utterly inadequate labor force for its vast new lands and a modest central government, the United States spent little time patrolling its borders or worrying about limiting the number of newcomers. After a brief flurry of anxiety about foreign influences in the new nation, embodied in the Alien and Sedition Acts of the 1790s, U.S. officials did little to discourage new arrivals. Anti-slavery sentiment did help choke off the official trade in enslaved Africans in 1808. People from the Atlantic shores of western and northern Europe provided the bulk of immigrants through the Civil War era.

Demographic changes in the late 1800s brought nativist reactions and restrictive policies in their wake. Tens of millions of migrants from southern and eastern Europe brought new cultures and new languages to American shores. Mostly Roman Catholic or Jewish and coming from hierarchical or even feudal societies, the new immigrants seemed more foreign than the previous German or Irish immigrants. The poet Thomas Bailey Aldrich warned that "so of old / The thronging Goth and Vandal trampled Rome," a fate Americans—the modern Rome—must avoid by using a "hand of steel" to bar the door. The arrival of large numbers of Chinese laborers on the West Coast produced a fiercely xenophobic and racist backlash culminating in the 1882 Chinese Exclusion Act, the nation's first significant legislative restriction on immigration and the only one to target a single country. The banning of Chinese workers added an international element to earlier deportations within U.S. borders of fugitive slaves to the South (1850–1861) and Native Americans to the West and initiated a new era of restrictionist policy making.[20]

Tighter border controls required a more vigorous enforcement bureaucracy. The new Census Bureau after 1902 provided statistical data about the U.S. populace, including immigrants, and after 1917 foreigners arriving in the United States were required to have a passport and visa. The 1907 Marital Expatriation Act revealed a crucial gendered character to the new effort to restrict and control who was considered fully American. Under the new law, an American woman who married a foreign man lost her U.S. citizenship. This was an era when women were widely considered, both legally and culturally, to be dependent upon their closest male relative, usually a husband. The law was not applied consistently, but it revealed a period when even U.S. citizens, if female, could be quickly rendered foreign. Only after women won the nationwide right to vote in 1920 did Congress undo this loss of female citizenship, beginning with the Cable Act of 1922.[21]

The nativist sentiments visible in the late 1840s and growing since the 1880s reached a peak between 1917 and 1924. World War I and the imminent entry of the United States into that conflict stoked anxieties about negative influences from abroad. In 1917 Congress passed a new immigration law creating an "Asiatic Barred Zone" that extended to the rest of Asia (except the Philippines, still a U.S. territory) the prior ban on China and, by diplomatic agreement in 1907, Japan. The success of the Bolshevik Revolution in Russia and growing public dismay about the U.S. intervention in World War I pressed policy makers to go further to exclude potentially subversive elements. Congress passed two laws to drastically limit immigration from southern and eastern Europe, first in 1921 and then in fuller form in 1924.

The 1924 Johnson-Reed Immigration Act marked the apex of anti-immigrant sentiment in shaping U.S. public policy. The language used was often florid. "There is little or no similarity," Congressman Fred Purnell (R-IN) declared, "between the clear-thinking, self-governing stocks that sired the American people and this stream of irresponsible and broken wreckage that is pouring into the lifeblood of America the social and political diseases of the Old World." George Creel, Wilson's prominent former head of the Committee on Public Information, argued that recent immigrants were "little more than human wreckage" that was "gathered thick on the shores of the Old World, swarming like flies at every European port of embarkation." Francis Walker, MIT's president, considered the newcomers from Italy, Russia, and the Austro-Hungarian Empire to be "vast masses of peasantry, degraded below our utmost conceptions . . . beaten men from beaten races, representing the worst failures in the struggle for existence." Rural and small-town Americans in the 1920s identified urban crime and newly prominent gangsters such as Al Capone as rooted in recent Italian, Jewish, or Slavic heritage. Nativists believed the demographic composition of the nation should not change from what Creel called the "clear-eyed, clean-limbed men and women" of the "old immigration."[22]

Controlling immigration required identifying and labeling people. This involved a confusing combination of race, ethnicity, and nationality. It meant drawing up discrete boxes with firm boundaries—"Asian," "Hebrew," "Polish"—out of a continuous spectrum of human diversity across the Eurasian landmass. In particular, the Asiatic Barred Zone painted a bright line through the center of the Middle East. Chinese or Japanese might be generally seen as Asian, but what about Arabs? U.S. court decisions in the 1910s found Syrian newcomers to be sometimes Asian and sometimes Caucasian or white. The same held true for Armenians, Turks, and even Indians. The U.S. Supreme Court in the *Ozawa* (1922) and *Thind* (1923) decisions cited both scientific and cultural criteria in an effort to clarify who was actually "white." The legal system sought to pin down artificial racial boundaries on a global map even as scientific and commonsense understandings of race remained in flux.[23]

Even within Europe, the Austro-Hungarian Empire challenged Americans' race-based sense of how to categorize people. In 1909, at the peak of immigration from southern and eastern Europe, the U.S. Bureau of Immigration published a list of "races and peoples represented by those from Austria-Hungary." Austria-Hungary was a place one could be from, but Austrian was not considered a race, although Hungarian was—along with Croatian, Slovenian, Bosnian, German, Romanian, Hebrew, Ruthenian, Moravian, and another half-dozen ethnolinguistic identities. The historian Alison Frank Johnson calls this the "magical process of transformation by which one person could leave Europe as an 'Austrian' but arrive in the United States only as a 'Pole,' 'Italian,' or 'Croat.'" Americans wrestled with how to understand such newcomers as they tried to either exclude or incorporate them.[24]

The Second World War reshaped many of the crucial contours of American life, including how Americans thought about other peoples. The United States sent millions of its citizens around the globe, while the course of the fighting left the nation in a dramatically new and dominant position in the economy and politics of the postwar world. The geopolitical imperatives of the war sprang leaks in the U.S. restrictionist dam limiting immigration by race and region. Then the Cold War competition for good relations with the newly independent nations of the Third World eventually swept the dam away. U.S. soldiers brought home tens of thousands of foreign brides, and Congress allowed in large new numbers of displaced persons from World War II and refugees from the communist regimes in China, Hungary, Cuba, and Vietnam during the Cold War.[25]

Restrictionists in Congress used the anticommunist anxieties surrounding the Korean War to preserve temporarily the discriminatory 1924 national-origins system in the 1952 McCarran-Walter Act. But they had to do so over President Harry Truman's spirited veto. Competition with the Soviets about the nature of freedom and equality now undercut the use of openly racist logic in U.S. policy making. Within a few months of its passage, the war ended in Korea, and public support for the McCarran-Walter Act largely disappeared. By 1964 Secretary of State Dean Rusk told Congress that the use of race-based quotas was "indefensible from a foreign policy point of view." The Hart-Celler Immigration and Nationality Act of 1965 eliminated the national-origins system and gave priority to new criteria such as family reunification and skilled labor. Though not anticipated in 1965, this change led in a few years to a new wave of immigration from Latin America and Asia, while European numbers dropped off, thanks to political stabilization and economic recovery on that continent.[26]

The Hart-Celler Act must be understood in the context of two other crucial pieces of legislation passed in the same period. The Civil Rights Act of 1964 brought a formal end to three centuries of racially discriminatory public policy, and the Voting Rights Act of 1965 finally placed the power of the federal government behind the casting of ballots by American citizens of color. Hart-Celler would prove similarly momentous in reshaping the nation's demography and identity. No longer would future

Americans be assumed to be white. Invidious ethnic and racial distinctions began to retreat—not to disappear, but to retreat—in public life. A once essentially black and white society became rapidly more multiracial. Latinos constituted 4.5 percent of the U.S. population in 1970; by 2013, they had quadrupled to 18 percent. People of Asian lineage made up less than 1 percent in 1970; by 2013, they more than quintupled to almost 6 percent. Increasingly, in the last third of the twentieth century, foreigners from all lands could become Americans. In 2018, the United States continued to have by far the largest number of immigrants, more than 44 million, four times as many as any other single nation.[27]

Religion

Native-born American views of immigrants were often closely linked to the issue of religious diversity and toleration. The importance of religious liberty and separation of church and state in the nation's founding can be traced back to Western Europe's Christian heritage and its emphasis on individual consciousness and autonomy. But the United States had nonetheless started out as an overwhelmingly Protestant society. The arrival of the first large flows of German and Irish Roman Catholics in the 1840s aroused nativist fears, as did even more so the larger numbers of Catholics and Jews who arrived from the 1880s to World War I. The immigration restrictionists of the 1910s and 1920s were primarily anxious Protestants.[28]

World War II and the Cold War brought a transformation of mainstream American attitudes and behaviors regarding religious diversity. The United States had remained a more avowedly religious nation than other industrialized Western countries, even if its people's religious knowledge did not always keep pace with their professed piety. One thinks, for example, of the recent poll indicating that less than one-third of Americans knew that Jesus delivered the Sermon on the Mount or that 10 percent of Americans believed Joan of Arc was Noah's wife. For more than three centuries before World War II, and despite a constitutional emphasis on religious freedom, the nation's large Protestant majority had regarded Roman Catholics and Jews with tolerance at best, with skepticism at almost all times, and with often-violent disdain at countless moments. In the face of deeply antireligious totalitarian enemies, however, first Nazi Germany and then the communist Soviet Union, religious differences among Americans lost their motivating power. In their place emerged a newly public tri-faith culture under the banner of the still-fresh term "the Judeo-Christian tradition," typified by Will Herberg's prominent 1955 study entitled *Protestant-Catholic-Jew*. Mainstream American understanding of what was foreign in terms of religion—a key American concern—shrank dramatically.[29]

Anti-Catholicism had previously served as a rich seam in the mine of the American past. For the Protestant majority, the Church of Rome tended to embody the warping of religious truth, the practice of magic, and the sway of blind loyalty to authority over individual reason and conscience. "Oppression has blotted out their reason and conscience and thought," the inventor of the telegraph and leading nativist Samuel Morse explained about Catholic immigrants. As a result, "their liberty is licentiousness, their freedom, strife and debauchery." Nativists played on Protestant doubts that members of such a hierarchical church could function as independent citizens of a democratic republic. In 1928, opponents of the first Catholic presidential nominee aimed to tamp down voter turnout in the heavily Democratic South by distributing a photograph of Democratic New York Governor Al Smith cutting a ribbon for the opening of a Manhattan subway tunnel, relabeled as a secret passageway to the Vatican.[30]

Then came rapid changes. The Great Depression turned Americans' worries away from cultural and religious matters and toward economic survival. The cutting off of new immigration with the restrictive 1924 law led to the accelerating assimilation of Catholics as mainstream Americans, where they settled in as one-quarter of the nation's population. This was followed by Catholic soldiers' patriotic service in World War II, the fervent Cold War anticommunism of prominent Catholics such as Senator Joseph McCarthy and Cardinal Francis Spellman, and the election of John Kennedy to the White House in 1960. By the 1970s, even fundamentalist Protestants—traditionally the nation's fiercest anti-Catholics—were finding common ground with conservative Catholics in the New Christian Right. In 2010, the U.S. Supreme Court consisted of six Catholic justices and three Jewish justices—not a single Protestant among them. One of the most important stories of modern U.S. history is the change in perception of Roman Catholics from being essentially foreign to being instead quintessentially American.[31]

Anti-Semitism followed a similar path. An influx of Jewish immigrants in the years before World War I stimulated traditional Christian prejudice and discrimination, which actually crested only late in World War II. Then came a series of blows to that ugly tradition: the patriotic service of Jewish Americans in the U.S. military, the revelations of the full horror of the Holocaust, the Cold War imperative of equality and inclusion, and the creation of the modern state of Israel. The success of Israel, in particular, recast Jews in the minds of gentile Americans as no longer helpless victims of the Nazis but tough, virile pioneers making the desert bloom as successful farmers, despite hostility from non-European indigenous neighbors—a story that sounded, to white American ears, a lot like the story of the United States. Harry McPherson, President Lyndon Johnson's special counsel, reported back to the White House from the Middle East, where he had just observed Israel's overwhelming victory in the 1967 Six-Day War against its Arab neighbors: "Incidentally, Israel at war destroys the prototype of the pale, scrawny Jew. The soldiers I saw were tough, muscular, and sunburned." For Americans deep in war in Vietnam at the time, these were their kind of people.[32]

Discrimination against Jews in the United States, while not disappearing, declined rapidly from 1945 on. An incident early that year among American prisoners of war in Germany suggested the coming inclusiveness toward Jewish fellow citizens. Several hundred GIs had been captured in the Battle of the Bulge and were imprisoned in a Nazi POW camp near Ziegenhain. The German guards instructed all Jews among the POWs to identify themselves. Master Sergeant Roddie Edmonds of Knoxville, Tennessee, was the senior U.S. officer. He ordered all several hundred American prisoners to step forward. "They cannot all be Jews!" snapped the startled German camp commander. "We are all Jews," Edmonds insisted, citing Geneva Conventions on not identifying prisoners by religion. Enraged, the camp commander pulled out his Luger pistol, pressed it to Edmonds's forehead, and threatened to shoot him if Jewish POWs did not identify themselves. Fellow troops described Edmonds as pausing and then saying, "If you shoot, you'll have to shoot us all," which the commander chose not to do. "Although 70 years have passed," one of those Jewish POWs recalled in 2015, "I can still hear the words he said to the German camp commander."[33]

The shift away from anti-Jewish sentiment could be measured by a range of variables from university admissions processes to employment opportunities. Another was the perception of physical attractiveness. Just days after Japan's surrender ended World War II, Bess Myerson, the daughter of a house painter from the Bronx, was crowned the first Jewish Miss

America. In that era, the designation of Miss America still captured the nation's attention and granted a kind of heroine status. The nation's most fervent acclamation of female beauty did not, by definition, go to an outsider. It went to the clearest embodiment of the society's own ideals. Myerson's selection suggested that anti-Jewish sentiment in the American public, while recently broad, was evidently shallow. In their most intimate lives of romance and partnership, gentile Americans were clearly moving away from seeing Jews as significantly different from other white Americans. The percentage of Jewish Americans marrying non-Jews leapt from less than 10 percent before 1960 to more than 50 percent by 1990.[34]

Officially members of the "Hebrew race" under the 1924 national-origins system, Jewish citizens became increasingly identified in mainstream American life in the 1950s and 1960s as simply "white." The Catholics and evangelical Protestants of the New Christian Right emerged as fierce defenders of Israel by the late 1970s, and Israelis and Americans developed myriad intimate ties. While Jews remained less than 2 percent of the U.S. population, the United States nonetheless was home to roughly 40 percent of the world's Jews, similar to the percentage who lived in Israel. By 1996, Benjamin Netanyahu, Israel's new prime minister, sounded and acted precisely like an American—because he had lived extensively in the United States, where he attended high school and college and began his career. In 2015, as anti-Jewish sentiment grew more visible in Europe and festered widely in majority-Muslim countries, the columnist David Brooks noted, "this country remains an astonishingly non-anti-Semitic place." Even the resurfacing of neo-Nazi and anti-Jewish violence that followed Donald Trump's election, including the 2017 white-nationalist march in Charlottesville and the 2018 killing of eleven congregants at a Pittsburgh synagogue, could not unwind the remarkable success of Jews in American life. Both events were followed by massive public outpourings of solidarity with the victims.[35]

What the historian Peter Novick called "the rapid collapse of anti-Semitic barriers to Jewish ascent in every area of American life" came at a cost to Jewish collective identity. It was logical but also ironic that the assimilation of Jews into mainstream American life undercut the preservation of Jewish consciousness and culture. This was the enduring loss that accompanied the gains of every immigrant community. It was impossible both to be fully incorporated and to retain a fully separate identity. Demographically, Jews were literally less foreign than ever: by the 1950s, three-quarters of Jewish Americans had been born in the United States, and most were now third-generation citizens. The prominent *Jewish Daily Forward* editor Abraham Cahan noted with resignation that "the children are becoming Americanized, and it is only natural; they live in this country and it treats them as its own."[36]

The new tri-faith culture and the idea of a Judeo-Christian tradition had its skeptics, particularly at first. Some fundamentalist Protestants, who often doubted the faith of even mainline Protestants such as Episcopalians, continued to find Roman Catholics and Jews mysterious and strange. Some liberal intellectuals, for their part, worried that Catholics might be a bit like communists in their adherence to an all-encompassing hierarchical faith with an overseas leader. While Jewish and Catholic Americans shared a common goal of ending Protestant domination and exclusivity, they occasionally eyed each other with suspicion. Some American Jews considered Catholics as having been a little too comfortable with fascism, while some American Catholics suspected that Jews might be a bit too accommodating of socialism. As president during most of the 1950s, Dwight Eisenhower sought to encourage Americans' religious faith and instituted the first-ever prayers to open Cabinet meetings. But the new practice required practice. Eisenhower's secretary recalled him once leaving a Cabinet meeting, only to exclaim: "Jesus Christ, we forgot the prayer!"[37]

Americans continued to wrestle with issues of religious diversity even after the successful mainstreaming of Catholicism and Judaism. Most Protestants and other Americans had long seen members of the Church of Jesus Christ of Latter-day Saints—more commonly known as Mormons—as not quite Christian and a little peculiar. Dislike of Mormon theology, particularly polygamist practices, had led to repeated incidents of violence against Latter-day Saints during the nineteenth century, which encouraged their original flight to then-remote Utah for safety. The original platform of the new Republican Party in 1856 then aimed to keep the "twin relics of barbarism—Polygamy, and Slavery" out of the nation's western territories.[38] Modern evangelical and fundamentalist Christians still regarded Latter-day Saints, with their devotion to the Book of Mormon, as a cult, one with Christian trappings but heretical content, even as they admired Mormons' strong family ties and relative economic success. Most Americans thought of the Mormons as a remote group mostly isolated in Utah's high-desert country. Eschewing both alcohol and caffeine, practicing Mormons seemed more communal and even a bit clannish to outside observers, with an air of strangeness lingering from reports of multiple marriage still occasionally practiced on the fringes of the American Mormon sphere.

But Utah's economy and demography changed rapidly in the years around 2000, bringing outsiders in and sending Utahns out. Tourism emerged as an important industry, driven in part by the development and expansion of downhill ski areas at Park City, Deer Valley, and other resorts in the snowy Wasatch Mountains. Salt Lake City hosted the successful 2002 Winter Olympics, overcoming serious security concerns just a few months after the September 11 attacks. The once-overwhelmingly Mormon population of Salt Lake City became more than half non-Mormon. State and local governments eased their restrictions on serving alcohol in bars and restaurants, further encouraging the tourism industry. At the same time, young Mormons engaged in mission work around the world, expanding the rolls of church membership so much as to become half foreign. America's most homegrown and insular faith community was now, in some ways, its most cosmopolitan. The Republican Party's choice of Mitt Romney in 2012 as the first Mormon major-party presidential candidate confirmed the mainstreaming of Mormonism in American life.

The central question about religion and inclusion in the contemporary United States regarded Muslims. With some two billion adherents around the world, centered in a crescent spanning from Morocco across the greater Middle East to Indonesia, Islam was the second-largest religious identity, just behind Christianity. Other than the tiny number of their fellow citizens who had spent time in Muslim-majority areas, non-Muslim Americans knew little about Islam before the Iranian hostage crisis that began in 1979. Radical supporters of the Islamist regime of Ayatollah Ruhollah Khomeini seized control of the U.S. embassy in Tehran, in response to the U.S. welcome of the deposed Shah Reza Pahlavi for cancer treatment in New York. The Islamists—and many others—considered the shah a thief and mass murderer who should be returned to Iran for trial. They held some fifty-two American embassy personnel as hostages for more than a year, parading them in front of news cameras, venting their frustration with long-standing U.S. support for the shah, and hoping to use the hostages as a bargaining chip for his return.[39]

The overthrow of the shah and the establishment of the Islamic Republic of Iran marked a major turn in modern world history. This was the first modern theocratic state and the first and only case of radical Islamists taking control of a major national government. But developments in Iran in the late 1970s were not peculiar to the Muslim sphere. They fit a broader pattern of religious resurgence across the monotheistic parts of the globe. Evangelical and fundamentalist Protestants in the United States built bridges to conservative Catholics in a novel Christian Right coalition epitomized by the new organization Moral Majority. The elevation of the charismatic Polish Pope John Paul II in 1978 helped inspire a Catholic revival in Europe, particularly in the Soviet-dominated eastern half of the continent. Christian communities underpinned the new wave of dissent that challenged communist authorities in Czechoslovakia, visible in the Charter 77 human rights movement (1977), and Poland, manifest in Solidarity (1980), the first labor union in a communist state, an oxymoron that pointed to the imminent demise of the USSR. In Israel, a resurgent Orthodox Jewish settler movement claimed Palestinian lands and helped elect a Likud government in 1977, the first non-Labor government since the state's modern founding. The secular promises of both capitalism and communism seemed to be falling short in this decade in much of the world, while religious alternatives were gaining popular support.[40]

The overthrow of the shah, by itself, might have made little impression among the American populace, but the seizure and parading of American hostages was an entirely different matter. Americans had little interest in the reasons for Iranian anger, but they were enraged by this first encounter with Islamist revolutionaries. The U.S. defeat in Vietnam was still fresh, and the economic recessions and oil crises of the 1970s amplified American bitterness toward defiant Third World nations. The failure of a U.S. military rescue mission into Iran in 1980 deepened the sense of humiliation. Close ties between Washington and the governments of such important Muslim-majority nations as Saudi Arabia, Jordan, and Egypt had little traction with the broad American public. With relatively few Muslims living in the United States, the overwhelming majority of U.S. citizens knew almost nothing about Islam. Iranian revolutionaries' flaunting of blindfolded hostages and chants of "Death to America!" provided a starkly negative introduction to the third great Abrahamic faith.

The shah and his supporters had been nominally Muslim but largely secular and pro-Western. American policy makers found these elite, urbane monarchists easy to understand and work with. Many such Iranians had studied in the West and often spoke English. By contrast, the pious followers of Ayatollah Khomeini were typically poorer and less cosmopolitan. They distrusted the United States and other Western nations as enablers of the shah's great injustices at home. Javad Zarif was the rare Iranian to bridge these two camps. He first came to the United States at age seventeen in 1977 to attend high school in San Francisco, staying on to earn an undergraduate as well as master's and doctoral degrees in international relations. Like many Iranian students abroad, he supported the Iranian Revolution from afar. When the new revolutionary Iranian ambassador to the United Nations purged the mission staff of its monarchist supporters, he hired Zarif, then a young graduate student, in 1982. "At the time," Zarif recalled, "anybody who [both] prayed and knew English was a rare commodity." Zarif later went on to become the Iranian foreign minister responsible for the 2016 agreement freezing his country's nuclear program in exchange for reduced Western economic sanctions.[41]

After 1979 U.S. relations with Muslim-majority nations remained fraught. American support for the Iraqi regime of Saddam Hussein during its long 1980s war with Iran deteriorated when Hussein sent his army into Kuwait in 1990. President George H. W. Bush responded by organizing a large multinational force to drive the Iraqis out. He did so with several Arab allies and in defense of Saudi Arabia, but the First Gulf War of 1991 pitted U.S. forces against a majority-Muslim nation. It also stimulated the growth of al-Qaeda as a Sunni Islamist group, outraged by what they saw as infidel American troops guarding Saudi Arabia, home of the holiest sites in Islam, Mecca and Medina. Ten years later, al-Qaeda's September 11 attacks on the United States brought Americans into an open-ended war against Islamist foes in Afghanistan, followed in 2003 by the U.S. invasion and occupation of Iraq, which created its own Islamist backlash. Many Americans wondered, in President George W. Bush's black-and-white language, "Why do they hate us?" A Defense Department study concluded that any regional dislike for the United States stemmed from specific U.S. policies rather than an inevitable cultural clash. Whatever its causes, anti-American sentiment in many Muslim-majority areas of the world was strong and persistent in the twenty-first century.[42]

On the other hand, the 1965 immigration reform that eliminated the national-origins system eventually brought new Americans not only from Latin America and Asia but also from the Middle East. By 2015, 3.3 million Muslims lived in the United States, making up roughly 1 percent of the nation's people. Estimates predict slow, steady growth to about 2 percent by 2050. Islam was more present in some places than others. The metropolitan Detroit region, for example, is home to a substantial Arab American community, most but not all of it Muslim in religious affiliation. The first significant Arab migration to the United States had unfolded a century earlier, when roughly two hundred thousand Syrians, mostly Christian, settled on the East Coast. Later Syrian and Lebanese immigrants moved further afield. In 1929 some of them built one of earliest mosques in North America in the tiny community of Ross in far western North Dakota, where the first Muslims had arrived in 1895. Theirs was a familiar immigrant story of individuals integrating into the surrounding community, at the cost of losing a distinct identity. The two hundred early Muslim migrants who joined other farmers out on the prairie eventually married into non-Muslim families, and the last regular Arabic speaker and Quran reader at the mosque died in 2004.[43]

The 2016 presidential campaign highlighted continuing tensions in the United States regarding Muslim immigrants. The Republican candidate Donald J. Trump spoke harshly of the supposed dangers of such migrants and promised "a total and complete shutdown of Muslims entering the United States." He considered all Muslims as potential jihadist terrorists. Among his first steps as president was to issue two executive orders restricting immigrants from several Muslim-majority nations. Federal courts promptly overturned those orders, stimulating further legal skirmishes. It was clear that Americans were deeply divided over how to view Muslim immigrants and refugees. Trump's supporters represented the resurgence of an older nativist perspective, while other Americans, including a significant percentage of Republicans, welcomed Muslim and other immigrants as merely the latest element in an ongoing American saga of newcomers making their way into the future.[44]

Latinos

People from Latin America made up the bulk of the newcomers to the United States in the half-century after the 1965 immigration reforms. The large majority of these came from Mexico. Its long U.S. border was the steepest economic gradient of any national boundary in the world and thus exerted a steady magnetic pull on Mexican workers. But Latino migrants varied enormously in their backgrounds, which ranged from northern

Mexico all the way to southern Chile and Argentina. New arrivals to the mainland from Puerto Rico came already armed with U.S. citizenship, thanks to earlier U.S. imperial annexation of the island and subsequent legislation regarding its legal status as a U.S. commonwealth.

Why call them "Latino"? Some people preferred "Hispanic," and the two terms were widely interchangeable. "Hispanic" emphasized the Spanish linguistic heritage shared by most but not all of Latin America. For some Americans, particularly in places such as northern New Mexico, "Hispanic" highlighted their roots in Spanish settlement in the region dating back to the 1500s, well before the first permanent English settlements on the East Coast. "Latino" pointed in a different direction, to Latin America rather than Europe. It carried a geographical emphasis that included the Spanish-language majority but also Portuguese-speaking Brazil (the most populous nation in the region) and the small French-, English-, and Dutch-speaking Caribbean nations. In the 1960s and 1970s, young Mexican American political activists preferred the term "Chicano," which appropriated and reversed a once-pejorative usage. But for most Americans whose heritage traced to other parts of the Western Hemisphere besides Canada, either "Latino" or "Hispanic" worked best.[45]

Animated debates about large migration flows from Mexico in recent decades obscured an older U.S. identification with the rest of the hemisphere to its south. The American Revolution and particularly its reprise in the War of 1812 took place in the same context as the Latin American colonies fighting against Spain to win their own independence. A robust feeling of inter-American unity reinforced Americans' belief that the anticolonial and republican ideas of 1776 were universal in nature. The historian Caitlin Fitz has shown that U.S. observers imagined the Western Hemisphere as "a happily independent republican community at a time when Europe seemed to be crumbling under the weight of dynastic alliances and monarchical tyranny." Traces of this legacy could be seen in the shift toward greater identification with Christopher Columbus, a Genoese Catholic sailing for Spain, as a way of demonstrating cultural as well as political independence from England. Americans placed their new capital city in the District of Columbia, for example, and King's College in New York was renamed Columbia College (later University) in 1784. In 1792 New York City hosted the first recorded celebration of Columbus's initial landing in the Caribbean three hundred years earlier. Hopes for a common political future of liberty allowed the mostly white Protestant Americans to hurdle traditional religious and racial concerns.[46]

In a later era, identification with Columbus came to be seen, ironically, as a relatively conservative cause. The federal Columbus Day holiday in October, which was established in the twentieth century, gestured politically, in large part, to the burgeoning Italian American community. But it conflicted with rising Native American activism that highlighted the genocidal impact of the European invasion of the Americas. South Dakota, for example, moved to celebrate Native Americans Day instead. The legendary Genoese sailor now symbolized Europeans in opposition to what Canadians call First Nations peoples. Lost in this newer political contest over symbolism was how Americans had originally used Columbus to identify with Latin Americans in opposition to what they viewed as corrupt, monarchical Europe. Long before the arrival of multitudinous Italian newcomers on American shores, the Columbian connection had served as an inclusive and democratic link.[47]

The first Latino Americans did not come to the United States. The United States came to them. Residents of Mexico's northeastern province of Tejas, without moving, found themselves swept into the Lone Star Republic after Anglo settlers declared the province's independence in 1836. Nine years later those Tejanos were suddenly made American residents after the United States annexed Texas. They had not crossed the border; the border had—twice—crossed them. The same came true for residents of the remaining northern half of Mexico when it was seized and then annexed by the United States under the 1848 Treaty of Guadalupe Hidalgo ending the U.S.-Mexican War. Between 75,000 and one hundred thousand Mexicans did not move but changed countries nonetheless. Many of these first Latinos had roots older than settlers in Jamestown or Plymouth on the soil that became U.S. land, stretching from San Diego to Santa Fe to Galveston Bay.[48]

How did other Americans feel about these relatively few early Mexican Americans? This was not always clear. Mexican residents lived in what was then the remote Southwest, far from centers of white population. In an era before airplanes or even highways, places such as California and South Texas were distant from most Americans' experiences or consciousness. On the one hand, Americans in the late nineteenth and early twentieth centuries had a deeply racialized view of demography, and Mexicans defied easy categorization. They were a people of blended European and indigenous American heritage, with appearances ranging from highly European to quite Indian. But the common one-drop rule placed anyone of visible mixed racial heritage into the nonwhite box. In the social practices of daily life, this meant that Latinos in the Southwest were mostly segregated in schools and elsewhere and lived under the burdens of white supremacy.

On the other hand, the international agreement of 1848 granted U.S. citizenship to Mexicans who lived in lands annexed by the United States. They were, in a legal if not social sense, white. In 1897 a federal district court upheld the right of a Mexican immigrant, Ricardo Rodriguez, to naturalize as a U.S. citizen, thus confirming rights by treaty over strict racial requirements. Mexicans' nationality trumped their race, at least legally. This also happened in the social sphere at times. Since the early nineteenth century, American men had married the daughters of affluent ranchero owners in California and the rest of the Southwest. The practice stemmed from both the proximity of romantic and sexual partners and the pursuit of land ownership. For most Americans the archetype of this remote and exotic world was the fictional Zorro, a swashbuckling Robin Hood figure created in 1919 by the pulp writer Johnston McCulley and made famous in a series of novels as well as film and television adaptations. The reality of white-Mexican intermarriage from a colonial era had a parallel in early Virginia in what the historian Peggy Pascoe called the "Pocahontas exception," in which segregation-era elite whites proudly claimed a small bit of Native American heritage.[49]

Latinos occupied an intermediate status in the American racial landscape. Not black and not Asian, but also neither fully white nor fully Native American, they were, for the most part, legally white but socially nonwhite. Racial ideology in the United States hardened in the decades around 1900, with greater emphasis on Mexicans as a blended and therefore supposedly degraded combination of Spanish and Indian heritage. The turmoil of Mexico's revolutionary decade of the 1910s exacerbated tensions on the border, and a brief failed uprising in south Texas by Mexican American residents in 1915 was crushed with great brutality, as Texas Rangers and vigilantes killed thousands of Latinos. After the immigration reforms of the World War I era, U.S. government officials tried to draw up more clearly racialized categories. In 1930 the Census Bureau enumerated Mexicans as a separate race, but with the imprecise definition of "persons who were born in Mexico and are not definitely white, Negro, Indian, Chinese, or Japanese."[50]

Latinos spent much of the next four decades, from the 1930s to the 1970s, struggling to claim their official status as white. To some degree, they succeeded. A landmark case was the U.S. federal appeals court decision in 1947 striking down segregated schools for Latinos in Westminster, California. The *Mendez v. Westminster* case set the precedent for the more well-known U.S. Supreme Court decision in *Brown v. Board of Education* (1954) that banned racial segregation in education. In 1980, the U.S. Census began using the terms "Hispanic" and "non-Hispanic white," indicating that being Latino was increasingly seen, at least officially, as merely another form of white ethnicity. It was similar to being Italian American, Irish American, or Jewish American. It was still somewhat more racialized, however, since there was no such category as "non-Jewish white," for example. In other words, Latinoness was still seen as a quality that was a little more permanent or at least more firmly bordered than other white ethnicities. But Hispanic or Latino was at least not a fully racial identity under the official categories such as white, black, Asian, or Native American.[51]

Part of the challenge for Mexican immigrants stemmed from being seen by the U.S. government and American employers, particularly in agriculture, as a flexible source of labor. They could be welcomed when needed and blocked or even removed when not. During the Great Depression of the 1930s, with unemployment soaring in the United States, authorities in Los Angeles rounded up Latino residents, both citizens and noncitizens, and packed them onto trains for deportation to Mexico. Then in World War II, as American laborers were drafted into the military by the millions, Washington and Mexico City arranged the "Bracero" program to bring north temporary workers to take their place. The historian Deborah Cohen notes that "crowds of men, women, and children supportive of Mexico's efforts would meet arriving trains and cheer as braceros disembarked."[52]

Such a radical shift from deportation to being embraced recalls the closing scene of the satirical film *A Day Without a Mexican* (2004), in which Californians wake up one day to find that all persons of Mexican descent have disappeared. Some initial enthusiasm is quickly swamped by the state's economy—and daily life—grinding to a complete halt, as little work gets done. It's a nightmare. The film ends with Border Patrol agents, normally feared and even loathed by undocumented migrants, finally discovering two Mexicans coming across the border in the dark of night. Rather than arresting them, the agents embrace the bedraggled migrants, hoist them on to their shoulders, and parade them around as heroes as the credits roll. One looks over at the other, stunned disbelief in his eyes: "Damn, these gringos are fuckin' cool!"[53]

One could almost get whiplash keeping up with the changes in U.S. policy toward Mexican immigration. During World War II, the reception remained warmly positive. "Citizens of Mexico, you have come to help us in our most difficult . . . [and] important wartime task," Governor John Moses of North Dakota announced in August 1944: "harvesting our crops . . . [and] starting them on their way to provide food and clothing and necessary equipment for our fighting men." That service symbolized Mexico's commitment to the "full share of the burdens of this war" and the defense of "all men of good will . . . to live as free men in a free world" that "knows no boundaries of nationality, race, or creed." In light of the decidedly mixed treatment of Americans of Mexican heritage, Governor Moses was putting a very positive spin on American social practices of the 1940s. But the war experience did accelerate more egalitarian and inclusive trends in American life.[54]

Mexican workers who came north under the Bracero program often gained an acute sense of national identity only once in the United States. Despite efforts at national consciousness building by the revolutionary Mexican government since the 1910s, poor rural people still understood themselves primarily through local and regional identities. Then in the United States, they were often thrown together with people from other parts of Mexico and treated as a single group by U.S. authorities, employers, and citizens. They thus became, in a sense, Mexican. This same process held true for Sicilians and Calabrians, who really learned to feel Italian only after arriving in the United States. Similarly, U.S. draftees in World War II trained and served around the country and abroad together with others from all over the nation, a process that helped break down regional distinctions in identity. During the war, people from Mexico who had long identified as a *norteño* or as a resident of a particular village were often invited to participate in local holiday celebrations such as July 4 or Thanksgiving and marched together as Mexicans to the applause of U.S. citizens. Becoming Mexican turned out to be a key step on the road to becoming American.[55]

After World War II, the greatest flow of Latino migrants to the mainland United States came not from Mexico but from Puerto Rico. Residents of this easternmost Greater Antilles island, lying between Hispaniola and the Virgin Islands in the Caribbean Sea, had exchanged Spanish colonial rule for American colonial rule as a result of the Spanish-American War in 1898. Puerto Rico shared the common Caribbean history of an economy rooted in sugar production and linked to the African slave trade. So Puerto Ricans tended to be even more racially composite than Mexicans, with African as well as European and indigenous heritage. But they also had U.S. citizenship after 1917. Few moved to the mainland before the migration of several million following World War II, who came mostly by airplane, in what has been called "the world's first migration by air." By 1970, one-third of all Puerto Ricans lived on the mainland. The eight hundred thousand in New York City made it the largest Puerto Rican city in the world. Other Americans viewed these Spanish speakers much like previous European ethnic immigrants, finding initial niches in New York that included rough working-class edges, such as the gang conflicts portrayed by the Sharks and the Jets in the hugely popular Broadway musical of 1957, *West Side Story*, and the subsequent film version four years later.[56]

Cubans fleeing the 1959 revolution led by Fidel Castro and its aftermath added another important stream to the Latino population in the United States. Refugees from the island just ninety miles off Key West tended to be educated and relatively affluent. Some left as soon as the U.S.-backed dictator Fulgencio Batista fled. Others departed over the next few years, disillusioned as the revolution turned leftward in the face of U.S. opposition, with Castro declaring his government to be communist and pro-Soviet by late 1961. Cuban émigrés settled primarily in the Miami area, where they became a powerful anticommunist force in Florida politics and U.S. foreign policy. The U.S. government eagerly wielded the Cold War propaganda advantage of welcoming refugees from a communist nation. In this, Cuban migrants were like refugees from Hungary after the 1956 Soviet crackdown on dissidents there, identified more by their politics and socioeconomic status than by ethnicity or race. Cubans from the 1960s onward helped define newcomers from Latin America as mainstream Americans.[57]

The same opportunities in postwar America that drew Puerto Ricans and Cubans appealed to other Latin Americans. Their numbers rose sharply after the 1965 immigration reforms. In 1970, there were 750,000 immigrants from Mexico living in the United States. By 2015, there were 57 million

Latinos in the United States, which included many millions from other parts of Latin America. The rapid growth of the U.S. Latino population slowed dramatically after the economic recession that began in 2008, and migration from Mexico actually reversed slightly, with more people moving south than north across the border—a pattern obscured by anti-immigrant rhetoric and policies during and after the 2016 elections. Future migration patterns were difficult to predict, but sharply declining birthrates in Mexico for the past several decades suggest a different future, regardless of U.S. border policies. Latinos in the twenty-first century became the largest minority in the United States, even as they continued to occupy an intermediate status in the nation's formal and informal categories of race and ethnicity.[58]

Incorporation and Its Challenges

In 1891 George Price, a Jewish physician and immigrant to the United States, published a book in Yiddish in Odessa, a major Black Sea port city in what was then part of the Russian empire and is today Ukraine. *Jews in America* was a guidebook for Jews planning to migrate to the United States. "A bit of advice for you," Price wrote of this different land across the Atlantic Ocean. "Do not take a minute's rest. Run, do, work and keep your own good in mind." He offered one other suggestion. "A final virtue is need in America—called cheek. . . . Do not say, 'I cannot; I do not know.'" Instead, he advised, have a little chutzpah and promote yourself in order to succeed.[59]

A century later a young Jewish boy named Gary Shteyngart and his family managed to leave Russia in the last years of the Soviet Union and moved to New York City. In a later memoir, Shteyngart joked that his grades at Stuyvesant High School in Manhattan were not strong enough to earn him admission to an Ivy League college, which meant that his family "may as well have never come here." Immigrant parents often had very high expectations of what their children could achieve in the new land. His mother apparently nicknamed him "Failurchka," or "Little Failure," because he spent his youth "as a kind of tuning fork for my parents' fears, disappointments, and alienation." Shteyngart had been expected as a boy to succeed rapidly and wildly "in a country we thought of as magical, but whose population did not strike us as being especially clever." Here was some of the chutzpah promoted in George Price's guidebook a century earlier: we immigrants were pretty talented, more so than a lot of natives, and we could make it quickly in a country as large and full of extraordinary opportunities as this one.[60]

Newcomers everywhere wrestle with how and how much to fit in to their surroundings, and natives try to figure out who these new people are. It is a very old story, one renewed all the time across the world as people move. The American version of this story happened to be, by far, the largest version of the tale: more than 40 million immigrants now live in the United States. For all the nativist anxieties thrown up in the 2016 presidential campaign and the early years of the Trump administration, recent studies indicate that immigrants are assimilating, integrating, or being incorporated into—equivalent terms with different emphases about the process for newcomers—American society as well or better than in the past.[61]

The timeframe is crucial for considering the project of immigration and incorporation. The political analyst Alvaro Vargas Llosa observes that full assimilation takes two or three generations, "a period [that] when viewed from a distance is short, but when viewed from an immediate perspective feels like an eternity." A person may not change cultures overnight, but families do so over a generation or two. A major analysis in 2015 by the National Academies of Sciences, Engineering, and Medicine found that while only 25 percent of first-generation Latino adults spoke English well, 88 percent of their children did. The children and grandchildren of immigrants lead entire lives in the United States, which gives them very different experiences than those of their progenitors, who came from elsewhere. The historian Tony Judt recalled his parallel situation as a youngster in London from a family that had come from Eastern Europe: "In my world, all grandparents had accents. That's what a grandmother or grandfather was: someone whom you didn't quite understand because they would unpredictably slip into Polish or Russian or Yiddish." Or Spanish, in the United States.[62]

For both migrants and others, how and what people eat reveals a great deal about what they are comfortable with. Native-born Americans, like most people everywhere, tended to look askance at the odd-tasting foods that newcomers brought with them. This disdain recalled the view of locals in what is today southeastern France expressed by Sidonius Apollinaris

(430–489 CE), an elite Gallo-Roman bishop and diplomat, who described "Burgundians as reeking of garlic and onion, and as giants who spoke an unintelligible tongue and who groomed their hair with rancid butter." Italians seemed equally off-putting to some Americans in the early twentieth century. But this view could change. After all, immigrants were sometimes amazed—and dismayed—by what locals ate. One Italian immigrant boy in the early 1900s pitied the people he called "Med-e-gons," who only got to have turkey on Thanksgiving and just did not seem to eat as well as the typically poorer Italian newcomers they so often looked down on. "It never occurred to me that just being a citizen of the United States meant that I was an 'American,'" he recalled many years later. "'Americans' were people who ate peanut butter and jelly on mushy white bread that came out of a plastic package."[63]

Pizza and spaghetti, however, soon joined the evolving menu of mainstream American food. Hector Boiardi facilitated the process by selling canned spaghetti to A&P stores by the late 1930s. He supplied the same to the U.S. Army during World War II as millions of GIs moved around the country and the world, being exposed to new foods in new places. This helped build the taste and customer base for the popular brand Chef Boyardee after the war. Once-exotic Italian food was domesticated into cuisine no longer seen as ethnically distinctive. The same story unfolded in the 1930s and 1940s with Oscar Mayer, whose original marketing of sausages to German immigrant customers shifted to selling hot dogs to everyone with the famous advertising jingle "I wish I were an Oscar Mayer wiener." The process of making the exotic familiar continued in the twenty-first century with many other cuisines. Mexican food was the most important of these; tacos and salsa are now mainstream comfort foods for Americans of many heritages.[64]

How Americans understood newcomers could also be estimated by the latter's engagement with the U.S. military. Polls regularly report that the armed forces remain the most trusted and respected institution in the contemporary United States, far more so than Congress, corporations, schools, or churches. The U.S. military was also remarkably successful in diversifying its ranks and its leadership over the last several decades. Consider these prominent recent army generals: General Colin Powell, the son of Jamaican immigrants and chairman of the Joint Chiefs of Staff and secretary of state; Lieutenant General Ricardo Sánchez, the son of Mexican immigrants and commander of coalition ground forces in Iraq in 2003; General Peter Pace, the son of Italian immigrants and chairman of the Joint Chiefs of Staff; General John Abizaid, the Arabic-speaking grandson of Lebanese immigrants and head of the U.S. Central Command; and Major General Antonio Taguba, born in the Philippines and author of the key report on abuses of prisoners committed by U.S. personnel at the Abu Ghraib prison in Iraq. Taguba's report is particularly telling: the U.S. military, the quintessential symbol of American patriotism, gave a Filipino immigrant the responsibility of holding it to the highest moral standards of civilization.[65]

In the United States, ethnic or racial nationalism had ceded the moral high ground to a more powerful form of civic nationalism.[66] The emotional center of nationalism centered on the sacrifices of people who had suffered and died for the nation, most commonly those who served in the military. Since its desegregation between 1948 and 1953, the U.S. armed forces became in many regards the model of a successfully diverse and racially integrated institution, with people of color, if anything, slightly overrepresented.[67] This did not mean that racism had disappeared from the ranks of the military, but it did underline the strong association of the American flag with people of all backgrounds and heritages. Against this potent civic nationalism, those who would have flown the Confederate battle flag, for example, have fought a losing campaign, as was evident in the continuing removal of that flag and associated symbols from positions of prominence in Southern states in recent years.[68]

Anxiety about newcomers did not disappear, of course, particularly among those fearful of economic decline or nervous about their own cultural status. The U.S. presidential campaign of 2016 was a startling reminder of this fundamental truth. It was hard to imagine a starker shift from the two previous elections, in which a significantly larger number of Americans voted into the White House the son of a visiting Kenyan student. Most concerns about immigrants centered on their staying in the United States and the effect that might have there. But nativists also worried about and resented the reverse: the prospect that newcomers might *not* remain. There was grumbling about sojourners earning money in the United States and then taking it home, something Americans who worked abroad in China or Saudi Arabia or elsewhere and then returned home also did. Such remigration suggested to nativists that migrants did not value the United States highly enough and were failing to see it as the best place to live.[69]

At the height of European migration to the United States in the years before World War I, as many as one-third of those who crossed the Atlantic did not remain permanently. Nationalists back home in Polish or Czech areas hoped this substantial share of returners might signal the end of the exodus from their lands. Migrants did often experience a rise in their own ethnic consciousness by traveling abroad, but they mostly returned, when they did, for more personal or familial reasons—or after World War I with the onset of Prohibition, in the words of one Czech official, because "it's better to earn less and at least be able to drink again." The experience and seasoning in the United States left many returners empowered and wealthier and thus more resistant to arbitrary authority. Such returners included future prime ministers of Norway, Finland, and Latvia and a future president of Ireland, Éamon de Valera, who was born in New York but moved "back" to Ireland with his Irish mother when he was just two years old.[70]

Some Americans worried about immigrants coming; others worried about them leaving. Degrees of anxiety ebbed and flowed, as they always had. The prevalence of Latinos and particularly Mexicans among immigrants since the 1970s renewed the prospect of people sojourning but not staying permanently, since Mexico was so close by. A century earlier, Italians in particular had tended to crisscross the Atlantic, coming and going in a seasonal pattern. The same was often true with migrants from south of the border. Santiago Enriquez, for example, was splitting time at the turn of the millennium between meatpacking work in Norwalk, Wisconsin, and his hometown in Cheran, south of Guadalajara: "I don't think I'll spend too many more years up north. Maybe ten more. Then I'll come back here [to Cheran] to enjoy what I've made, if God grants me the years." And retiring in Mexico or Central America was not unique to Latinos. More and more other Americans were making the same choice in the twenty-first century, motivated by a combination of lower costs of living and warmer weather. Immigrants seemed to be, yet again, much like other Americans.[71]

The United States was hardly the only nation to receive large numbers of immigrants in recent decades. Some comparison with other major receiving nations, such as Canada and those in Western Europe, sheds light on the American situation. At 20 percent, Canada was one of the nations with the largest share of its population consisting of immigrants, while some 20 million immigrants settled in Western Europe between the mid-1960s and the mid-1990s. Regarding the European guest-worker programs of the 1960s that initially encouraged that flow, the Swiss writer Max Frisch famously observed, "We asked for workers, and got people." The results, that is, were complicated and helped reveal the distinctive elements in the U.S. approach to newcomers.[72]

A primary concern of Americans less sympathetic to immigrants was that newcomers might not work hard at fitting into American society. Some feared they would stick to themselves and not learn the English language and American ways of thinking and behaving. In European countries such as France, new arrivals clustered in densely concentrated immigrant neighborhoods of large metropolitan areas. Newcomers in the United States also tended at first to live among people familiar to them—in Little Italy, Chinatown, the barrio—but over time they moved out into the wider American society to a much greater degree. The sociologists Richard Alba and Nancy Foner conclude in a major recent study, "The idea that immigrant-origin groups are establishing 'parallel' societies that evolve separately beside, and apart from, the mainstream seems wildly overstated when confronted with the empirical evidence." Racial discrimination remained an impediment, particularly for immigrants of African descent, but immigrants in the United States on average experienced greater incorporation into American life than did their counterparts in most of Western Europe.[73]

National identities in such countries as Germany and France were not structured to be readily hyphenated. In France, immigrants were expected to become part of the French nation as individuals rather than as part of a group—to assimilate and feel French and not to display in public distinctive ethnic characteristics. A bright boundary between being French or German and being anything else put pressure on people to choose. In North America this worked somewhat differently. Americans as well as Canadians had a long tradition of newcomers remaining hyphenated in their identity: Irish-American, Cuban-American, French-Canadian. Particularly for the second generation, Alba and Foner conclude, "Americans are comfortable with hyphenated identities. You can be American and 'ethnic' at the same time." Western Europeans, for their part, were slower to incorporate newcomers because "they tend to imagine their societies as derived from a core majority population that has occupied the national territory for centuries." Recurring bursts of nativist activity in the United States could not hide the fundamental image that Americans, like Canadians, held of themselves as a nation of immigrants. British, Dutch, and other Europeans did not typically understand their countries in the same way.[74]

Religion played a critical part in the generally warmer reception of immigrants in the United States than in Western Europe. Europe's recent immigrants were primarily Muslim, given the geographical proximity to the greater Middle East and North Africa. But Western Europe had become a deeply secular place by the late twentieth century. This made the significant new numbers of relatively devout Muslims in France, Germany, the Netherlands, Sweden, and the United Kingdom stand out even more clearly. Anti-Muslim discourse fused elements from the Right— xenophobia and cultural pride—and elements from the Left—liberal and feminist critiques of Muslim patriarchal fundamentalism—with overarching security concerns about jihadist terror networks. Contemporary Western European skepticism about religious faith made pious immigrants seem particularly foreign.[75]

In the United States most immigrants were Christian rather than Muslim, particularly Roman Catholic Latinos. Previous immigrant groups had typically been defined, in part, by their religious faith—Protestant Norwegians, Catholic Italians, Russian Jews—which had not usually been seen by most Americans as quite the same fundamental threat to U.S. institutions and American identity as in twenty-first-century Europe. Instead, the United States remained by far the most religious of modern Western nations, which were the primary receivers of large numbers of immigrants. So newcomers to the United States entered a culture where personal piety was widely admired rather than considered odd, particularly on the conservative side of the political spectrum. Indeed, polling in the 2010s indicated that many more Americans would disapprove of a child marrying an atheist than marrying a Muslim. It did not hurt that Muslim migrants to the United States tended to be well educated, more so on average than native-born Americans, and to fare reasonably well in economic and professional terms.[76]

The greatest challenge to reading patterns of political and cultural development over time is the difficulty of rising above the pressing concerns of one's own political and cultural moment. The first years after the 2016 election of an openly nativist and evidently racist U.S. president recalled the xenophobic reaction to U.S. military engagement in Europe in World

War I. Pundits leapt to cheer or, mostly, bemoan this seeming turn against immigrants and refugees. The pendulum from openness to exclusion continues to swing, as it has throughout the American past. How far and how wide it will swing in the future is unclear.[77]

Hostility to outsiders was not the dominant color in the American tapestry, however. A balanced reading of the past indicates that the United States had been and remained a nation and culture remarkably open to outside influences and foreign peoples. The vast majority of people who had migrated to the United States remained and became absorbed into the country's multihued material. Perhaps the most distinguishing feature of American society was its relentless absorption of varied peoples, pulling them into its wildly productive and materially creative economy. This has been truer than ever over the last half-century, after the 1965 immigration reform that eliminated the four-decade-long discriminatory national-origins system.

Just how powerfully assimilative American culture could be was sometimes clearer to outsiders than to Americans. Some native-born U.S. citizens feared that newcomers would not fit in, but authorities back in migrants' home territories rightly suspected that they might fit in all too well. This had been true throughout U.S. history. Eastern European officials in the late nineteenth century, for example, often sought to hold on to their people by slowing down emigration across the Atlantic. In 1889 at the town of Auschwitz, later the site of the infamous Nazi extermination camp but then a Polish-speaking town near the convergent borders of the Russian, German, and Austro-Hungarian empires, authorities put two Jewish travel agents on trial for illegally encouraging such departures. The prosecutor asked if "we can be indifferent to the loss of over a million Polish brothers," as these migrants to America were there "dispersed in all of the businesses, mines, and factories, and crushed by foreign elements, and in time they cease to be Poles. This denationalization takes place in the course of only a few years." Ceasing to be Poles, they became Americans, "crushed by foreign elements" of the potent American culture.[78]

Even those migrants who came only for a sojourn in the United States before returning home sometimes left an impact far greater than expected. A few decades later, at the end of the 1950s, one of the smart and ambitious young foreigners who sought better opportunities was a young man from a Muslim family in Kenya who won a fellowship to study at the University of Hawai'i and then Harvard University. He returned to Nairobi

in 1964 and eventually became a senior economist in the newly independent government there. In Honolulu, he had been married for three years
to a young woman of Kansas background, and they had a son together.
Barack Obama Sr. did not ultimately remain in the United States, but his
son grew up to become its president in 2009, elected twice with his African heritage and his middle name of Hussein, the same as the surname of
the dictator of Iraq whom the United States had just gone to war to depose.

CHAPTER IV

Lurking

Communists and the Threat of Captivity

F oreigners, for Americans, often failed to remain foreign. Former
external enemies—Germany, Japan, Italy—became close allies.
Once suspect internal exotics—Roman Catholics, Jews, Latinos—
became mainstream Americans. A defining feature of modern American
society has been the tendency to absorb diversity and even dissent in a resil-
ient, expansive popular culture, just as U.S. foreign policy has regularly
adjusted diplomatic relationships with other nations based on changing perceptions of geostrategic interests. This cultural inclusiveness and diplomatic flexibility even held true with the greatest perceived threat to the
United States in the twentieth century: communism. Americans would
subvert the subversives, eventually.

No challenge to the United States proved as sustained and elemental as
that of socialism. While Americans understood themselves as a people
defined by liberty and opportunity, socialists of different stripes saw instead
in American society class exploitation, unfreedom, and lost opportunity
for the vast working majority. Left-wing organizers infused the labor union
movement with energy and passion, which helped bring such humanizing
reforms as the eight-hour workday, the minimum wage, and a steep reduction in child labor. As an organized force in American electoral politics,
socialism did not have the kind of impact that it had in much of Europe.
But leftist radicals in the United States fought with measurable success at

least to reduce the human damage caused by the churning forces of capitalist production.[1]

The collectivist values of socialism found their most powerful expression in the Russian Revolution of 1917. Out of the destruction of World War I and civil war arose the vast Union of Soviet Socialist Republics (USSR), a communist state that grew to offer the most challenging alternative to American democratic capitalism. After World War II, the Soviet Union seemed poised to perhaps surpass the United States in global influence. Soviet leaders promised newly independent peoples of the emerging Third World greater justice and equality than what Western capitalism offered. Americans in the subsequent Cold War decades feared that communists—seen as clever, devious, relentless—might even burrow into the U.S. government and American society and subvert them from within. They could imagine nothing more foreign—more "un-American"—than the collectivist vision of Soviet communism, embodied in the sprawling Soviet gulag of slave-labor camps for political prisoners. The terms "un-American" and "subversive" became rhetorical touchstones of American anxiety after 1945.[2]

But such worries had it precisely backward. It turned out that American acquisitive values and individualist culture proved more alluring and helped eventually undermine communism around the globe. The crumbling of the Berlin Wall in 1989 and the unraveling of the USSR in 1991 demonstrated, in part, the durable attraction of consumer capitalism and liberal democracy. Soviet promises of capitalism's imminent demise, meanwhile, rang hollow as the late twentieth century unfolded and a wave of globalization spread market forces in every direction. The mental enslavement of communist "brainwashing" that Americans feared never materialized. Instead, Americans, not Russian or Chinese communists, turned out to be the true subversives of the modern world. They would seek to render familiar even the most foreign of people.[3]

From Socialist Theory to Soviet Reality

The processes of industrialization reshaped Europe and North America in the second half of the nineteenth century. The dramatic growth of large-scale manufacturing, rapid transportation, vast cities, and the use of electricity created enormous wealth. The American writer Mark Twain famously referred to this period as the "Gilded Age." But just beneath the gold-plated surface yawned a chasm dividing the affluent from the new industrial working class, or proletariat. So much wealth and so much immiseration, cheek by jowl, troubled and sometimes outraged observers. The most influential of these observers was the exiled German philosopher, sociologist, and journalist Karl Marx, who along with other socialists of various stripes anticipated a coming redistribution of the wealth that had been produced with the labor of the Industrial Revolution's working men and women. In *The Communist Manifesto* (1848) and *Capital: Critique of Political Economy* (1867), Marx laid out a class-based analysis of industrial capitalism and a prediction that it would be merely a necessary stage on the road to eventual socialism. Capitalism was required for the industrial advancement of human society and the creation of wealth, Marx believed, but the coming higher stage of socialism would then *distribute* that wealth in a much more just and humane future. Precisely how this would unfold remained uncertain.

Few expected the revolution to begin on the semifeudal eastern edge of Europe. World War I created a crisis in tsarist Russia, and Vladimir Lenin and his Bolshevik comrades seized the opportunity to establish the world's first communist government in 1917. With a tiny industrial proletariat and primarily agrarian economy, Russia did not at first glance fit Marx's model. He had expected revolution to come initially in the most industrialized nations, such as Germany or England, where capitalism and the industrial working class had advanced the farthest. The Bolsheviks' boldness, however, had changed history. Put into action, Marxism became Marxist-Leninism. The new Union of Soviet Socialist Republics inherited the Russian empire's vast landscape, covering one-sixth of the earth's dry land, and Europe's largest population. But revolutionary fervor could not immediately overcome certain structural deficiencies. The tsar's limited development of modern transportation systems meant that the empire had little capacity to project power beyond its borders. It could go only as far and as fast as its soldiers could walk. "Russia was a very large man with very short arms and slow feet," the historian Joshua Sanborn writes: "impossible to ignore, very dangerous at close range, but able to be neutralized if one maintained a respectful and wary distance."[4]

How much of a threat did the Soviet Union pose to the United States and other capitalist nations? In the immediate military realm, the communist victory in Russia had the potential to change the entire outcome of World

War I. The Bolsheviks signed a separate peace with imperial Germany in February 1918, allowing the Germans to turn all their forces against their remaining enemies on the Western Front. The final German spring offensive in northern France nearly succeeded, turned back only by stout French and British resistance and by the support of the first U.S. troops. That small stream of American "doughboys" widened to a river of personnel as 1918 progressed and promised to become a flood of men and materiel. German commanders surrendered that fall, the opportunity lost from the Soviet withdrawal.

At the level of ideas, the Soviet threat was potentially more dire to Western capitalists. U.S. policy makers feared that the Bolsheviks might seize the moral high ground of democratic self-determination. They published the Allies' secret treaties, deposited in the tsar's vault, which showed British and French plans to take more territory for themselves during the war, rather than promoting what U.S. president Woodrow Wilson had called a war to "make the world safe for democracy." Lenin asked European workers pointedly if this is what they were fighting for: to extend British rule into Mesopotamia, replacing the Ottoman Empire with the British Empire? Capitalism, for the Bolsheviks, was irredeemably, relentlessly exploitative of working people and had to be replaced.[5]

Wilson swiftly announced his "14 Points" for postwar peace in an effort to regain the moral high ground from the Russian revolutionaries. Wilson and Lenin were competing directly for the future of a world emerging from the long era of European imperial dominance. They each offered a version of democracy, but in different forms. While Wilson believed in a world of self-determining capitalist nation-states, Lenin saw working people shaping a socialist future across the globe, the embodiment of Marx's call: "Workers of the world, unite!" The president warned his allies and followers during the Paris peace negotiations in 1919 that "we are running a race with Bolshevism and the world is on fire." Socialism had to be contained, and Wilson cooperated with the British and French in supporting the anti-Bolshevik forces within Russia during the civil war from 1917 to 1920.[6]

Socialist egalitarianism also attracted support within the United States. The U.S. Congress worried enough about this to pass the Alien and Sedition Acts, and the Wilson administration used the statutes to imprison the American socialist leader Eugene V. Debs for his public opposition to the war. More moderate Progressive reformers also sometimes pointed to the Russian revolutionaries as models of more democratic behavior. American feminists during World War I were deeply engaged in the struggle for women's suffrage—that is, for letting the majority of U.S. citizens actually vote, which they could not do in most states—and suffragists pointed to the Bolsheviks' formal equality for women after they took power in 1917. Most American activists backed away from identifying publicly with the Soviets once the anticommunist repression of the First Red Scare ramped up in 1919, but they had highlighted the truth that the United States was not yet as democratic as it liked to think. The Nineteenth Amendment granted women the right to vote after it was ratified in 1920.[7]

Lenin and his comrades were going where no one had gone before, and their strategy evolved in response to their circumstances. Theory did not always work out as anticipated in practice. Most fundamentally, the Bolsheviks hoped and expected that other communist revolutions would follow swiftly, as nearly happened in postwar Germany and Hungary. They did not consider their new Union of Soviet Socialist Republics as a normal nation-state that would engage in typical diplomatic relations with other states. Other governments were to be overthrown, not negotiated with. Capitalism's apocalypse was imminent, and the once-ailing Russian empire was now the model for the world's future.

As commissar of foreign affairs, Leon Trotsky initially expected to eliminate his department. He represented the Soviets in the ceasefire negotiations with imperial Germany in early 1918, and he at first attempted unsuccessfully to override the diplomatic process by speaking not to the German diplomats but directly to the German people, particularly the German soldiers on the Eastern Front. He wanted to encourage them to make their own revolution. The Bolsheviks believed the revolution in Russia could only survive if followed by similar uprisings in the advanced capitalist states. The failure of communist efforts elsewhere in the chaotic conditions of 1919, amid the wreckage of World War I, forced them eventually to adapt to a future they had not anticipated. They would have to be patient. Only gradually did they come to accept the idea of managing their new revolutionary state's external relations by acting diplomatically as a more or less normal government.[8]

Americans have rarely been among the most perceptive observers of the Soviet Union. As products of a deeply anticommunist society, Americans have tended to dismiss the Bolsheviks' experiment as a murderous, totalitarian spectacle of abuse of Russians and their neighbors. But the Soviet claim to being a socialist society, despite the Terror of the 1930s and other traumas of Soviet history, the historian Stephen Kotkin reminds us, "continued to make sense and motivate people the world over until the very end in 1991—a circumstance that the historian may or may not find abhorrent but has no right to dismiss and every obligation to explain." The story of Soviet socialism was, Kotkin argues, "a fable of a new person and a new civilization, distinct because it was not capitalist, distinct because it was better than capitalism." *Pravda* in 1936, for example, contrasted "the popularity of gangsters like Al Capone" in capitalist countries with the Soviet celebration of "heroes of labor." Widespread faith in building socialism among the Russian people led decades later to great disillusionment, but it remained powerful as long as capitalism was mired in crisis in the 1930s and as long as fascism directly threatened them in the 1940s.[9]

The Impact of the Cold War

The 1917 Bolshevik Revolution established the great modern alternative to liberal capitalist society, but for a quarter-century communism remained more theoretical than real to Americans. The Soviet Union was poor, rural, and remote after World War I. A threat in theory, it was weak and isolated in practice. The Bolsheviks were focused inward, trying to build the world's first socialist society. Even steady economic growth and industrialization during the 1930s, while the rest of the world was mired in depression, were just barely sufficient to steel the nation for its titanic struggle in World War II against Nazi Germany. It was the defeat of Germany and the Red Army's advance into Central Europe that made the Soviets a force with which the West had at last to contend. The ideological challenge of 1917 became a tangible strategic challenge in 1945.[10]

U.S. policy makers still did not consider the USSR primarily a military threat after World War II. Although the Red Army occupied Eastern Europe, the Soviet Union had been devastated by the course of the fighting. The German army had occupied the western third of the country in its initial invasion in 1941 and plundered it mercilessly. Horrific fighting over the next four years had killed more than 25 million Soviets. What President Harry Truman's administration most feared after 1945 was not Red Army troops marching west to invade Western Europe but their mere presence in the heart of Europe encouraging local leftist radicals. In the chaotic, impoverishing aftermath of World War II, with conservatives dispirited and delegitimated by wartime collaboration with fascism, voters in France, Italy, and Belgium shifted significant support to socialist and communist parties. What scared U.S. policy makers was not so much an unlikely Soviet invasion of Western Europe. What worried them more was the possibility that Western Europeans might choose communism on their own, in democratic elections.[11]

Just as troubling for some American political leaders was the idea of communists working inside the United States. The concern here was not that communists might get elected in deeply anticommunist American elections. American Communist Party organizers had gained some real respect in the 1930s for their commitment to labor unions and civil rights, and they were shielded to some extent by the U.S. alliance with the Soviet Union from 1941 to 1945. But the start of the Cold War between the two countries led to the onset of the Second Red Scare by 1947 and swift repression of radicals of all stripes. The number of American Communist Party members, always small, dropped precipitously. The Second Red Scare merged into McCarthyism in 1950 with the emergence of the witch-hunting junior Republican senator from Wisconsin and the onset of the U.S. war in Korea, and it lasted until at least the end of that war in 1953 and the Senate's censure of Joseph McCarthy in 1954.[12]

American Cold Warriors worried not about communists in the United States being popular but about them being treacherously clever. Spies were the primary concern. Agents of the Soviet Union indeed worked in both Britain and the United States and occasionally gained access to valuable classified information. They were not nearly as prevalent or successful as some U.S. leaders feared, but congressional and Justice Department investigators sought them out and hounded many other suspects who turned out to be innocent. McCarthy made his name chairing the Senate Internal Security Subcommittee, while over on the House of Representatives side of Capitol Hill, Richard Nixon and others manned the House Un-American Activities Committee (HUAC). Established originally to investigate disloyalty and subversion from right or left in the run-up to World War II, HUAC quickly shifted to focusing on communists and those sympathetic to Marxism.[13]

HUAC's very name suggested some uncertainty about what constituted "American" activities and anxiety about Americans acting in "un-American" ways. Among other industrialized democracies, a comparable national legislative investigation of, say, "un-British," "un-French," or "un-Swedish" activities would have been unlikely. Regardless of the wishes of some nativists, the United States had never been an ethnostate or a nation whose ancestors had lived on the same land for centuries and millennia, back into the mists of prehistory. Instead, Americans bonded in a common commitment to certain political ideals of liberty and constitutional self-government. So "un-Americanism" referred to subversion of those ideals. Un-American behavior could be seen as stretching all the way back to the resistance of British Loyalists during the American Revolution, whose rejection of independence and republican government rendered them the first un-Americans. In the early Cold War, HUAC's brief period of political prominence revealed anew an enduring concern about foreignness and whether foreign influence might gain traction with some U.S. citizens.[14]

Concern about communist influence in the late 1940s and early 1950s derived in large part from a crucial expansion of how Americans defined their "national security." From independence in 1776 to the 1930s, U.S. citizens rarely used this phrase. They considered security a matter of simply defending the nation's borders from military attack. Protected by oceans to the east and west and nonaggressive neighbors to the north and south, Americans enjoyed something close to free security. Only in the lead-up to World War II did this change. Japanese imperial expansion in the western Pacific conflicted with far-flung U.S. interests there, including the American-controlled Philippines, and Nazi Germany's aggressions in Europe threatened important U.S. trading partners and liberal democracies, particularly France and Britain. The Franklin Roosevelt administration began to recalculate the factors that assured American security in a world trending toward autarchy, closed trading blocs, and war. Could the United States survive as a wealthy democratic country isolated in such a hostile world? Roosevelt thought not. "National security" stretched beyond mere border defense to the shaping of geopolitics abroad.[15]

The course and outcome of the Second World War recast Americans' understanding of their nation's place in the world. If U.S. interests were global, then so too were potential threats. The onset of the Cold War confirmed and deepened the U.S. commitment to shaping a world order that would allow the United States to thrive as a free-trading liberal democracy. Americans had helped vanquish the threat of totalitarianism from the right in the hot war against Nazi Germany. Now they turned to the longer struggle of defeating totalitarianism from the left in the Cold War against the Soviet Union, their former ally.[16]

The fascist project and the communist project were hardly the same. Fascists aimed for a kind of vertical solidarity: all the people of a single ethnic state, unified and bound together by blood and soil, following a charismatic leader and pressing outward to conquer and dominate other, lesser peoples. By contrast, communists sought a kind of horizontal solidarity: all workers of the world united against their class exploiters, with no national, ethnic, or racial barriers to divide them. These were very different kinds of revolutionaries. Fascists and communists understood that they were each other's truest opposites and opponents, as the fighting in Europe in the 1930s and 1940s often demonstrated, from Spain to Poland.[17]

For most Americans, however, such ideological differences seemed less important than certain obvious similarities in behavior. Both fascists and communists in practice embraced absolute government control of individual citizens. The United States had its own evident limitations on citizens' liberty, particularly for citizens of color, but the large majority of Americans considered such totalitarian behavior to be anathema. Both fascists and communists were associated with walls and confinement, with mass death and vast prison camps: the Nazi extermination facilities such as Auschwitz and the Soviet gulag of grim political prisons across Siberia. Fascists and communists might see themselves as standing at opposite ends of a linear political spectrum, as far apart as they could be. But Americans tended to view that spectrum as bending more into a circle, with the rightist and leftist opponents of liberal democracy going opposite ways around the circle and meeting at the shared point of totalitarian rule. Some observers used the term "Red Fascism" to describe the USSR.[18]

Mainstream American views of communism were interwoven with understandings of Russia. For the quarter-century before 1945 and to the Bolsheviks' dismay, communists had succeeded in just one land. They had seized control of the vast territory of the Russian empire, which incorporated Ukrainians, central Asians, and many other non-Russian peoples, as well as dominance of Mongolia. Americans, like other Westerners, wrestled with Russia's geographical and therefore cultural identity. Was it European or Asian? Could it be both?

The most important American explanation of Soviet behavior in the early Cold War came from the diplomat George Kennan, whose "Long Telegram" home from the U.S. embassy in Moscow in 1946 presaged the following year's Truman Doctrine of containing communism around the globe. Kennan blamed much of Soviet despotism and tyranny on the country's being half-Asian. Its leaders' suspiciousness and inscrutability were "the results of century-long contact with Asiatic hordes," which resulted in an "attitude of Oriental secretiveness and conspiracy." Kennan believed the "westernized upper crust" of the old czarist elite had promoted healthier European values and behaviors, and their removal by the Bolsheviks revealed the Russians as "a 17th-century semi-Asiatic people" at heart. Leslie C. Stevens, the naval attaché in the U.S. embassy in Moscow from 1947 to 1949, agreed, referring to Russians' "half-Asiatic minds."[19]

The newly independent nations of what was just beginning to be called the Third World were skeptical of such an interpretation of Russianness. For them, Soviet leaders might sometimes provide useful economic or military assistance, but they were unquestionably white and European. The USSR was not included in the 1955 conference of the nonaligned nations of the Third World, held in Bandung and hailed by President Sukarno of Indonesia, the host nation, as "the first international conference of colored peoples in the history of mankind." From an Asian or African perspective, the Soviets represented one side in an intramural competition among the industrialized nations of the global North.[20]

Americans were not so sure. In its coverage of the Soviet occupation of Hungary in 1956, *Time* magazine described the "big new tanks . . . protected by trotting groups of Asian-Russian infantrymen." These were outsiders—Asians, "trotting" like animals—invading Europe. This is what the Iron Curtain was all about. Soviet communists were often described by Americans in language implying inhuman relentlessness or animalistic devouring. Kennan's Long Telegram depicted the regime in Moscow as exerting "insistent, unceasing pressure for penetration and command" over Western societies. Other observers spoke and drew images of the USSR as a large and aggressive bear, armed with powerful teeth and claws and intent on seizing, tearing, chewing, and swallowing other nations and peoples. Thus Truman and his successors sought to contain the Russian bear, down through President Ronald Reagan's famous 1984 reelection campaign advertisement that warned, "There's a bear in the woods . . . Isn't it smart to be as strong as the bear?"[21]

Or was it equally important to be as clever as a coyote? Communists during the Cold War were also frequently depicted as scavengers. They were too weak or cowardly to hunt for prey in a straightforward fashion, instead slinking around to attack the most vulnerable targets, in this view. Scores of relatively poor, agrarian new nations won their independence from colonial rule between 1945 and 1965 and became the focus of Soviet and American campaigns to win their loyalty. While communists spoke the language of revolution and centralized control of economic development, American analysts developed instead a theory of economic and political modernization. From the modernizers' perspective, all successful nations would follow the American path of free trade and private investment to reach the takeoff point for industrialization and affluence. Modernization theory viewed communists as trying to pick off the poorest and weakest of the new nations, deceiving them with false promises of rapid economic growth and greater social justice.[22]

Ultimately, communism and Russia did not remain synonymous for Americans as the Cold War era developed. Communists had come to power in Eastern Europe and North Korea on the backs of the advancing Soviet army in 1945. But that was it for "Red Army socialism." Elsewhere, indigenous communists gained control on their own in several lands, including Yugoslavia, China, Vietnam, Cuba, and Cambodia. This pattern frustrated Moscow's desire to assert its own unquestioned authority. Marxist sympathizers who called themselves socialists rather than Communist Party members also governed, at least briefly, in such countries as Iraq, Syria, Chile, Angola, Mozambique, Ethiopia, and Nicaragua.

At the start of the Cold War, Americans had widely believed that any kind of communist or socialist organizing, anywhere in the world, was controlled by master puppeteers in the Kremlin. Assistant Secretary of State Dean Rusk told a large gathering in New York in 1951 that the revolutionary government of the new People's Republic of China, with whom the United States was then at war in Korea, "may be a colonial Russian government. . . . It is not the government of China. It does not pass the first test. It is not Chinese." This would surely have startled Mao Zedong and the other proudly Chinese leaders whom Rusk was describing. American thinking evolved to see the possibility of Chinese as well as Russian hands behind communists elsewhere, such as in President Lyndon Johnson's blaming "the deepening shadow of Communist China" in 1965 for the crisis in South Vietnam in which he chose to intervene. But Americans continued to assume that communists were only successful when empowered by outsiders. Top communists in Moscow and Beijing were conspirators who hoodwinked others.[23]

The Cold War had one other effect on commonplace American thinking about other peoples in the face of communist expansion. Neutrality, long the cherished U.S. position toward conflicts abroad, became anathema. No one could remain neutral given this global crisis. With the Soviets threatening freedom everywhere, Cold Warriors demanded that the United States lead and engage everywhere. "The assault on free institutions is world-wide now," U.S. policy makers declared in the definitive 1950 analysis known as NSC-68, which shifted U.S. policy from merely containing communism as it was to instead seeking to roll it back. "In the context of the present polarization of power a defeat of free institutions anywhere is a defeat everywhere." No more ground could be given. U.S. national security now encompassed the entire globe, and Americans expected every nation to choose between what they saw as U.S.-style freedom and Soviet-style slavery. Neutrality was no longer an option.[24]

Americans who came of age after the 1940s, when World War II and the Cold War pulled the United States into its modern role as the most powerful and globally engaged nation, had no memory of the much longer era of American neutrality toward great-power conflicts. From 1941 onward, American leadership became a given and was framed as a moral necessity, from defeating totalitarianism to defending freedom around the globe. But with the brief exception of U.S. belligerency in World War I in 1917–1918, regretted thereafter by many citizens, the longer tradition of U.S. neutrality had also been understood in moral terms from the beginning. The New World of republican rule should have no "entangling alliances" with the corrupt monarchies of the Old World, George Washington had warned. Europeans and others would continue their unjust imperial wars, Thomas Jefferson had observed, and the United States should "fatten on the follies of the old" nations by trading with all and fighting with none. American leadership in the world, as the Puritan leader John Winthrop had suggested even earlier, should flow from serving as a "city upon a hill," a model of just and peaceful behavior in a corrupt and wicked world. And the United States had sought strenuously to avoid being pulled into either World War I or World War II.[25]

The virtues of neutrality depended on how one evaluated the nature of the conflict being avoided. For U.S. leaders in the early Cold War, this seemed clear-cut: a total global emergency with the direst implications for the future of humanity. From this perspective, Washington's impatience and occasional anger at the efforts of Third World nations to avoid choosing sides was not surprising. Such sentiments sometimes reflected cultural or racial condescension. George Kennan told U.S. officers at the National

War College in 1952 that nonwhite leaders needed to be seized "by the scruff of the neck" and made to defend their newly independent nations from potential Soviet incursions. In a 1956 commencement address at Iowa State College (today University), Secretary of State John Foster Dulles declared that "neutrality has increasingly become an obsolete conception, and, except under very exceptional circumstances, it is an immoral and shortsighted conception." In a crisis of freedom versus slavery, as U.S. leaders understood the Cold War, refusing to stand up for freedom was immoral—regardless of the irony of the American historical legacy as the greatest slaveholding society.[26]

But freedom turned out to be a complicated issue in the mid-twentieth century. The majority of the world's people lived in lands long dominated by European imperialists, and their primary political goal was national independence. Their most immediate problem was colonialism and its twin burden of racial discrimination against nonwhite peoples. For Asians and Africans, colonialism and racism, not communism, were the great moral injustices that had contorted their lives and the lives of their ancestors for generations. They knew that the United States had its own considerable legacy of racial inequality and continuing alliance with the Western European colonial powers. The U.S. State Department acknowledged in an internal study that Third World neutralism was often defended on the grounds that "the racial intolerance of the Western powers is just as bad as anything that might be practiced by the Communist bloc." Just as anticommunists disdained or mistrusted neutralism regarding the Soviet Union, the Central Intelligence Agency reported to the White House in 1963, antiracists saw "no room for nonalignment in this dispute" over colonialism and racial inequality.[27]

The Nature of the Communist Threat

The dream of a better socialist future was the siren song that most Americans feared above all others. The Soviets might outsell the Americans in a world recovering from the devastation of World War II. As closed societies, the nations of the communist bloc offered little ammunition to would-be investigative critics; they avoided the Western albatross of formal Jim Crow discrimination and lingering colonialism. The United States, the ultimate society of salespeople, might thus—ironically—lose out to the marketing of the great antimarket nation, the USSR. U.S. leaders believed they could not afford to forfeit the great prize of the Cold War competition: the loyalty of the world's newly independent, majority-nonwhite nations.[28]

Some of socialism's enduring allure in the late 1940s stemmed from the physical and psychological trauma across Europe, from the Red Army's remarkable success against the Nazis, and from revulsion at capitalism's close cousin, imperialism, and the brutalities and racism associated with it. Some of socialism's attractiveness arose from its focus on social justice and greater economic equality. And some of its appeal derived from the apparent Marxist logic of moving from a necessary, materially productive but exploitative stage of capitalist society to a now higher, more humane, redistributive stage of socialist society. From the English Channel to the South China Sea, socialists and communists were gaining adherents.[29]

Capitalists, religious devotees, and nationalists all felt threatened. For capitalists, the alternative system of socialism posed a perilous form of apostasy, a false promise of even greater freedom and justice. Rather than simply rejecting private property and free enterprise, communists were convincing people to replace them with something better. For religious believers, Marxism offered only scorn. As the "opiate of the masses," religion for these secular revolutionaries was a false distraction from the immediate material reality of life. And for vigorously nationalistic Americans, communism was about as foreign as one could get, with the aim of uniting all workers of the world and erasing the very national boundaries that literally defined America as America. What could be less American than that? Communists seemed the most foreign of foreigners.[30]

Since the first communist success in Russia in 1917, opponents of socialism had sought to explain the identity and allure of Marx's most revolutionary followers. Observers of the Russian revolution noted the imperial German government's efforts to undermine its czarist enemies on Germany's eastern front. Berlin cleverly arranged for the charismatic Vladimir Lenin to return to Russia from exile in Switzerland in order to foment greater radicalism among the diverse opponents of the czar. The Germans were usually described as ushering Lenin through wartime Germany on a "sealed train" from the Swiss border and then on to Russia via Sweden and Finland. Winston Churchill referred to Lenin as the "plague bacillus" injected by the German kaiser into the fluid body politic of Russia, a deadly bacterium that could potentially destroy a government. The goal was to keep the infection of Bolshevism from leaking out on German soil and set it loose instead in a destabilized Russia.[31]

U.S. policy makers often used a carceral rather than biological metaphor. Obsessed with the notion of individual liberty, they saw the Soviets and their allies as jailers. Communists locked innocent people up. Eastern Europeans and North Koreans had joined Soviet peoples in this kind of high-walled captivity by 1948, and Americans feared that Western Europeans could be next. The establishment of the People's Republic of China in 1949 shocked Americans, who had long believed their country had a special role to play in China through missionary and educational work. "With God's help," Senator Kenneth Wherry (R-NE) had reportedly declared just a few years earlier, the United States could "lift up Shanghai up and up, ever up, until it looks just like Kansas City." Instead, young men from Kansas City and young men from Shanghai were soon killing each other by the thousands on the Korean peninsula, as the United States and China sent troops to aid their respective allies in the Korean War in 1950.[32]

Developments in Cuba a few years later stoked similar fears. Fidel Castro's revolution there in 1959 soon seemed to Americans another demonstration of a formerly free people being taken captive and enslaved, now worrisomely close to American shores. American observers loathed the idea of a communist government just ninety miles across the Straits of Florida from Key West, and President John Kennedy's administration tried repeatedly to subvert or overthrow the Castro regime. Anticommunist Cuban refugees settled in south Florida and provided steady publicity about the communist captivity of the island and its people. In Europe, the communist government of East Germany stanched the outflow of young émigrés to the West by building the infamous Berlin Wall in 1961, sealing in East Germans. Kennedy visited West Berlin in 1963 to demonstrate U.S. solidarity with city residents, more than half of whom turned out to hear him declare in front of the wall, "I am a Berliner!" Two days later, the high priest of socialism, the Soviet leader Nikita Khrushchev, visited this starkest symbol of communist captivity and announced to an East German crowd of half a million: "I love the wall."[33]

For Americans, who tended to think of their own culture as the freest and highest expression of human nature, the idea of captivity was peculiarly repugnant. Physical captivity, such as being taken prisoner in war, was bad enough. But the prospect of mental captivity—of Americans losing their minds to the false lures of apostasy—was simply evil. It was *unnatural*. Fears of captivity dated back to the earliest English settlers in North America and their encounters with indigenous peoples—the original subversive, communitarian "Reds"—which gave rise to abiding anxieties about frontier captives "going native," that is, losing who they really were by going along with their captors and converting, willingly or not, to a Mohawk or Powhatan culture.[34]

The central story of captivity in the United States, of course, had been that of tens of millions of enslaved black workers, a centuries-long gulag whose deep scars remain visible. Captive Africans and their African American offspring and descendants labored on Southern plantations and in towns and cities, from 1619 until slavery's abolition in the Civil War by 1865. They built the wealth that underlay American economic success, while having the fruits of their labor—along with their freedom—stolen from them daily. The end of formal slavery soon led to its de facto reinstitution during the Jim Crow century (1870s–1960s) through the widespread use of state vagrancy laws and convict gang labor. The historian Douglas Blackmon called this "slavery by another name," while the historian David Oshinsky labeled it "worse than slavery."[35]

Americans, in other words, had a great deal of experience with slavery and captivity by 1945. More than any other great power, they had been modeling it for the world. The irony of a still-segregated United States leading what it called the free world in the Cold War eventually gave rise to several library shelves' worth of historical literature. It also stimulated resistance from many new Third World leaders and provided a field day for Soviet propagandists in the late 1940s and 1950s. The seemingly endless story of white violence against African Americans received renewed attention with the highly publicized torture and murder of fourteen-year-old Emmett Till, down from Chicago to visit relatives in rural Mississippi in the summer of 1955. The Pulitzer Prize–winning Mississippi novelist William Faulkner responded that "if we in America have reached the point in our desperate culture where we must murder children, no matter for what reason or what color, we don't deserve to survive and probably won't."[36]

Unlike Faulkner, most white Americans did not pay much attention to events such as the Till murder. The common American blindness regarding race in the early Cold War years suggested instead the prevalence of the psychological mechanisms of denial and projection. NSC-68, the central U.S. strategic plan of 1950, depicted a globe starkly divided into a "free world" and a "slave world." "The implacable purpose of the slave state," the authors concluded, "is to eliminate the challenge of freedom." Three years later, Secretary of State John Foster Dulles reworked a proposed "Resolution on Enslavement of Peoples" in order to position the United States as perpetually abolitionist, in contrast to the enslaving Soviets. "The People of the United States, in fidelity to their tradition and heritage of freedom," Dulles wrote, "have never acquiesced in such enslavement of any people."[37]

Such denial of 250 years of American slavery by the nation's top foreign policy maker deserves a moment of contemplation. Seeing themselves as a liberty-loving people, white Americans, at least, so despised captivity that they could write it out of their history. Something similar happened in the nation's history classrooms, where the antebellum South and the Civil War had long been treated with kid gloves. Only the rise of the civil rights movement and the subsequent blossoming of the fields of black history and bottom-up social history brought American slavery into clearer focus in the later 1960s and 1970s. At the time some critics tried to dismiss this as "revisionist history," but of course all history worth writing is revisionist— that is, seeing the past anew, or re-visioning. Anything else would be just mindless copying of traditions without reconsidering them. And the failure to grapple with the history of American slavery surely demanded revision.[38]

The apparent obtuseness or hypocrisy of John Foster Dulles, the chief American diplomat in 1953, suggests how readily people adjust their pasts to fit their needs. We pick and choose and reimagine in order to construct a narrative that makes sense to us, and we leave a lot out. Political needs can encourage particularly selective uses of history. The dominating feature of the political landscape was the Cold War, and American troops were still deadlocked in a grinding hot war on the Korean peninsula. Dulles's boss, President Dwight Eisenhower, made clear in his inaugural address a month earlier that "forces of good and evil are massed and armed and opposed as rarely before in history." This was not a time for subtle distinctions, Eisenhower insisted: "Freedom is pitted against slavery; lightness against the dark."[39]

Soviet behavior had plenty of dark to it. After the use of Soviet troops and tanks to help crush an uprising in communist-ruled Hungary in 1956, Eisenhower proclaimed a "Captive Nations Week" to call attention to the lack of freedom in Eastern Europe. In their focus on Soviet authoritarianism, U.S. policy makers were genuine. But to some observers Washington seemed also selective in its understanding and use of the idea of captivity. Algerians were not included as a captive nation, although they were fighting desperately at the time against foreign French control. Kenyans were also not included as a captive nation, although they were at the time being rounded up and jailed in concentration camps by their imperial British overlords. European victims of foreign captivity enjoyed much greater concern from the U.S. government than did Asian or African victims.[40]

With the Cold War at high tide, however, most Americans paid relatively little attention to decolonization and the rise of the Third World. Like most people everywhere, Americans focused primarily on their own lives. This was particularly true in the consumer-friendly decades following World War II, as a rapidly expanding middle class engaged with issues of family, homeownership, and an abundance of material goods from automobiles to bubblegum. When they did attend to international events, citizens tended to see them in terms of the black-and-white Cold War struggle that their leaders articulated. A large majority of Americans by the 1940s and 1950s were not black and did not live in the South, and for them race slavery seemed increasingly a story of a distant past, even as segregation remained.[41]

Brainwashing and the Korean War

Captivity now seemed to reside elsewhere. The twentieth century had witnessed the rise of two great totalitarian empires that had literally locked up their own people, the German Third Reich in concentration camps and extermination factories and the Soviets in the labor camps of the gulag. Anne O'Hare McCormick wrote in the *New York Times* in 1952 of this "grim century of the homeless man," in which Russians and Eastern Europeans were now "the saddest people on earth" and "homeless at home," forced against their wills "to live under a system so alien to their own instincts and desires." Their "own instincts and desires," in this view, were to live freely, like Americans—or at least like white Americans. This was natural. But instead "their homelands are strange prisons," and "their spiritual exile is far worse than physical deportation." This was unnatural.[42]

The spread of this "system so alien" into China during the civil war there from 1945 to 1949 filled many Americans with dread. Communism had now seized control of the most populous nation in the world, a symbol of the nonwhite global majority, who were rapidly shedding colonialism.

China had also long been seen by American missionaries as the most fruitful field for Christian evangelism. And here the Chinese were turning starkly against American political and religious values. The Chinese revolution seemed a portent of the future of the Third World, particularly when the United States and China went to war with each other less than a year later in Korea, in defense of their respective Korean allies.

When American soldiers then began to be taken as prisoners of war, a new concern swept through the U.S. military command and the American public: the fear of "brainwashing." Edward Hunter, a CIA officer operating undercover as a journalist, apparently first used the term publicly in a September 24, 1950, *Miami News* article entitled "'Brainwashing' Tactics Force Chinese Into Ranks of Communist Party." The term encapsulated American concerns that the communists in China had developed devious new methods of psychological torture and mind control, used first on Chinese citizens and then on American POWs, which supposedly enabled them to reprogram the minds of their victims. The *Wall Street Journal* explained this phenomenon in an editorial under the expository title: "The Silent People: Communists Brainwash the Once-Individualistic Chinese Into Gloomy Conformity, Fear, and Mental Atrophy."[43]

The negative image of "washing" a person's brain was a little surprising, given the positive value of personal hygiene in American society. Frequent handwashing and regular bathing and tooth brushing were seen as particularly American habits. But this metaphor provided a useful way to explain enthusiasm for communism as the result of an external intervention. If American-style individualism was in fact the normal cultural setting for healthy peoples, then hostile action against people's minds offered a convenient explanation for the disturbing interest in socialism in the emerging Third World.

Communists as brainwashers fit with the belief that followers of Karl Marx were fundamentally deceptive. "The Communist does not look like the popular conception of a Communist," declared Thomas F. Murphy, the federal prosecutor in the 1950 trial of the suspected Soviet agent Alger Hiss. "He does not have uncropped hair, he does not wear horn-rimmed glasses nor carry the Daily Worker. He doesn't have baggy trousers." Mainstream Americans imagined communists as sneaky and dishonest, in contrast to the assumption that normal U.S. citizens dressed, spoke, and acted openly and directly. Communists were not who they seemed to be. If they scavenged amid the detritus of modernization, it showed that they could not win an open, honest argument. Instead, they picked off the weakest members of the historically poor Third World with false promises.[44]

Going to war in Korea sharply ratcheted up American anxieties about communism. Soviet and American negotiators had agreed late in World War II that they would share postwar occupation of the Korean peninsula, once it was surrendered by the Japanese colonial forces who had controlled it since 1905. Soviet troops arrived in Korea well before U.S. troops in 1945, and the Soviets lived up to their agreement, even accepting a U.S.-suggested border at the 38th parallel, which kept Seoul, the capital city, in the south. Each side allowed politically compatible Koreans to establish governments and withdrew their forces from the resulting independent communist North Korean and anticommunist South Korean states by 1949.[45]

A divided peninsula satisfied neither side. Hostile border skirmishes and large-scale leftist uprisings in the South killed one hundred thousand Koreans even before the outbreak of the main "Korean War" in late June 1950, when the North launched a massive attack across the border. The North Korean army swept southward and seized all but a small redoubt around Pusan. The Truman administration sent U.S. troops from neighboring occupied Japan to save the South Korean regime from annihilation. U.S. forces turned the tide and forced the North to retreat. Three years of horrific warfare followed, with the People's Republic of China sending in reinforcements to help the North after U.S. troops neared the Chinese border. The fighting bogged down in a bloody stalemate close to the original dividing line at the 38th parallel.

The Korean War put U.S. troops for the first time into combat against communist forces. In World War II, the Soviet Red Army had been a critical ally of the United States, and fascism had been the common enemy, so this was radically different. The military correspondent for the *New York Times*, Hanson Baldwin, wrote in December 1951 that the imprisonment of U.S. troops by communists in North Korea embodied "the essential tragedy of our times." Far beyond mere power politics, Baldwin believed, this was an elemental struggle of free men to hold on to their very souls. Broader anxieties about communist influence around the globe took concrete form on the ground in Korea, even as the nature of the war remained largely mysterious to an American public with little knowledge of Northeast Asia. Once the fighting front between Chinese and American troops stabilized in 1951, the war dragged on for two more years, largely over the question of how to handle the repatriation of prisoners of war.[46]

The Chinese insisted on the terms of the Geneva Convention amendment directing that all POWs be "released and repatriated without delay." The Truman administration, seeing a confluence of moral principle and political advantage, demanded instead that all POWs be given the choice of going where they wanted to go. U.S. officials genuinely believed that soldiers in the Chinese People's Liberation Army (PLA) should not be forced to return to communist rule if they did not wish to. Such personnel could go instead to Taiwan, to which the Chinese anticommunist forces of Chiang Kai-shek had retreated from the mainland just a few years earlier after being driven out by the PLA. Washington hoped for a huge propaganda coup by having tens of thousands of Chinese soldiers refuse to be returned to communist hands—to slavery, as Americans saw it.[47]

It was in Korea that communism as captivity became fully clear to Americans. GIs were now literal prisoners of actual communists. Surely, U.S. policy makers assumed, many Chinese would not go back to Mao Zedong, while of course all captured American GIs would be thrilled beyond measure to return home. But a few handfuls of American prisoners complicated this clear-cut moral and political expectation. Twenty-one U.S. POWs refused to be repatriated and chose instead to go to China. Chinese authorities paraded them before the international press corps. For U.S. authorities, the best explanation for such treason was brainwashing. Only some kind of devious mental torture and manipulation could lead a patriotic American soldier to reject his own liberty. Over the next decade and a half, almost all of the twenty-one eventually found their way quietly home to the United States, living in an anonymity quite different from their brief moment of international notoriety in the fall of 1953.[48]

By contrast, nearly fifty thousand Chinese and North Korean POWs also refused repatriation. Vetted by neutral Indian military guards, they remained instead in U.S.-allied South Korea or chose passage to U.S.-allied Taiwan. They seemed to represent a vigorous confirmation of the natural aspiration of all peoples to live freely, like Americans. But this choice also reflected the recent political turmoil in Northeast Asia, including the founding of two new Korean nations and defeat of the anticommunist Guomindang government of China by the communists. More than half of the Chinese POWs had previously served as soldiers for Chiang Kai-shek's Guomindang, and a large fraction of the North Korean POWs were originally captured South Korean soldiers. Political allegiances were up for grabs. The ranks of the prisoner-of-war camps in South Korea thus became fiercely politicized, and "the defection issue transformed the camps into a war zone," in the words of the historian Charles Young. Such circumstances inhibited individuals in trying to make a fully free choice.[49]

Was it actually true: did brainwashing happen? Certainly American POWs in North Korea did a lot of hard thinking while incarcerated under often-extreme duress, surrounded by disease, hunger, cold, violence, and death. No doubt many of them questioned everything they knew in the face of their own possible imminent deaths. U.S. Army commanders were worried enough about the first returning POWs, released in April 1953, that they isolated twenty of them in a medical facility in Valley Forge, Pennsylvania, for a period of observation. It quickly became clear, however, that the veterans showed no signs of psychiatric reprogramming. Indeed, despite the brutalities of the POW camps, they had evidently resisted their captors when possible. Forced to sing revolutionary songs in order to receive supper, for example, they subverted the lyrics of the Communist Internationale, "arise ye wretched of the earth" becoming "arise ye red shit of the earth." The Pentagon concluded there was "no evidence of any of them having been subjected to 'brainwashing' techniques." A 1956 U.S. Army training manual on interrogation confirmed that not one "conclusively documented case of the actual 'brainwashing' of an American prisoner of war in Korea" existed.[50]

The extent of concern about brainwashing suggests the central place of psychological warfare in the Cold War. With nuclear weapons on both sides, wars were necessarily limited, in contrast to the total war of World War II. Yet the nature of the conflict seemed utterly black and white to Americans: if freedom was poised against slavery, how could such a total conflict be limited? This dilemma profoundly frustrated Americans, just as the stalemated fighting frustrated U.S. soldiers on the Korean peninsula. Allowing all POWs to go where they wished after the ceasefire offered an opportunity for at least a clear moral victory, demonstrating to the world that people overwhelmingly preferred U.S.-style democratic capitalist freedom to Soviet- or Chinese-style communism.

Pointing out the absence of such freedom under communist rule remained a primary theme of U.S. leadership throughout the Cold War. Revolutionary Cuba's proximity to American shores particularly riled American policy makers, as did Fidel Castro's strident denunciations of U.S. behavior. Gone were the days of Havana as a center of pleasure tourism, famous for its casinos and brothels, annually hosting some three hundred thousand visitors, mostly Americans. One of those had been a handsome and sociable young U.S. senator from Massachusetts, John Kennedy. Castro believed he and his fellow revolutionaries had finally freed their country from foreign control and debasement. U.S. leaders thought exactly the opposite. In an October 1962 speech announcing the discovery of Soviet nuclear missiles installed on Cuban soil, Kennedy, now president, reiterated this message about enslavement: "Finally, I want to say a few words to the captive people of Cuba. . . . I have watched and the American people have watched with deep sorrow how your nationalist revolution was betrayed—and how your fatherland fell under foreign domination." Kennedy warned that "your leaders are no longer Cuban leaders inspired by Cuban ideals. They are puppets and agents of an international conspiracy." The struggle against captivity continued.[51]

The myth of brainwashing outlived the Korean War and drifted into many corners of Cold War American culture and beyond, from the early novel and film *The Manchurian Candidate* down to the popular contemporary Showtime television series *Homeland*. American social critics worried about the rise of what they called "mass society" and the conformity of a vast, homogenized popular consumer culture. How might this affect the individualism that the United States was supposed to sustain? Could Americans continue to develop as free individuals? Metaphors of brainwashing spread widely by the mid-1950s, from how the burgeoning advertising industry affected potential customers to how police interrogators sometimes extracted false confessions from suspected criminals. In a 1957 television broadcast, Walter Cronkite, the nation's most trusted newsman, declared that brainwashing jeopardized "our preservation as human beings" and was thus "one of the underlying themes" of the twentieth century.[52]

Brainwashing dominated the science-fiction films that proved widely popular in the 1950s. In these movies aliens regularly infiltrated and replaced Americans' minds while leaving them apparently normal and unchanged on the surface. "Suddenly, while you're asleep," warned the 1956 movie *Invasion of the Body Snatchers*, "they will absorb your minds, your memories, and you'll be reborn into an untroubled world" of collectivist calm, without individuality or meaning. Later generations of filmmakers used technological innovations for the same purpose. The hugely popular Jason Bourne series of films of the early 2000s hinged on traumatic techniques of supposed mind control as a way to train elite CIA operatives. Whether at the hands of socialists, aliens, or rogue U.S. government scientists, the individualism that Americans believed defined their culture seemed to them at risk.[53]

Concerns about preserving Americans' individuality and essential personhood dovetailed with the rapid and dramatic expansion of psychology as an academic discipline directly after World War II. Psychology's boom derived in part from the overall growth of American universities in the postwar era. But the interest in figuring out the sources of individual human behavior also arose from the specific challenges facing the United States in the 1940s and 1950s: the vast bureaucracy of the military during World War II, the spread of homogeneous suburbs across the American landscape, the existential threat of nuclear war, and the collectivist challenge from global communism. The psychological warfare central to the Cold War stimulated a demand for psychological expertise.[54]

The healthy cognitive and emotional development of children emerged as a particular theme in the competition with the Soviet Union for the loyalty of the rest of the world. "The great weakness of dictatorships is that they enslave the minds and the characters of people over whom they rule," President Harry Truman told the Mid-Century White House Conference on Children and Youth in December 1950. "And the effects of this enslavement are most serious in the case of children." Kids deserved what the prominent conference organizers Margaret Mead, Benjamin Spock, and others called "a healthy personality for every child." A similar meeting toward the end of World War II had aimed to change German childrearing and education after the war in order to disrupt a return path to Nazism. "Driving these scholars' interest in children was the conviction that human difference was rooted in culture rather than blood," the historian Sara Fieldston writes. They "rejected the claims of eugenicists who understood personal characteristics as governed by heredity." Rather than seeing individual personality as genetically hardwired at birth, they believed it "bore the indelible stamp of early childhood experiences." From the perspective of American social scientists, children everywhere could be raised to be like Americans—that is, as free individuals.[55]

Learning to Live with Communists

In the long run, even supposedly brainwashing communists could not remain completely foreign to Americans. From the beginning in 1917, of course, some Americans had been sympathetic to the Bolshevik project. American communists had cheered for and sometimes traveled to the new Soviet Union in order to help bring on what they saw as humankind's better future. Members of the Communist Party of the United States of America (CPUSA) were not rejected and loathed by all their fellow citizens, particularly in the dark days of capitalist failure during the Great Depression of the 1930s. Party members, few as they were, often proved to be unusually courageous organizers of working people and promoters of racial equality, for which they won some real admiration, at least until the onset of the Cold War.[56]

Even those Americans who were highly unsympathetic to communism sometimes learned to live with it, often quite profitably. The Ford Motor Company, for example, sold plenty of tractors and other machinery to the Soviets in the 1920s, well before official U.S. diplomatic recognition of the new regime in Moscow. Fred Koch was an MIT-trained chemical engineer who established the family oil business underpinning Koch Industries, later run by his sons Charles and David, libertarian-leaning conservatives and perhaps the two most influential political contributors in modern U.S. history. A fierce Oklahoma anticommunist, Fred Koch nonetheless made much of his early wealth helping Josef Stalin's regime establish its first modern oil refineries and training Soviet engineers to manage them. More inclined to admire the fascist and militarist regimes coming to power in Italy, Germany, and Japan, Koch pivoted to work with the Nazis in building similar petroleum-production facilities in Germany in the 1930s.[57]

Capitalists were typically practical people, not ideologues. U.S. companies were perfectly comfortable working with Soviet communists when doing so promised to be profitable, even before Franklin Roosevelt opened formal diplomatic relations with the government in Moscow in 1933. Official U.S.-Soviet relations remained cool at first, particularly after the Soviets signed a nonaggression pact with the Nazis in 1939. But Hitler's forces broke that agreement in spectacular fashion by invading the USSR two years later, and six months after that Japan attacked the United States at Pearl Harbor. From late 1941 to 1945, as the United States and the Soviet Union fought together against the Axis powers in the largest military conflict in human history, the democratic capitalists in Washington promoted warmly positive views of the Russian people and their communist rulers.[58]

Even the onset of the Cold War in 1946 and 1947 did not completely eliminate U.S. collaboration with communists abroad. Historians and laypeople alike still tend to equate "communism" and "the Soviet Union," at least until the later falling out between the USSR and the People's Republic of China. This was the logic of Moscow as the supposed puppet master controlling Marxist revolutionaries everywhere, an image that remained powerful in the United States right down to President Reagan's 1983 denunciation of the Soviet Union as "an evil empire" and "the focus of evil in the modern world." But U.S. policy makers successfully supported some communists *against* Moscow from the very beginning of the Cold War.[59]

The advancing Soviet armed forces occupied Eastern Europe at the end of World War II and oversaw the installation by 1948 of communist governments from Poland in the north to Bulgaria in the south. Some observers called this "Red Army socialism": a system created by outside liberators-turned-occupiers. The one exception was Yugoslavia, where leftist partisans seized control from the retreating Germans without the assistance of Soviet troops. The new communist government of Josip Broz Tito in Belgrade remained determinedly independent of Moscow, even as tensions mounted. In 1948 Stalin broke off communication with Tito and expelled the Yugoslavs from the Communist Information Bureau, or Cominform, and Yugoslavia never joined the subsequent Warsaw Pact alliance of Eastern European communist governments. The U.S. response was strategic, not ideological. It recognized a national communist government independent of the Soviet Union. The Truman administration swiftly built a constructive relationship with Belgrade involving trade and military assistance. A wedge had been inserted into the communist sphere.[60]

Americans, clearly, could work with communists when they chose to. The wedge expanded and helped crack open the entire idea of a communist bloc by 1969, when Soviet and Chinese forces engaged in a brief firefight along their shared border on the Ussuri River. The clash followed years of growing diplomatic acrimony between the two largest communist governments. The Soviets found that the Chinese, like the Yugoslavs, asserted their own national and international interests rather than obediently follow Moscow's guidance. Communists in power turned out also to be nationalists. Mao Zedong's regime pivoted to the United States to balance its deteriorating relationship with the USSR, and President Richard Nixon's triumphant visit to Beijing followed in 1972. Even the iciest U.S. relationship with a communist regime could thaw; even the most fiercely anticapitalist government could be turned. After Mao's death in 1976, Deng

Xiaoping, the new Chinese leader, believed that the still-agrarian People's Republic, long mired in the internal chaos of its Cultural Revolution, must move decisively to start catching up with the industrialized West. He was willing to take risks to do so. In 1978, the Marxist Deng initiated reforms allowing in the first subversive elements of private enterprise—the Trojan horse was now inside the gate.[61]

The persistent threat of nuclear war gave Americans the most persuasive reason for working with communists: simple survival. U.S.-Soviet confrontation over the placement of Soviet nuclear missiles in Cuba in the fall of 1962 brought the world its closest brush to date with nuclear holocaust. In the months that followed that wrenching crisis, American and Soviet leaders began to work harder to avoid similar risks in the future. Part of this required dialing back some of the demonization of communists. "No government or social system is so evil that its people must be considered as lacking in virtue," President Kennedy announced to the graduating class of American University in June 1963. "As Americans, we find communism profoundly repugnant as a negation of personal freedom and dignity. But we can still hail the Russian people for their many achievements—in science and space, in economic and industrial growth, in culture and in acts of courage." A direct telephone "hotline" was established between the White House and the Kremlin. In July 1968, Pan American and Aeroflot each began nonstop flights between New York and Moscow. In 1972, President Richard Nixon visited Moscow and initiated several years of formal détente. A decade later, Mikhail Gorbachev, the new Soviet leader, began the processes of *glasnost* (political openness) and *perestroika* (economic restructuring) that ushered in the eventual demise of the USSR in 1991.[62]

American dissidents helped prepare this path to détente and the eventual disappearance of the Soviet Union. The intensity of Cold War anticommunism had long troubled many Americans, particularly liberals and leftists. Some had courageously criticized the witch-hunting excesses of the Second Red Scare as it unfolded in the late 1940s and 1950s. When the United States went to war in Vietnam to defend an unpopular anticommunist regime, failing to secure a victory but inflicting massive destruction on that land and its people, a nationwide protest movement swelled at home. New Left organizers, particularly Students for a Democratic Society (SDS), were central to the eventual success of the antiwar resistance campaign. SDS's own orientation can be best understood as anti-anticommunist: they saw Cold War U.S. anticommunism itself as the engine of injustice in much of the Third World. For the New Left, communism seemed a red herring, a false diversion from the real American problems of imperialism abroad and racism and poverty at home. Anticommunism was thus part of the problem, not the solution. It kept Americans focused on the wrong target. The dramatic U.S. failure in Vietnam encouraged a wide swath of the American public, far beyond the ranks of antiwar protesters, to question the virtue of simple anticommunism. This skepticism continued down to the end of the Cold War.[63]

After the USSR disappeared in 1991, reverting to Russia and more than a dozen smaller neighboring countries, the anticommunists had to adjust to a new era. Four years later, the United States opened formal diplomatic relations with communist Vietnam, establishing a new relationship that warmed rapidly. Indeed, within a few months, the new Vietnamese ambassador-designate to Washington found himself invited to dinner with the most obdurate and powerful American anticommunist (and longtime racial segregationist): Jesse Helms (R-NC), chair of the Senate Foreign Relations Committee. Helms represented North Carolina's tobacco farmers, who were facing declining domestic smoking rates and negative publicity at home and were seeking to make gains in more tobacco-friendly markets abroad, particularly in Asia. Helms was pleased with the dinner and later explained to reporters: "I was with some Vietnamese recently, and some of them were smoking two cigarettes at the same time. That's the kind of customers we need!"[64]

In the popular and critically acclaimed FX network television series *The Americans*, whose first season broadcast in 2013, two Soviet spies are inserted into the United States in the 1960s as a supposed young married couple, Elizabeth and Philip Jennings. They run a travel agency in Washington, DC, live in the suburbs, and have two children. The fictional show offered plenty of racy and unlikely plot lines that guarantee action and excitement for viewers. But it also wrestled with serious questions of how to blend raising children with managing careers, how to balance the use of unsavory methods with the pursuit of greater ends, and how to work closely with a spouse in a stressful job. The show particularly highlighted the challenge that the material comforts of American capitalism created for communists during the Cold War. After all, Soviet theorists had always expected capitalism to fail and socialism to supersede and replace it.

The two spies seem well matched and develop a real affection and even love for each other. But Philip seems more taken with the quality of affluent life in the United States, while Elizabeth burns more brightly in her zeal for serving the Soviet Union—"our country"—and building a socialist world. She resists the temptation of American material comforts. At one point, Philip, impatient with her puritanical resistance to enjoying the good life they have, asks if she does not like "any of this": their nice house, their handsome clothes, the ease of their American life in contrast to how they had grown up in the Soviet Union. Elizabeth responds: "It's nicer. It's easier. It isn't better." She remains focused on social justice and the Soviet version of how to pursue that end. But in one of the first scenes after their summertime arrival in humid Washington, she and Philip walk into a typical 1960s motel room. She moves over to the window-unit air conditioner and holds out her hand, bewildered at the cool, pleasant air in contrast to the hot mugginess outside. She is wrestling with the magical allure of capitalist innovativeness.[65]

In principle, Marxism predicted that the socialist future would be materially richer, not poorer, and available to all, not just the bourgeoisie. The British writer and historian Francis Spufford evokes this expectation brilliantly in a fictionalized version of Nikita Khrushchev's 1959 visit to the United States. "If communism couldn't give people a better life than capitalism, he personally couldn't see the point," Spufford writes of Khrushchev. The Americans "had a kind of genius for lining up the fruitfulness of mass production with people's desires. . . . They were magnificently good at producing things you wanted—either things you knew you wanted, or things you discovered you wanted the moment you knew that they existed." Spufford has the Soviet leader ruminate that "America was a torrent of clever anticipations. Soviet industries would have to learn to anticipate as cleverly, *more* cleverly, if they were to overtake America in satisfying wants as well as needs." Khrushchev concludes that the Soviets "too would have to become experts in everyday desires."[66]

They did not. The Soviet economy prioritized military hardware. It produced a remarkable amount of steel and a stunning number of nuclear and other weapons. Soviet central planners minimized homelessness and kept their people mostly fed. But they never developed a socialist path to the kind of creativity and efficiency of the market-based economies of the West, particularly the United States. They did not become "experts in everyday desires." By the 1970s and particularly the 1980s, thanks to détente and accelerating global communication and transportation, the Russian, Ukrainian, and other peoples living under Soviet rule were well aware that their material existence paled in comparison to that of middle-class Americans. That knowledge undercut communist legitimacy. The project of making socialism stumbled on the resilience and cleverness of democratic capitalism. Communist rulers ultimately could not match the profit motive of market economies, so they either disappeared or, as in China and Vietnam, adapted to the incentive of citizens working for themselves and accumulating private property. Marx would have been dismayed. But Americans had proven more clear-eyed about individual freedom and private property and their attractiveness to all peoples, even communists. They had subverted the subversives.[67]

CHAPTER V

Outbound

U.S. Expansion Into Foreign Lands

Many Americans spent the second half of the twentieth century, at the apex of their nation's global power, worrying about the possible spread of communist captivity. Yet the entire sweep of U.S. history from the colonial era onward had been defined, above all else, by expansion and the occupation of new lands and other peoples. The capturing of others and their natural resources formed a central theme of the nation's history. From the first European sailors exploring the North American coastline in the 1500s and the earliest Spanish, English, Dutch, and French settlements ranging from the Florida Straits to the St. Lawrence River to the seizure of the Philippine islands in 1898 and the establishment after World War II of hundreds of military bases around the world, the development of the United States was an outbound story structured by expansion and occupation. When a capturing people worried about being taken captive themselves, it looked a lot like what psychologists call projection.[1]

The scope and speed of expansion in American history were remarkable. This is evident in the growth of population from a few million at independence to more than 330 million today. It is visible in the territorial sovereignty that ballooned from a few small settlements on the sandy shores of the James River in today's Virginia and Cape Cod Bay in today's Massachusetts (and small Spanish communities in St. Augustine and Santa Fe) to the fourth-largest nation on the earth in square mileage. Whether one counts from the first Europeans and Africans to walk on North American soil or from the establishment of the United States as an independent nation, Americans proved to be a restless people eager for new land. The only fully comparable tales of national growth in the modern era were Canada, Australia, and Russia, all important but none as large in population, wealth, or influence. Contemporary Russia may include a few more time zones in its east-west sprawl, but the United States not only straddles an entire temperate continent but also remains the only country with lands that are both arctic (Alaska) and tropical (Hawaiʻi, Puerto Rico, the U.S. Virgin Islands, Guam, the Northern Mariana Islands).

How one should feel about such breadth is a different question. It seems safe to say that most Americans simply considered it normal, their country's size and power a mostly positive reality that reflected well on them. Native Americans and their sympathizers took a different view, one of relentless loss of their lands and disruption of their cultures. Citizens of Mexico shared the perspective that U.S. expansion came at the cost of their diminution. Canadians who knew their history tended to be at least slightly wary of the United States, aware of earlier American efforts to seize lands north of the common border and of ongoing American cultural influence. But most U.S. citizens cheered at least for growth of an economic kind. Growth carried associations with healthfulness in the natural world, such as with gardens and forests. Only a small minority of critics questioned the consequences not only of appropriating others' lands and building military bases abroad but also of unconstrained economic expansion and exploitation of natural resources. They found wisdom in the Western writer Edward Abbey's observation that "growth for the sake of growth is the ideology of the cancer cell."[2]

Assumptions about the perceived virtues of American democracy and American culture helped ease expansion. In common American thinking, self-rule, individual liberty, and a market economy were natural sources of happiness, and other peoples would only benefit from such blessings. While this view seemed commonsensical by the middle of the twentieth century, it was not entirely original to the Cold War period. The revolutionaries of the 1770s had expected other peoples to emulate their actions and in fact had watched as most of Latin America did so in the following generation. The subsequent story of U.S. expansion had awkwardly balanced outright conquest with attempts at cultural conversion, from Powhatan and Pequot Indians in the 1600s to Afghani and Iraqi civilians in the 2000s.

A letter sent by the Continental Congress to the inhabitants of Quebec in 1774 captured perfectly the contradiction of an expanding empire presenting itself as a center of freedom. The letter was translated into French and printed for general distribution north of the border. It began by recalling the Canadians' bravery in their recent shared "previous fortunes of war" during the Seven Years' War—then got to the point. The letter invited the Québécois to join the anti-British union of colonial troops marching north with these words: "You [will] have been conquered into liberty, if you act as you ought." It went on to warn that "you are a small people, compared to those who with open arms invite you into a fellowship."[3] While Quebec and the rest of Canada managed to avoid being "conquered into liberty," others were not so fortunate—or unfortunate, depending on one's political views. Through the nineteenth century, U.S. dominion ranged from Liberia in the east to Hawai'i in the west, from Alaska in the north to Nicaragua in the south. By the twentieth century, U.S. forces had leapt the oceans on the way to global hegemony, with a growing emphasis on influencing Asia. The early twenty-first century found thousands of American soldiers hunkered down in central Asia and the Middle East.

Americans Abroad

Some Americans have ventured abroad in every era, but historians and others have not always paid much attention to those who did. From the beginning, American society was viewed as a receiver—*the* receiver, even—of immigrants from elsewhere, and the numbers have certainly supported this perspective. Commentators have used the images of melting pots and salad bowls, among other things, to frame their understanding of how people came to and lived in the United States, but there were few if any prominent metaphors for those who left. Places that sent out large numbers of émigrés were often described in terms of diasporas, such as the African diaspora or the Eastern European Jewish diaspora. Migrant-exporting countries such as China, Ireland, and Italy since the nineteenth century acknowledged and paid attention to their national or ethnic compatriots abroad, often with forms of governmental tracking and support, including encouragement to return. But there was little talk of an American diaspora, even with nine million U.S. citizens living elsewhere by 2015 (enough to constitute the twelfth-largest state, ranking between New

Jersey and Virginia). Other than the U.S. government requiring them to continue to file and pay U.S. taxes, few noticed when people left the United States, in contrast to the ample focus on immigrants landing on American shores. Departing folks seemed to be walking off the stage and out of the American story, which was supposed to be all about arriving.[4]

Americans abroad nonetheless remained part of the U.S. story. Some left for good, building new lives elsewhere, pulled by love or opportunity or curiosity or pushed by previous troubles or persecution. Some went abroad temporarily, as soldiers, diplomats, entrepreneurs, missionaries, students, and tourists and often had significant impacts in other lands before returning home. All carried with them American culture and values, traces of their earlier lives and relationships that formed webs of connection between the United States and the rest of the world. They were wildly diverse: British Loyalists fleeing to Canada or British Caribbean islands after the Revolution, tall-ship traders to East Asia, formerly enslaved African Americans in Liberia, former Confederates in Brazil, miners to Australia, Methodist missionaries in Chinese treaty ports, artists and socialites in Paris and London, World War II soldiers and sailors on every continent and every ocean, oil-industry workers in Saudi Arabia, Vietnam War draft evaders to Canada, Navy SEALs in Cameroon and Somalia, and retirees in Mexico and Nicaragua. In addition to the vast collection of narratives of newcomers to the United States are tens of millions of human stories of Americans who lived abroad. "Isolationism" offers little guidance for understanding the full tapestry of U.S. history.[5]

The United States of America was born out of one empire and immediately became another. The historian Daniel Immerwahr notes that the new nation's name was, from the beginning, never quite accurate: "From the day the treaty securing independence from Britain was ratified, right up to the present, it's been a collection of states *and territories*," starting with the then-western lands of the Ohio River Valley.[6] To imagine the United States as a naturally configured product of democracy requires ignoring a great deal of history. Territorial expansion shaped the American story, beginning with continental territories to the west and continuing with overseas territories, along with foreign military bases built in the west and overseas to facilitate the process. How long lands might remain under U.S. control but in the legal limbo of territorial status was unclear. For California it lasted only two years, for Oklahoma 104. For Puerto Rico and the other inhabited overseas territories (American Samoa, the U.S. Virgin

Islands, the Northern Marianas, and Guam), it remains an open question. A few years after helping negotiate the peace terms for ending the War of 1812, including rejecting a British proposal to create an Indian republic to the west of U.S. borders, future president John Quincy Adams wrote in his diary, "The United States and North America are identical."[7] Canada managed to dodge its relentless southern neighbor, but Mexico lost the northern half of its territory.

Some Americans hoped that the seizure of new lands might create opportunities to resolve some of the new nation's stickiest dilemmas. Western lands provided space for relocating Indians from desired property in the eastern states, most infamously the Cherokee and other southeastern tribes driven on the fatal Trail of Tears in the early 1830s to what later became Oklahoma. White antislavery pioneers since the 1760s talked about sending emancipated black slaves to their own colonies between the Allegheny Mountains and the Mississippi River, and the prominent Philadelphia physician Benjamin Rush in 1794 purchased twenty thousand acres in southwestern Pennsylvania's Bedford County as part of a colonization plan for the Pennsylvania Abolition Society.[8]

The main black colonization effort aimed east across the Atlantic instead. In 1819 and 1820, as the first New England Congregational missionaries set sail for the Sandwich (Hawai'ian) Islands in the Pacific, the first African American settlers departed for Liberia on Africa's west coast. Black attitudes toward colonization varied widely, and the motivations of the few who actually traveled to Liberia ranged from missionary work among indigenous Africans to finding better economic opportunities. They shared a common desire to live free of discrimination and violence at the hands of white people and a hope that Africa might feel more like home. It rarely did. African American settlers and their "Americo" descendants identified culturally with the United States and tended to look down on indigenous Liberians as less civilized, who in turn resented the newcomers as arrogant exploiters, whom they called "whites" or "black white men."[9] Americans did not have to be white to feel disappointed in poorer peoples abroad. Similar local attitudes toward other African Americans who showed up in Africa highlighted the greater significance of culture than race. The diplomat Ralph Bunche learned that Congolese in the early 1960s considered him just another European, and even Malcolm X, the very symbol of black nationalism and pride in the United States, found himself referred to as white in Kenya.[10]

Like other peoples, Americans often experienced a heightened sense of their own national identity when they traveled or lived abroad. Going among strangers clarified who they were. U.S. citizens living in other lands also figured centrally in major U.S. military interventions to defend them or their property. The historian Brooke Blower has suggested a partial list, which includes Americans on Indian lands across the continent, in Canada before the War of 1812, in Texas before the Mexican-American War, in China leading up to the anti-Boxer intervention, and in Caribbean islands and Central America before multiple incursions, not to mention some forty thousand Americans living in Mexico on the eve of the 1910 revolution there that brought two U.S. interventions or the 15,000 mostly affluent Americans residing in London on the cusp of World War I.[11] Residence abroad defended by imperial troops when necessary represented a still larger shared reality at the height of imperialism across the nineteenth century and into the twentieth. White settlers (and Japanese settlers, in the cases of Korea and Taiwan) did not always have the same interests as the metropolitan government back home, as the Rhodesian renegades of 1965 demonstrated, but they usually counted on empire's reach to save them when the chips were down. Americans were no different.

Certain European empires imagined themselves to be utterly and unbreakably tied to their colonies. France did not consider Algeria, its nearest and most important colonial holding, to be an overseas colony, even if it lay across the Mediterranean Sea. The government in Paris instead held Algeria to be simply another province of France, solidified by the presence of a million French settlers.[12] Portugal imagined something similar with its more distant African colonies. Lisbon in the 1940s sought to bolster its imperial claims by promoting the theory of "luso-tropicalism," in which a supposedly historically unique absence of racism among the Portuguese people had allowed Portuguese colonization in tropical lands to develop without the racial discrimination so evident in the colonies of other European powers. Luso-tropicalism underpinned Portugal's claim that Angola and Mozambique were not actually colonies but overseas provinces of a single "Greater Portugal."[13] Such positive views of exceptional imperialisms did not survive the upheavals after World War II in Asia and Africa. American imperialists in warmer climes generally did not go as far as the French or the Portuguese, rejecting the Philippines as unassimilable and keeping Puerto Rico, Cuba, and the Panama Canal Zone in various conditions of dependent status. With a small nonwhite population, a growing white community, and unusual strategic importance in the mid-Pacific, Hawai'i was different, suggesting, after a long delay, the abiding American belief that other parts of the world might really want to be like—or even become part of—the United States.[14]

Part of the challenge of understanding the influence of Americans abroad is to not be overly impressed by actual U.S. borders. Such boundaries could have great meaning, of course, including full legal and military control, but they could also serve to obscure inward and outward flows of people and influences, a transnational story to which historians have paid considerable attention in recent years. Formal U.S. colonies and territories were supplemented by a vast realm of informal American empire—that is, areas mostly nearby that were significantly penetrated and even dominated by U.S. influences. Were such lands—technically independent and foreign but economically, politically, militarily, and often culturally pervaded by Americans and their power—best understood as truly foreign? Hawai'i, Alaska, Puerto Rico, Guam, the Panama Canal Zone, the U.S. Virgin Islands, the Northern Mariana Islands, and offshore U.S. military bases were one thing. But other neighboring lands may not have been as different as they appeared on a map. Cuba after 1898 fell under American dominion, marked by Cuban nationalists decrying Havana as America's brothel before the 1959 revolution and then by Washington's decision to continue using Guantánamo thereafter as a military base and an offshore prison for keeping jihadists separated from U.S. legal protections (and, earlier, Haitian refugees who might have been HIV positive). Canada built and preserved a robust national identity but also kept a wary eye on its ten-times-more-populous neighbor to the south, since Canadian foreign trade was dominated by the United States and the vast majority of Canadians lived within one hundred miles of the U.S. border. Mexico remained more exotic to Americans, as it was much larger than Cuba and more persistently independent, but it was still intimately linked to the United States through trade, tourism, migration, and Americans retiring south of the border. The influence of American culture and language was felt around the globe, and even more so close by.

Historians have long debated the precise significance of the U.S. acquisition of a large empire abroad in the 1890s. Many scholars emphasized the common patterns of warfare and administration evident in both continental expansion to the west coast of North America and overseas expansion to the south and particularly to the west across the Pacific. The change to using oceangoing ships did not seem as significant as the conti-nuities with marching and riding over land, which was how expansion had primarily proceeded over the previous three centuries. Historians also noted the much earlier white settlements in Hawai'i and acquisitions of Alaska and the Midway Atoll west of Hawai'i; Americans had already been shipping out for decades.[15] Regardless of some patterns of continuity with previous seizures of new lands, the results for the United States of the brief, successful war with Spain in 1898 did nevertheless represent a bold new step toward world power. Hawai'i and Guam were annexed, as was Puerto Rico, and Cuba became a de facto dependency. Largest and most impor-tant was the densely populated Philippine archipelago, which the United States took and held until 1946, making it instantly a major force in the western Pacific. Filipinos had hoped for independence after helping defeat Spain, and they fought for years against a ferocious counterinsurgency cam-paign by the new American occupiers. "There must be two Americas," the acerbic anti-imperialist Mark Twain wrote: "one that sets the captive free, and one that takes a once-captive's new freedom away from him."[16]

Imperialists won the vigorous debate in Congress in 1899 over whether to annex the Philippines. Senator Albert Beveridge (R-IN) led the annex-ationist charge, which he declared a noble and exalted cause for the "English-speaking and Teutonic peoples" who were called by God to be "the master organizers of the world." Americans, he believed, like their English cousins, had "the blood of government" in their veins.[17] While opponents of annexation warned that democracy and empire could not be successfully blended, annexationists had no interest in resolving that dilemma by having the archipelago evolve into an eventual U.S. state. In 1900, Manila would have been the seventeenth largest city in the United States, just after Newark, and the densely populated Philippines as a whole would have created the most populous state in the Union, just ahead of New York. Statehood would have catapulted several dozen nonwhites into the U.S. Congress, an unimaginable possibility early in the century, when European imperialism abroad and Jim Crow segregation at home were still at their peak.[18]

For better and worse, U.S. practices went abroad with Americans. When the Philippines became U.S. territory, U.S. laws excluding Chinese immi-grants took effect there, as Secretary of State John Hay confirmed to an outraged but impotent Chinese minister to the United States, Wu Tingfang. This was true despite China's close proximity to the archipelago (just four hundred miles, versus 7,500 to California) and the presence there already of thousands of residents of Chinese descent, composing more than 10 percent of Manila's population.[19] On the other hand, young American servicemen on duty in the islands had no problem engaging in the most intimate manner with local women of whatever race or ethnicity. U.S. commanders recognized this reality and installed a formal system of military-colonial regulation of prostitution in order to try to control the dramatic spread of venereal disease among their troops. Such practices were standard fare for experienced European military commanders in their colonies. But Americans back home liked to imagine that U.S. soldiers would somehow behave differently than older imperialists. Social reformers from the United States who visited the Philippines during the U.S. war there were appalled by the thorough Americanization of the local red-light districts, complete with U.S. flags inside and outside brothels and official licensing and inspection by U.S. officials.[20]

While occupying and annexing new lands, Americans had long wrestled with how to treat the people they conquered. Within the continental territory that became the first forty-eight states, relatively small Indian populations suffered catastrophic decline: they were most often defeated in battle and driven onto small reservations of less desirable land. Congress did not clarify their status as U.S. citizens until 1924, and four more decades were required to guarantee their right to vote in some states.[21] With overseas territories acquired from Spain in 1898, the U.S. government took different approaches. The 7.5 million residents of the distant Philippines were no longer legal aliens but also did not receive U.S. citizenship, just as their lands remained bound for eventual independence. The 1.2 million residents of the small nearby island of Puerto Rico did gain U.S. citizenship in 1917, in time to be included in the military draft for World War I, but the island as a whole would be kept at arm's length as a quasi-independent commonwealth. These varying policies reflected uncertainty about how to manage the identity of colonial subjects who had been swept up into the American empire.

The modern United States was often compared to the ancient Roman Empire. Each was the expansive superpower of an era, whose reach extended across much of the known world. Each was also noted for the diversity of its peoples, for the inclusion of others originally seen as foreigners, and for the opportunities available to them once inside the imperial system. The historian Mary Beard reminds us that the myth of Rome's founding had

Romulus establishing the city in 753 BCE "by offering citizenship to all comers, by turning foreigners into Romans." Almost exactly a thousand years later, the emperor Caracalla fulfilled that promise by declaring all free inhabitants of the Roman Empire, from Scotland to Syria, to be Roman citizens. More than 30 million provincials became legally Roman overnight, perhaps the largest grant of citizenship ever. This momentous erasure of the legal distinction between rulers and ruled previewed a similar trend two millennia later in the late-twentieth-century United States. So, too, did the growing gap between wealthier and poorer Roman citizens (*honestiores* and *humiliores*), a challenge that also continued to echo on American shores.[22]

In territorial Hawai'i the United States took a decisive turn toward bringing its legacy of overseas conquests into alignment with egalitarian and inclusive democratic promise. The location was crucial. The Hawai'ian Islands lay almost halfway across the Pacific Ocean, a strategic crossroads of immense military value. White American settlers and their descendants controlled the lucrative sugar and fruit economy, whose plantations were manned by a diverse workforce of Japanese, Chinese, Filipinos, native Hawai'ians, and even Puerto Ricans. The timing was equally critical. Japan attacked Pearl Harbor in 1941, and the U.S. military spent the next four years projecting its successful war effort across the Pacific from bases in Hawai'i. Once an exotic archipelago remote from Americans' experience and understanding, Hawai'i emerged in the 1940s as familiar terrain for the hundreds of thousands of sailors and soldiers who spent time there. For the nation as a whole, it became both a sacred ground of military sacrifice and a fantasy spot of warm weather and beautiful beaches. It was now seen as more fully American, as were its residents.[23]

After 1945, the United States never retreated from the world. U.S. troops remained stationed throughout Asia as well as elsewhere, as the peoples of that region negotiated away from or threw off their colonial overlords, beginning with the Philippines in 1946. During these epic struggles for national independence and racial equality, the United States fought major wars in Korea and Vietnam. Hawai'i, with its majority Asian and Hawai'ian population, became a crucial Cold War symbol of American leadership in a mostly nonwhite world. Hawai'ian statehood might have seemed hard to imagine for Americans before World War II, but in the Cold War era that followed it quickly became logical and geopolitically necessary. Much less populated Alaska and Hawai'i entered the Union as the forty-ninth and fiftieth states in 1959, and two Asian Americans, Senator Hiram Fong and Representative Daniel Inouye, joined the U.S. Congress. Hawai'i's diverse population—including a future president born there in 1961, Barack Obama—thereafter made it a forerunner and model for the trajectory of the nation as a whole, as the size of the white majority continued to shrink. A majority of new births by 2016 were infants of color.[24]

Personal Contact

There was never a time when Americans were not engaging with foreigners. From the colonial-era foothills of the Appalachian Mountains to the twenty-first-century slopes of the Hindu Kush in Afghanistan, U.S. citizens, particularly young men, met and interacted with other peoples. As the United States grew in size and power into the twentieth century, those contacts inevitably increased. Not even widespread disappointment at the results of World War I and the Paris Peace Conference, which stimulated a backlash against formal international involvement, kept Americans from traveling abroad. Strong U.S. economic growth during the 1920s underpinned a robust tourism industry, much of it focused on escaping the newly created Prohibition regime at home. The party was offshore, and cities such as Tijuana, Havana, Shanghai, Berlin, and Paris served as symbols of libertine nightlife and freedom, including alcohol and sex tourism. After U.S. states in the 1980s established a uniform minimum drinking age of twenty-one, Mexico, Canada, and European countries, with their lower age restrictions, would hold a similar allure for affluent underage Americans.[25]

In the years after World War I, a new mass tourism, enabled by the booming U.S. economy, gave Americans more personal contact with foreigners than ever before. Paris in the 1920s became a particular mecca for middle-class visitors from across the Atlantic. Some were veterans of the recent war, returning to see the country they had helped defeat Germany. Most famously, American artists, jazz musicians, and writers took up residence in the City of Light, finding there a freedom from the constraints of what they saw as a staid, moralistic, and materialistic society at home. Many African Americans, including the singer Josephine Baker and writers from the Harlem Renaissance, were among them. A certain tension separated the older image of Paris as the apex of high culture and civilization from the developing reputation of one of its tourist-filled neighborhoods as "Cedar-Rapids-let-loose," in the words of one observer. French traditionalists also distrusted the profusion in their capital city of automobiles, a quintessential American product that they considered a "moving house of debauchery," a perspective shared by conservative Americans at the time and some parents of young adults ever since. The historian Victoria de Grazia has demonstrated the pervasive reach of U.S. consumer products and practices into Europe across the first half of the twentieth century and their influence in reshaping the routines of daily life on the continent.[26]

Having helped defend French independence in 1917–1918, U.S. troops returned in 1944 with British, Canadian, and other allies to liberate France from German occupation. Four years to the week after British and French forces had evacuated from Dunkirk under German assault, Allied soldiers on D-Day waded ashore onto the beaches of Normandy at a horrific cost of thousands of lives lost. In fairly swift fashion, they liberated Paris and drove the German army off of French soil, back across the Rhine River. Along the way, the demographic diversity of the American troops startled many French people they met. Daniele Philippe was astonished that the first two GIs he encountered were originally from Italy and Scandinavia. "What a mix of races!" Francoise de Hautecloque exclaimed in a letter. "It is common to meet a soldier whose father is Greek and mother German. And yet they come together under the star-spangled banner."[27] European ideas of racial diversity in the 1940s might have seemed amusingly limited to a later generation. But such observations captured the assimilating character of the modern American military as an institution, one that echoed the style of the ancient Roman imperial army.

American troops in France were young men far from home, and they were engaged in killing enemy soldiers. In other words, they had, on the one hand, considerable collective sexual desire and had, on the other, already broken free from the most elemental social restraint, regardless of often-tight military discipline. They had more provisions and were much more powerful than the sometimes desperate and disproportionately female civilians they encountered. Some GIs had grown up hearing tales from their fathers of sexual adventure in France in 1917–1918. They tended to expect French women to be sexually available, a view summarized by a journalist for *Life* magazine: "France was a tremendous brothel inhabited by 40,000,000 hedonists who spent all their time eating, drinking [and] making love." Such fantasies, even when taken with a grain of salt, derived both from the nearly universal interest of soldiers in sexual release and from specific American understandings of what went on in Paris. An understanding of the French as morally degraded was bolstered by widespread condemnation of French men for surrendering so swiftly to the invading Germans in 1940.[28]

Here were the ingredients for fraught encounters between American men and French women. The historian Mary Louise Roberts has traced the kinds of relationships that developed during the year between the D-Day landings and the end of the war in Europe. There were somewhat analogous situations with female civilians in other places occupied by American soldiers during the war, including the Italian peninsula and England in preparation for the cross-Channel invasion, so the story in France was suggestive of broader truths. Sexual relationships ranged across a spectrum from romance to prostitution to rape. Romance was real enough, and many marriages resulted, but it was perhaps the least common kind of liaison. Prostitution was pervasive, with GIs coming into more frequent contact with sex workers than any other kind of French person. Of course, romance and prostitution were not always fully discrete phenomena given the hunger and stress of wartime, and soldiers' access to food and cigarettes could mask the transactional aspects of some encounters. Rape was all too common, as in every war, and U.S. authorities tended either to ignore it or to cast it as a black crime, just as happened at home in the U.S. South. The vast majority of rape convictions of American GIs in France were of African American soldiers, themselves a small minority of the armed forces.[29]

Crucial for the shaping of relationships between foreign soldiers and local women in any war was military policy regarding "fraternization." Commanders had enormous influence over the behavior of their troops, and they set the guardrails within which human interactions unfolded. Infamous examples of brutal treatment of civilians by occupying armies in World War II included soldiers from Japan in China, from Germany in the Soviet Union, and from the USSR in Germany.[30] In the era of domestic racial segregation up into the 1960s, U.S. military officials wielded different policies in different theaters of war. In lands with poorer and darker-skinned inhabitants—the Philippines, Haiti, Mexico—they encouraged prostitution and discouraged public socializing such as dating. In richer places with lighter-skinned locals—England, Australia, New Zealand—they condoned public socializing and even marriage.[31]

The long tradition of conquering soldiers appropriating local women took a particular shape for the United States in World War II. American recruits were, on average, two years younger than in World War I—eighteen rather than twenty—and served much longer terms of deployment overseas. The historian Susan Zeiger has noted "the unprecedented scale of the marriage phenomenon in World War II" and found that 85 percent of those bringing home a foreign bride at the end of the war had been posted abroad more than two years. Shared cultural and linguistic backgrounds figured into the high percentage of Italian war brides, up to 40 percent, who were married to Italian-American soldiers.[32] But neither race nor ethnicity nor language was sufficient to prevent liaisons, romance, and marriage for young American men far from home, in every theater in which they were deployed.

U.S. military officials were particularly leery of fraternization with civilians after the fighting ended in Germany and Japan, the fiercest wartime enemies. The costs of the war had been astronomical, and they initially feared sabotage and prioritized keeping clear lines of authority and separation in the postwar occupations. But cooperative behavior by civilians eased concerns, and the developing Cold War divided the victorious Allies and sharply increased the value of occupied Japan and western Germany for the United States. Commanders steadily loosened regulations. In Germany, by June 1945 GIs were allowed to talk to "very small children," by October they could socialize with all civilians, and by December 1946 they could marry German women. Enemies had become allies.[33]

With the war over and anxieties rising about the Soviet Union, American soldiers in western Germany seized the opportunities available. Aware of their economic power in a devastated postwar society, they laughed off the diminishing nonfraternization program as a "nonfertilization" campaign. In comparison to the combined U.S.-British-Canadian sweep through France after D-Day, occupation duty in Germany was stable and open-ended in duration, and the ranks of healthy adult German males had been shredded by the war. In this impoverished landscape of the late 1940s, American soldiers not only ruled with the hard authority of weapons but also stood out for their good health, collective confidence, and casual American manners. Not all German women were positively impressed, and not all GIs were looking to impress, but relationships between them sprang up everywhere, and many of them lasted. Already by the spring of 1947, sixty thousand European war brides—mostly German and British, along with Italian and French—and their children had reached the United States to join their husbands.[34]

In the months and years immediately following World War II, the U.S. Congress carved out temporary exceptions to the country's tight immigration restrictions. These legislative acts allowed in both refugees and women who had married U.S. soldiers. The 1945 War Brides Act initially excluded Japanese women, in accordance with existing anti-Asian exclusions. But the world was changing very rapidly for U.S. officials in the mid-to-late 1940s: Asians were seizing their independence and becoming a primary target in the Cold War competition for influence, communists were winning control of China, and at home President Truman and the federal courts were taking actions to undo racial discrimination and segregation. On the ground in occupied Japan, American GIs were once again failing to remain aloof from local women, regardless of their race. In 1947 Congress amended the War Brides Act to permit Japanese women to accompany their uniformed husbands onto American soil. By 1950, more than 750 had arrived.[35]

How significant was this development? One year before the California Supreme Court in *Perez v. Sharp* overturned a state law against interracial marriage, and twenty years before the U.S. Supreme Court in *Loving v. Virginia* eliminated all remaining state racial limitations on marriage, the U.S. Congress was tacitly accepting and supporting the reality of extensive interracial marriage. The nation's own soldiers were forcing this process. They were declaring, in the most intimate way possible, that these foreigners were not foreign at all: they were life partners. No doubt this recognition was easier with mostly white men pairing up mostly with non-white women; such privilege based on sex and race had deep roots in the American past, quite unlike that of matches of white women with non-white men. Regardless of the gendered skewing of this new openness, another chunk of the glacial foreignness of Asia for Americans was breaking off and melting. The war in Korea that began in 1950 led to a similar result, with nearly one hundred thousand Korean women marrying U.S. military personnel and moving to the United States by the year 2000. Parallel U.S. approval of thousands of Korean orphan adoptions into white American families placed still more pressure on the leaking dam of U.S. segregation and exclusion.[36]

Asia as the Twentieth-Century Landscape
of U.S. Expansion

Far too often, "Asia" proved to be a conceptual maze in which non-Asian Americans got lost. Like the idea of races with which they were associated, continents were commonly seen as discrete entities, separate from one another, each with a distinctive history and culture. American commentators began in the 1980s to refer to "Asian values," usually with some combination of anxiety and admiration, as a way of talking about the impressive economic growth of specific countries, first Japan, then the so-called Asian Tigers (Hong Kong, Singapore, Taiwan, and South Korea), and later China. Observers emphasized what looked like a combination of hard work, self-denial, familial obligations, and rising education. It seemed, in other words, like Puritans in seventeenth-century Massachusetts, in contrast to what looked like contemporary American individualism and self-indulgence. Americans, who on average weighed twenty-five pounds more in 2000 than in 1960, appeared to be growing literally and metaphorically flabby.[37]

Like most stereotypes, anxious generalizing about Asia took certain observable facts and spun them into larger theories that did not hold together well under careful examination. Industrial growth rates in specific nations under particular historical circumstances did not necessarily indicate a coming "clash of civilizations." Such generalizing fit in a well-established pattern of declaring essential differences between West and East, as the literary scholar Edward Said famously illustrated in his groundbreaking 1978 study of what he called "Orientalism." The word "Orient," predecessor to "Asia," derived from the Latin for "East," reflecting the direction in which Asia lay for European imperialists. But Asia was not even a continent, much less a unified civilization. It was a label for the vaguely defined eastern regions of the Asian-African-European supercontinent or Eastern hemisphere. Did Siberians, Sri Lankans, and Filipinos share a culture? Hardly. Asia was home to well over half the world's population and spanned remarkable cultural diversity. It included four of the six most populous modern nations, three of whom—India, Indonesia, and Pakistan—did not readily fit popular American images associated with so-called Asian values, which highlighted people with East Asian features.[38]

If South and Southeast Asians already complicated the picture, western Asia revealed still more variety. Was the Middle East, sometimes called the Near East, part of Asia? Without a clear border, it was hard to know for sure. Americans did not lump Middle Easterners in with Africans nor usually with Europeans, yet there also was no discrete Middle Eastern continent. In the decades preceding the establishment of the 1924 national-origins system for limiting immigration, U.S. courts heard many cases regarding the racial status of immigrants from the eastern borderlands of Europe. At issue was their whiteness and thus whether they were eligible for naturalization as U.S. citizens. Finns, for example, won definitive status as whites in 1908. Syrians figured prominently in other cases in this era of racial sorting. As the first Arabs to emigrate in significant numbers to the United States and the largest group of Arab Americans before World War II, Syrians in the United States worked assiduously as individuals and in organizations to lobby for status as white persons. Unlike immigrants of Indian and Japanese descent, Syrian Americans succeeded with their cases and were included as white in 1924.[39]

Closely related to the question of who and where Asians were in the world was how to think about them on American shores. Who were they when they showed up as permanent residents in the United States, often with children who were U.S. citizens by birth? China and Japan were the two most important Asian countries for most Americans. The fundamental issue in this arena for non-Asian Americans, whether explicit or implicit, throughout the nineteenth and early twentieth centuries was this: were Chinese Americans and Japanese Americans simply extensions of the people in China and Japan, as though their culture were carried somatically in their skin and thus passed on permanently to their descendants? Or were they ultimately like other immigrants and their children and grandchildren, able to assimilate or be incorporated into mainstream American society, particularly over generations?

Such questions were more pointed with immigrants from Asia than with those from Africa. Black people in the United States, whatever their precarious legal and social status, tended to have further-back ancestors of less clear geographical origins, given the weaker polities of West Africa and the obscuring, poisonous legacy of the transatlantic slave trade. Black Americans therefore called themselves African Americans but rarely Angolan Americans or Wolof Americans. Americans from across the Pacific came eventually to use the conglomerate term Asian Americans after World War II, but previously they had mostly considered themselves Chinese Americans or Japanese Americans. Their origins lay not in an undifferentiated massive "Asia" but in specific nations and cultures that had often been at war with their neighbors. And the strength and status of those nations were directly linked to the prospects of particular Asian Americans in the United States. The history of immigration and the history of foreign relations, traditionally studied separately, were in fact thoroughly intertwined.[40]

Asians were, of course, the very first North Americans. By some 15,000 years ago, small numbers of people had migrated from Siberia across what was then the Bering land bridge. South of the ice sheets in what is now Canada, they found a vast unpeopled hemisphere teeming with toothsome animals for ready hunting. Over the next ten thousand years they spread southward to Patagonia at the tip of South America. Along the way they developed communities of great diversity in divergent environments, from high alpine valleys to sea-level jungles and from small nomadic bands to densely complex urban communities as large as any cities in Europe. These peoples whom later Europeans called Indians, natives, Native Americans, or First Peoples were, in a historical sense, Asian Americans. Contemporary racial categories, in other words, obscure as much as they reveal.[41]

In the more modern era following Columbus's voyages, Spanish galleons by 1565 were sailing regularly across the Pacific between Manila and Acapulco, exchanging silver mined in Mexico for Asian spices, furniture, porcelain, and silks. The sailors on those ships, both hired and impressed, included Filipinos and Chinese, some of whom jumped ship and found their way to Mexico City. By the 1760s some of these Filipino "Manilamen" had migrated northward to the bayous of Louisiana in what was still Spanish territory. There in the swamplands outside of New Orleans, the historian Gary Okihiro has observed, they "founded the oldest continuous Asian communities in North America."[42]

Prominent colonial Americans inherited from Europe a lively interest in China, the vast dominant empire of Asia. Benjamin Franklin referred to it as "the wisest of Nations." Tom Paine judged the Chinese a "people of mild manners and of good morals, except where they have been corrupted by European commerce." Ezra Stiles, Yale University's president, studied China as closely as any early American and declared it in a 1783 sermon to be "the wisest empire the sun hath ever shined upon." Such admiration was not, at first, mutual. The Chinese official negotiating the first diplomatic treaty with the United States in 1844 reported back to the emperor that it was "the most uncivilized and remote of all countries . . . solitary and ignorant. Not only are the people entirely unversed in the forms of edicts and laws, but if the meaning be rather deep, they would probably not even be able to comprehend." He concluded that "we must make our words somewhat simple." Reading these words may call to mind images of contemporary American tourists sometimes trying to communicate abroad in English by speaking more slowly and loudly.[43]

By the early twentieth century, China emerged as the foremost target of American Christian outreach work. One of the first steps in this process came in 1818, when the Cornwall Foreign Mission School in Connecticut began enrolling young Cantonese, in hopes of sending them back to China as missionaries. One year later the first shipload of missionaries bound for the Hawai'ian Islands left Boston under the aegis of the American Board of Commissioners for Foreign Missions, extending American influence into the Pacific. The most prominent early Chinese migrant was Yung Wing, who arrived in the United States in 1847 and studied at Yale, becoming in 1854 the first Asian graduate of an American university and traveling back and forth often between the United States and China for the rest of his life. More than a dozen states named towns or districts Canton or Pekin (as Beijing was then known in the West), including Canton, New York, home to both St. Lawrence University and the State University of New York at Canton. China's sixth-century Grand Canal, the world's longest artificial waterway, which connected the Yellow and Yangtze Rivers, served as an inspiration for the construction of the Erie Canal between 1817 and 1825, which provided the first crucial direct link of the U.S. East Coast to the vast North American interior.[44]

There had always been tension between anti-Asian sentiment among many Americans and the early cosmopolitan Sinophilia of racial liberals. The latter approved of Yung Wing's 1875 marriage in Avon, Connecticut, to Mary Louise Kellogg, a white American, eased by Yung's extensive Americanization as a Yale-educated, English-speaking, Western-dressing Christian businessman. Something similar prevailed in remote Hawai'i, where white men married into indigenous and particularly royal families as part of the consolidation of American influence there. But support for white-Asian marriages on the mainland was shrinking fast. While from the 1840s to the 1870s white American perceptions of Asians appeared to remain fluid and uncertain, they turned sharply negative thereafter, and states began stigmatizing Asians in antimiscegenation statutes. The major reason was the new influx of Chinese immigrants, who soon numbered more than one hundred thousand, a much larger Asian presence—concentrated on the West Coast—than in any other Western nation and one that fueled white racial and economic anxieties. The other important reason for the declining status of Chinese in the United States was the diminishing power of China in international affairs, beginning with its defeat by the British in the First Opium War of 1839–1842. The erosion of international respect for China continued steadily until the overthrow of the last emperor in 1912. White Americans had less to fear from mistreating Asians.[45]

While anti-Chinese sentiment in the United States grew markedly by the 1870s and led to the Chinese Exclusion Act of 1882, American missionaries in the same era paid increasing attention to Chinese people in China. Part of the attraction of China for them was its sheer size, which made it an obvious mission field. China also drew their attention in the nineteenth century because the declining strength of its government invited steady incursions from outside imperial powers, who began carving out spheres of influence. Like maple-sugar farmers tapping spouts into maple trees to drain off the sweet sap, Britain, France, Japan, and others built treaty ports and other installations that sucked much of the wealth out of the world's largest country. The imperialists had long controlled other parts of Asia, from the Dutch in the East Indies to the British in India to the French in Indochina. As they increasingly turned their guns and trading ships on China, many Americans hoped their representatives instead could be a more democratic and Christian influence there, while also keeping an "open door" for U.S.-Chinese trade and investment.[46]

U.S. missionaries grew to be the largest group of Protestant missionaries in China by the 1920s. Few had extensive theological training, and most went primarily as teachers. They had only limited successes in converting Chinese to the Christian faith, falling well short of the grandest dreams of turning China into a predominantly Christian country. But they contributed a great deal to China's modernization, particularly through the establishment of Christian schools, colleges, and hospitals. Through education and the provision of medical services they helped improve individual lives, and they emphasized teaching women as well as men and campaigned against such traditions as female foot-binding. After the establishment of the

People's Republic of China in 1949, these Christian colleges were absorbed into the new national university system under communist control.[47]

American and other Western missionary outreach efforts may have had only a modest impact in terms of the percentage of Asians who took up the Christian faith. But there were several prominent cases of conversion, which helped shape the twentieth-century political landscape of the region. The founder of the Chinese Republic, Sun Yat-sen, attended school in Hawai'i and converted to Congregationalism. Soong Mei-ling was a Wellesley College–educated Methodist whose marriage to Chiang Kai-shek helped lead to that key Chinese Nationalist leader converting to Methodism himself. Chiang was America's closest ally in Asia from the 1920s onward, and he and Madame Chiang, as Americans knew her, were particularly prominent in the United States in the 1930s and 1940s, landing twice together on the cover of *Time* magazine (Chiang appeared there by himself eight other times) and embodying American hopes for a future Asia modeled on the United States.[48]

After Chiang's 1949 defeat in the Chinese revolution, which led to communist rule on the mainland and the Nationalist retreat to Taiwan, the Christian identity of other leading figures in the region helped sustain American hopes for an Asia that would look and act more like the United States. Ngo Dinh Diem, a devout Roman Catholic, ruled South Vietnam from 1954 to 1963, thanks to U.S. support. Syngman Rhee, the close ally whom Washington put in power in South Korea after World War II, had studied at Princeton with Professor Woodrow Wilson and was a practicing Methodist. Korea turned out be the most fertile field for evangelization in the region, with some 25 percent of South Koreans identifying as Christians by the 1990s. Even Kim Il-sung, the Marxist-Leninist leader of North Korea with whom the United States went to war in 1950—and whose grandson, Kim Jong-un, continued in the 2010s to defy Washington and the world with tests of nuclear devices and ballistic missiles—had a Christian mother.[49]

The fullest expansion of U.S. influence into Asia came in the mid-twentieth century as a result of the aggressive imperialism of the other most important country in the region: Japan. The earliest American views of Japan had come from educated Europeans, who, from the 1540s onward, tended to see the Japanese through a positive racial lens, considering them a white people. Cosmopolitan Europeans in the eighteenth century shared the perspective of the Swedish scientist Carl Linnaeus, whose 1735 taxonomic treatise *Naturae Systema* referred to Japanese as having "fair skin, temperate habitat, and superior civility" and being "civilized, physically fair, strong, and worthy of their respect." Only later in the nineteenth century did Europeans and white Americans come to see the Japanese instead as "yellow" and thus an essentially inferior race.[50]

For the two and a half centuries from 1600 to 1850, while Europeans were busy conquering much of the world and Americans were seizing a continent, Japan was taking a radically different route. Under the military leadership of the shoguns, Japan became one of the most successful governments in the world in excluding foreigners and controlling migration within its own boundaries. Japan cut itself off from nearly all external influences, including the Portuguese merchants and missionaries who had previously been allowed entry since first appearing on Japanese shores in 1543. Only in the mid-nineteenth century did outsiders impinge again on the remote archipelago off the eastern end of Eurasia. European imperial navies circulated in the region, and then Commodore Matthew Perry led a U.S. naval expedition in 1853 that forced the Japanese government to open its ports to greater commercial contact. In 1860 Japan established its first hotel for foreigners, complete with wine cellar and billiards table. That same year it sent its first diplomatic mission to Washington. In 1868, in reaction to the growing dominance of Westerners in Asia and determined to avoid China's fate, the Meiji Restoration initiated a period of industrialization and modernization that turned Japan into the greatest economic and military power in Asia.[51]

By the first years of the twentieth century, President Theodore Roosevelt and many other prominent Americans openly respected and even admired the rise of the Japanese empire as a "civilized" and civilizing power in East Asia. The prominent U.S. writer and lecturer John Stoddard, father of the even more well-known nativist and racial theorist Lothrop Stoddard, proclaimed Japan "the pioneer of progress in the Orient." If other parts of Asia could be dismissed by Westerners as rural, poor, and colonized by outsiders, industrializing and increasingly affluent Japan was another matter. Roosevelt and others accepted Japan's incorporation of Taiwan in 1895, and Britain concluded an alliance with Tokyo in 1902. After Japan's defeat of Russia in 1905, the Western powers not only failed to object to its seizure of the Korean peninsula but even raised their legations in Tokyo to full-blown embassies as symbols of Japan's arrival as a first-rank international power. The U.S. adviser to the Korean government observed that Japan's actions in Korea were like those of the United States, which had done "something of the same sort in the Philippines," and David Starr Jordan, Stanford University's president, declared Japan's project in Korea "comparable to our sanitation of the Canal Zone of Panama." Japan represented the great exception to white dominance at the apex of global imperialism at the start of the twentieth century.[52]

World War I offered an unusual opportunity for the budding Japanese empire to continue to expand in East Asia and the western Pacific. The other great powers, their very survival at stake, were focused primarily on battles in and around Europe. As an ally of Britain and the other Entente powers, Japan seized the German-occupied Shandong peninsula in China, and its navy helped ferry Australian and New Zealand troops to the eastern Mediterranean for the epic battle at Gallipoli in modern-day Turkey. The Bolshevik Revolution in Russia provided a further unexpected chance for expansion, which Tokyo seized by sending a military expedition into Siberia in 1918. The postwar Paris Peace Conference granted Japan control of the Marshall, Mariana, and Caroline Islands as League of Nations Class C Mandates, adding legitimacy to the Japanese empire among the other great powers.[53]

Of course, anti-Japanese sentiment had not disappeared. Theodore Roosevelt negotiated the Gentlemen's Agreement with Tokyo in 1907 to end Japanese migration to the United States as a way to ease rising persecution of Japanese residents of California. A decade later, Woodrow Wilson and other white leaders at the Paris Peace Conference blocked Japan's proposal to include a racial-equality clause in the charter of the new League of Nations. The 1924 Johnson-Reed Immigration Act then capped two decades of tightening immigration restrictions, which now excluded nearly all Asians. Japanese resentment of such continuing insults flavored the ongoing strategic competition between the two rising powers of the Pacific area. With the onset of the global Great Depression in the 1930s and the strengthening of the militarist forces within the Tokyo government, the stage was set for the terrible showdown that began with the Japanese attack on Pearl Harbor in 1941.[54]

World War II in the Pacific is an oft-told tale, full of unspeakable cruelty and great bravery splashed across a significant portion of the earth's surface. Huge battles and epic atrocities punctuated the U.S.-Japan conflict. The historian John Dower and others have detailed the racially charged slaughter that took place on both sides and gave the fighting a nearly geno-cidal quality at times, particularly with the U.S. use of atomic weapons at its end. Greg Robinson, Roger Daniels, and other historians have laid bare the dismaying incarceration in the United States of U.S. citizens and resi-dents of Japanese descent; they have also pointed to their estimable resil-ience through that experience. Yet out of this exquisitely inhumane era came the beginning of a remarkable transformation of Asian Americans in the eyes of their white countrymen from the once-demonized "Yellow Peril" to a widely admired "model minority."[55]

Demonizing the enemy in war was standard practice across cultures and centuries, a process eased at first for Americans after Pearl Harbor by phe-notypical difference. Tapping into the long legacy of anti-Asian sentiment, U.S. military and cultural authorities identified Americans of Japanese heritage—unlike those of German or Italian descent—as potential traitors requiring confinement. The *Los Angeles Times* put it bluntly: "A viper is nonetheless a viper wherever the egg is hatched—so a Japanese-American, born of Japanese parents—grows up to be a Japanese, not an American." But this kind of racialized assumption ran smack into actual experience, which revealed its ignorance. Japanese Americans not only failed to spy for Tokyo; they even volunteered by the thousands for military service out of the camps in which their own government had locked them. Indeed, they manned the segregated 442nd Regimented Combat Team, which fought its way up the Italian peninsula and became the most decorated unit in the entire U.S. Army. Public recognition grew of the sacrifices made by Japanese Americans, including immigrant Issei "Gold Star Mothers" who had lost their sons for the defense of the United States.[56]

White Americans' sense of connection to Japanese occasionally pene-trated even the grim Japanese POW camps in the western Pacific, known mostly for their barbarity. Years later, the U.S. veteran Anton Bilek told the oral historian Studs Terkel about his time as a prisoner working in a Japanese coal mine just across the bay from Nagasaki. "Once in a while you'd find a good Jap. . . . One time, at the end of the day, while I was waitin' for the little train to take our shift out, I laid back against the rock wall, put my cap over my eyes, and tried to get some rest. The guy next to me says, 'God damn, I wish I was back in Seattle.'" Bilek looked around and was stunned to see the speaker was Japanese. The man continued very quietly: "I was born and raised in Seattle, had a nice restaurant there. I brought my mother back to Japan. She's real old and knew she was gonna die and she wanted to come home." But the war broke out and he couldn't return to the United States. "They made me come back down here and work in the coal mines." Similarly, a number of Kibei—U.S. citizens of Japanese descent who were born in the United States (that is, Nisei) but sent to Japan by their families for education before an anticipated return to the United States—were trapped in Japan by the outbreak of war.[57]

Fighting World War II changed the U.S. relationship with Asian peoples for two essential reasons. First, a million and a half Americans crossed the International Date Line en route to the western Pacific and East Asia, part of what the historians Ken Coates and W. R. Morrison have called "the fastest and most widespread dispersal of a country's citizens in the history of the human race." Victory in 1945 meant that tens of thousands of them remained afterward as occupation forces. The United States became a major Asian power.[58]

Second, for all the wartime demonization of Japan and the earlier history of anti-Asian discrimination, the U.S. military for the first time had critically important Asian allies. China alone kept some two million Japanese troops busy occupying the country's coastal regions and fighting Chinese insurgents. These were two million fewer soldiers shooting at American GIs in the island campaigns in the western Pacific. China's role as a key U.S. ally, which built on earlier missionary relationships, forced Americans to differentiate between "good Asians" and "bad Asians." The reputation of Chinese Americans rose. Bill Simons, a columnist for the *San Francisco Chronicle*, praised local citizens of Chinese descent for their activism as air-raid wardens, Red Cross volunteers, draft registrars, and military enlistees. "That's what Chinatown has been doing for America," Simons wrote on January 14, 1942. "Next time you're eating or drinking in the [Chinatown] district, don't let the fancy neon lights, the Cantonese talk or the Oriental architecture fool you. These people are American through and through." A year later Congress, with the support of two-thirds of the public, repealed the Chinese Exclusion Act. Asians were beginning to be widely seen as actual or potential Americans.[59]

Americans and Asians in the Cold War

The outcome of World War II forced Americans to assess anew who Asians really were. Asia has "exploded into the center of American life," James

Michener wrote in *Life* magazine on June 4, 1951. "Now it will stay there forever." An adaption of Michener's debut novel had recently opened on Broadway as the wildly popular musical *South Pacific*. He was writing in the context of the U.S. war in Korea, but it was World War II in the Pacific that had brought Asia and the United States together as never before. One indicator of the dramatic expansion of U.S. influence was a shift in Washington, DC, telephone directories across the second half of the twentieth century, where listings beginning with the world "International" grew almost three times as quickly as those starting with the word "National." Nowhere was the American footprint during the Cold War decades larger or more sustained than in Asia, and Asians had a similarly crucial impact on the United States.[60]

From 1941 to the early twenty-first century, Americans fought three major wars across the Pacific—against Japan, in Korea, and in Vietnam—and built the world's most important contemporary bilateral economic and strategic relationship with China. In these years, the United States gradually abandoned the exclusion of Asians from its own shores, first in 1943 with China, then in naturalization policy in 1952, and finally with the rejection of the national-origins system in 1965. From the 1940s to the 1970s and after, in other words, Americans were forced to reconsider and decide whether Asians were like Americans or could be Americans. This was a continuous process of reevaluating Asianness and Americanness and their possible overlaps. The historian Scott Kurashige has called the result a "paradigm shift in racial discourse." Long demonized as the quintessential Other, Asians turned out to be ultimately just like other peoples, for better and worse, at least in mainstream American thought by the late twentieth century.[61]

The end of the fighting in World War II left Asia battle scarred and in turmoil. Other than the United States, the region's long-time imperial overlords—Japan, Britain, France, and the Netherlands—were either defeated or gravely weakened. Nationalists organized for independence everywhere and won victories in the Philippines in 1946, India and Pakistan in 1947, Burma and Ceylon (Sri Lanka) in 1948, Indonesia in 1949, and northern Vietnam in 1954. Asia was setting the standard for the future: empires declined; nations rose. The remaining colonized lands of Africa and the Caribbean soon followed suit.

The U.S. government hoped for a gradual decolonization process that would bring pro-Western indigenous elites to power. Washington modeled this with the Philippines. The U.S. occupation forces assured the same in Tokyo, with the aid of a defeated and accommodating Japanese civilian population and political class. But the strategy failed with China. Just as Japan was being turned from bitter enemy to close ally, the communist victory in 1949 pushed China from ally to enemy. Nine months later the North Korean invasion of South Korea raised persistent civil conflicts within South Korea and along the border to the level of a major international war. U.S. troops from Japan landed anew on mainland Asia, just in time to defend the South from being overrun. The GIs' swift battlefield success, in turn, brought China into the war to defend its North Korean allies from imminent annihilation.[62]

The communist revolution in China and Chiang Kai-shek's hasty retreat to Taiwan had shocked and dismayed Americans, who had long viewed China as a place of unique American influence. Now it seemed the Chinese under Mao Zedong's leadership had betrayed Americans' faith in a pro-Western, democratic, Christian future for the world's largest nation. Instead, Chinese soldiers were busy killing American soldiers on Korean battlefields. Inclinations to view China in racially charged terms—"Chink" served commonly as both noun and adjective—were partially checked by having close U.S. Asian allies in Japan, Taiwan, South Korea, and the Philippines. But at least regarding Mao and his followers, American images of a racial "yellow peril" merged with those of a communist "red peril," and relentless U.S. bombing campaigns against North Korea bordered on the genocidal in sparing few noncombatants. "There's no such thing as innocent civilians," one U.S. pilot declared after strafing civilians. "They are all enemy."[63]

These developments across the Pacific helped provoke the political repressions of McCarthyism back in the United States. But they did more than that. Historians such as Cindy I-Fen Cheng, Meredith Oyen, Ellen Wu, Madeline Hsu, and Charlotte Brooks have recently explored the effects that the Chinese revolution and the Korean War had on Chinese Americans and other Asian Americans. Cheng has shown that very different narratives about Asian Americans competed in the public sphere: one viewed them as potential communist agents from abroad, while the other portrayed them as respected and assimilated Americans whose presence legitimated American democracy for the Cold War struggle in Asia. Chinese and other Asians, in other words, could no longer be dismissed in the old racist fashion of calling them "inscrutable." They had to be scrutinized—or at least considered and understood.[64]

What the U.S. government saw when it looked at Chinese living in the United States during the communist takeover in China were primarily assets. Ambitious, skilled individuals would be useful—and important to keep from helping Beijing build a new socialist society. Washington was alert for potential spies among Chinese in the United States, but what it found were 12,000 mostly elites, primarily students, engineers, intellectuals, and diplomats eager or at least open to remaining in the United States. Congress allotted $10 million to help keep highly skilled Chinese in the country, among them An Wang, later founder of the innovative computer company Wang Laboratories, and the architect I. M. Pei, later designer of Paris's Louvre pyramids, Cleveland's Rock & Roll Hall of Fame, Boston's Kennedy Library, and Washington's National Gallery of Art East Building. In the late 1940s and 1950s, the U.S. Asian population was reconfigured by such skilled Chinese refugees, along with Japanese and Korean brides of U.S. soldiers and Korean orphans adopted by American families. Americans in the Cold War had close allies in Japan, Taiwan, South Korea, the Philippines, and South Vietnam, and they had a growing number of fellow residents and citizens of Asian descent.[65]

One prominent example was Sammy Lee, a child of Korean immigrants, born in Fresno and raised in Los Angeles, where his parents operated a small grocery. Lee graduated from Occidental College and from medical school at the University of Southern California. An ear, nose, and throat specialist, he served as a major in the U.S. Army Medical Corps. He also won the Olympic platform-diving competition in 1948 in London, where he joined his fellow diver Vicki Manalo Draves, of Philippine descent, as the first two Asian Americans to win Olympic gold medals. Lee repeated his Olympic victory in 1952 in Helsinki and then won the Amateur Athletic Union's James E. Sullivan Award as the nation's outstanding amateur athlete. Just months after the stalemated end of the Korean War, the United States was holding up a Korean American as one of its heroes.[66]

In the fall of 1954, the U.S. State Department sent Lee on a goodwill tour of several Asian nations. His diving demonstrations produced warm responses as he presented a model Asian face—as athlete, physician, and officer—to American public diplomacy. His trip paralleled the "Jazz Ambassador" tours of prominent jazz musicians, black and white together, to what was then known proudly as the Third World. In an era of national independence unfolding across the non-European world, the State Department seized such opportunities to display the diversity of the American people and the success of at least some of its citizens of color. Lee recalled later that when people in Asia asked him how Asians were treated in the United States, "I told them the truth. I said Americans had their shortcomings, but they had guts enough to advertise them, whereas others tried to cover them up."[67]

Sammy Lee was no fool. He had experienced abundant discrimination growing up. After his retirement from the U.S. Army, he and his wife Rosalind tried to buy a home in 1955 in the booming Orange County town of Garden Grove, California, where he planned to practice medicine. But real estate agents were blunt. "I'm sorry, doctor," he later remembered one apologetically telling him, "but I have to eat, and I'd lose my job for selling to a nonwhite." Lee's prominence, including dining at the White House with President Dwight Eisenhower, led to media attention when word got out about his experience of housing discrimination. National and local leaders spoke out, and Orange County realtors changed their minds. The Lees bought a home in Garden Grove, and the county sponsored a welcome party for them. Other Asian Americans encountered similar efforts to prevent them from moving into white neighborhoods in the 1950s, just as African Americans did in cities such as Detroit and Chicago, but there were also cases of whites welcoming them, such as Freddie Wing and his family, who integrated a neighborhood in Sonoma, California, and held a house-warming party two hundred local residents attended. The struggle for inclusion continued.[68]

So did symbolic changes. Californians in 1956 elected Dalip Singh Saund, an immigrant from India, as the first-ever U.S. congressman of Asian descent. Three years later, Hawai'i, with its majority Asian-descended population, entered the Union as the fiftieth state, electing Daniel K. Inouye as the first Japanese American U.S. congressman and Hiram L. Fong as the first Chinese American U.S. senator. *Reader's Digest* identified an "amazing turnabout" of Japanese Americans, just a decade past their mass wartime incarceration, now "enjoying a prestige, a prosperity, and a freedom from prejudice that even the most sanguine of them had never hoped to attain within their own lifetime." The *Saturday Evening Post* declared that "Japanese residents of California have lifted themselves higher in a few postwar years than they had done in the preceding half century." Once imagined as unassimilable and utterly alien, Asian Americans during the Cold

War began to appear to white Americans as a so-called model minority, marked by strong values, economic and educational success, and rising rates of outmarriage.[69]

Certain U.S. allies in Asia were developing in parallel fashion into what might almost be considered model-minority nations. Like Asian Americans in the United States, such countries as Japan, South Korea, and Taiwan combined cohesive cultures with rapid economic growth and increasing integration with the global capitalist economy. These nations affected Americans directly. As late as 1969, the U.S. produced 82 percent of the televisions sold to its people; by 1988, one could hardly buy a domestically manufactured television set. TVs, like automobiles and other electronics, were coming increasingly from East Asia. The United States crossed a critical watershed in 1979, when total U.S. trade across the Pacific Ocean surpassed that across the Atlantic.[70]

The significance of this expanding engagement with Asia was sometimes missed in the backwash of defeat and withdrawal from Vietnam just a few years earlier. Indeed, histories of modern U.S. relations with Asia have often emphasized wars. Michael Hunt and Steven Levine in *Arc of Empire*, for example, traced the rise-and-fall narrative of U.S. military efforts in the region, from the seizure of the Philippines in 1898, to the peak of success against Japan in 1945, to the Chinese challenge in the draw of the Korean War, to failure and departure from Vietnam in the early 1970s. But in terms of trade, tourism, and all the resulting cultural influence and exchange, the U.S. relationship with Asia in the late twentieth and early twenty-first centuries was still building. While the last U.S. combat troops left Vietnam in early 1973, a few months earlier Richard Nixon had landed in Beijing to open the most important relationship of all, that of the United States and the People's Republic of China.[71]

The process at home of domesticating Asianness into Americanness was an ongoing one, not yet completed despite the optimism of *Reader's Digest* and other observers. Discrimination against people of Asian background came in many forms, from street violence to higher standards for elite college admissions, in which applicants appeared to be the so-called new Jews, the latest minority group to have a disproportionate number of its members be highly qualified but not admitted in according proportion.[72] The very idea of a "model minority" was constructed, in part, as a not-so-subtle rebuke to African Americans during an era of militant black protest against racial discrimination. "Chinatown, in short, was not Watts," in the historian

Ellen Wu's concise formulation.[73] The model-minority idea necessarily carried its own burden of prejudicial limits: expectations of being studious, orderly, hard working, and deferential.

But the old issue of whether Chinese Americans or Japanese Americans were really just extensions of China or Japan, as though their culture were carried somatically and inerasably in their skin or their bones (or their "blood"), had been decided in mainstream American life by the middle years of the Cold War. Vietnamese were reminded of this reality in 2009, when the USS *Lassen* docked in Da Nang for an official visit. The uniformed American commander strode down the gangway to a red carpet welcome. He was H. B. Le, once a five-year-old refugee from Vietnam back in 1975 and now the first Vietnamese American to command a U.S. Navy destroyer.[74]

The Chinese public demonstrated a similar awareness of changes in American life with the enormous attention they paid to the arrival in 2011 of Gary Locke, a former two-term governor of Washington State and U.S. commerce secretary, as the first U.S. ambassador to China of Chinese descent. During his two and a half years in Beijing, however, Locke failed to curry adequate favor with privileged Chinese officials, and major Chinese state media eventually responded to his imminent departure in 2014 by referring to him as a "rotten banana," a racial slur: "When a banana sits out for long, its yellow peels will always rot . . . revealing its white core." Thus did the government of the largest nation with an emigrant rather than immigrant tradition reveal its incomprehension of the integrating and hybrid character of what Cullen Murphy has called the world's "most successful multi-ethnic state," the United States. One factory worker reflected the Chinese public's warmer and more perceptive view of Locke: "He has Chinese blood, but American characteristics."[75]

American history told a story of expansion. Whatever uncertainties Americans had about other peoples, they rarely hesitated to go out to meet them—to seize their lands, to kill them, to trade with them, to have sex with them, to build alliances with them, to convert them, to marry them, to eat their food and see their sights, to talk to them (preferably in English), to become friends with them. The complexities of U.S. connections to other lands and peoples have allowed historians of U.S. foreign relations to fill a small library with their books. From a handful of minor coastal colonies along the shore of a vast continent to the great global power of the modern world, the United States, above all else, expanded.

At each step along that outbound way, Americans engaged with foreigners. In the course of the twentieth century, U.S. international power and influence soared to new levels. This presence abroad also helped stimulate significant human migration in the other direction, as foreign peoples became linked to the Americans in their lands and many of them sought to move to the United States, often as wives of U.S. soldiers, as other family members, or as students. Something similar could be seen in the histories of earlier burgeoning empires, such as those of France and Britain or Rome and China, exerting a migratory pull on many of their colonized peoples. The presence of Americans and U.S. economic and military power had dramatically affected nine of the ten countries sending the most migrants to the United States in the second half of the twentieth century. Immigration, in other words, was closely tied to U.S. involvement overseas. Mexico and Cuba offered primary examples, as did Korea, Vietnam, and the Philippines.[76]

Like nineteenth-century Europeans circumnavigating the Atlantic Rim, Asians in the nineteenth and twentieth centuries migrated around the entire Pacific Rim. With Chinese in the greatest numbers, they sought better economic opportunities and wound up everywhere from Indonesia and Australia to Canada and Peru. But also like Europeans before them, more Asians came to the United States, once allowed to after 1965, than to any other land. In the very same years, the United States was deepening its economic, political, and military ties across the Pacific. These links took the form of a competition with the Soviet Union for influence while the Cold War lasted, but even after the demise of the USSR, American ties to Asia only continued to grow.[77]

Such changes and connections became visible in many ways, including in the films of two prominent Hollywood figures, Bruce Lee and Clint Eastwood, both known for their tough-guy personas on screen. Born in San Francisco and raised in Hong Kong, Lee moved to Seattle to attend the University of Washington and spent much of his too-short adult life (he died at thirty-three) traversing the Pacific to make action-packed films in both Hong Kong and the United States. *Fist of Fury* (1972) and *Enter the Dragon* (1973) established him as a huge martial-arts star on the silver screen. Most interestingly, he modeled a new bare-chested, tautly muscled, straight-ahead style of Asian masculinity, the reversal of decades of American film portrayals of Asian men as more typically effeminate, servile, sneaky, drug addicted, or cruel. In the very same months that Nixon and Mao were thawing a quarter-century of U.S.-Chinese hostility and Vietnamese were ushering the last American troops out of their country in defeat, white Americans were learning to cheer for the first Asian American action hero.[78]

Perhaps no one embodied masculine toughness on screen in the late twentieth century more than Clint Eastwood. "Go ahead—make my day," his quasi-rogue cop Harry Callahan taunted criminals, hoping they would give him a reason to shoot them. In real life, Eastwood had impeccable Republican political credentials. As a director, however, he made several films that cast new and intriguing light on older, white-dominant nationalist narratives, including the revisionist Western *Unforgiven* (1992). His *Flags of Our Fathers* (2006) depicted the American experience of the iconic 1945 battle of Iwo Jima, which he paired with a Japanese-language (with English subtitles) *Letters from Iwo Jima* (2006), portraying the final days of the Japanese island's defenders. Having Clint Eastwood humanize the lives of some of America's fiercest enemies in its greatest war marked another milestone on the path to normalizing Asian cultures in American sensibilities.

It bears repeating, once again, that prejudice and insensitivity toward people of Asian heritage did not disappear from the United States. These realities were rarely funny, but they occasionally could be. At a White House reception in May 1981 for the visiting Japanese prime minister, Zenko Suzuki, the recently appointed U.S. secretary of state, Alexander Haig, was greeting those in the prime minister's party. Also present at the gathering was the Japanese American U.S. senator from Hawai'i, Spark Matsunaga, a twice-wounded U.S. World War II veteran and graduate of Harvard Law School. Haig, mistaking him for a member of the Tokyo delegation, asked Matsunaga if he spoke English. Well known for his sense of humor, Matsunaga replied with a smile, "Yes, Mr. Secretary, I do—and I had the honor of voting for your confirmation the other day." Discrimination and sometimes violence remained daily challenges for Asian Americans, even as they moved gradually from exotic outsiders to model minority to simply American citizens.[79]

CHAPTER VI

Subversion

The Power of American Culture in a Global Era

G lobalization made the exotic increasingly familiar. Systems of transportation and communication that had been gradually speeding up for centuries accelerated anew after the 1960s. Container ships, computers, and the internet pulled faraway places closer together. Across the last several decades, the contours of what was considered foreign in American life shrank steadily thanks to rising trade, information flows, cultural exchange, travel, and migration. In matters from food, music, and sports to disease, scientific education, and climate change, Americans became more engaged than ever before with non-Americans, a development eased by the rapid spread of English as a global language. Globalization reduced what was foreign in the American imagination.[1]

Increased contact, of course, did not always lead to understanding or good relations. Americans were both attracted to and repelled by foreigners, just as other peoples were both attracted to and repelled by Americans. Resistance to American-inflected globalization helped shape politics from Russia to China to the Middle East to Latin America. Thoughtful Americans, across the political spectrum, worried about manifestations of anti-American sentiment abroad, well before the attacks of September 11, 2001, and President George W. Bush's public wrestling with the question of "Why do they hate us?"[2] At the same time, polls revealed an often-wide gulf between Americans and informed knowledge of the non-American world. One example among many would be the Roper poll in late 2002, on the eve of the U.S. invasion of Iraq, which revealed that only 13 percent of young Americans aged eighteen to twenty-four could even locate Iraq on a map—although Garry Trudeau's cartoon strip *Doonesbury* had a U.S. officer respond that, unfortunately for Saddam Hussein, "all 13% are Marines." Widespread American ignorance of the outside world was perhaps no worse than parochialism in any other country, but it had greater impact because of the scale and intensity of American involvement beyond U.S. borders.[3]

A perpetual challenge for mostly monolingual Americans abroad was the chasm between their military, economic, and cultural might, on the one hand, and their linguistic limitations, on the other. "The Americans naturally gravitated toward Iraqis who could speak English," the journalist Dexter Filkins observed about U.S. forces in the Middle East in 2008. "There were never enough." The same had been true in Vietnam and every other non-Anglophone land where U.S. troops landed. "There were always two conversations in Iraq, the one the Iraqis were having with the Americans"—which was in English—"and the one they were having among themselves"—which was not. "The one the Iraqis were having with us—that was positive and predictable and boring, and it made the Americans happy because it made them think they were winning. And the Iraqis kept it up because it kept the money flowing, or because it bought them a little peace." Filkins concluded, however, that "the conversation they were having with each other was the one that really mattered. . . . That conversation was the chatter of a whole other world, a parallel reality which sometimes unfolded right next to the Americans, even right in front of them. And we almost never saw it."[4]

In the face of such challenges and limitations, the greatest advantage of the United States in engaging with foreigners in recent decades was its relentlessly absorptive popular culture and consumer economy. American society operated much as an amoeba does with foreign objects: after an initial encounter, it slowly surrounded and absorbed the foreign. What used to be outside became inside. This process happened, for example, with cuisine and the changing of popular tastes to absorb new ethnic traditions and styles. Some observers have suggested that the preferred initial American approach to a foreign culture was, in fact, to taste it.[5]

The same incorporating process was visible in the commodification of the counterculture of the 1960s and 1970s. Once foreign-seeming practices such as yoga or nose piercing and exotic items such as rock 'n' roll records or incense—and now marijuana, in several states—turned into profitable mainstream consumables.[6] Something similar happened with domestic once-feared black political radicals such as Paul Robeson and Malcolm X, each now long since granted his own first-class U.S. postage stamp, with a warm, smiling image. The United States, the Indian-American novelist Jhumpa Lahiri has suggested, "just absorbs everything. It accommodates differences but always extinguishes them in some way."[7]

Immigrant parents, in particular, experienced the power of this absorptive force on their children—with varying mixtures of regret, resignation, and satisfaction—and they understood that power better than did anxious nativists—and better than did observers, including historians, who focused too narrowly on the sound and fury of those nativists. Mario Puzo illuminated this dynamic in his 1964 novel *The Fortunate Pilgrim*. He described Italian American mothers gathering on their tenement stoops in early-twentieth-century New York City, recalling the rigid familial expectations they had grown up with in southern Italy and bemoaning the empowered behavior of their own Americanized children. They told stories of what they considered the younger generation's insolence and disrespect toward their elders. "But in the hot summer night their voices were filled with hope, with a vigor never sounded in their [Italian] homeland. Here now was money in the bank, children who could read and write, grandchildren who would be professors if all went well. They spoke with guilty loyalty of customs they had themselves trampled into dust."[8]

In the globalizing era that began in the 1970s, Americans had the most influential voice of any people. Their preeminent economic and cultural power helped shape the contours of a world that seemed smaller and more connected than ever before. But an accurate assessment of the impact of American-promoted market forces and individualist values requires first considering those who sought to impede U.S. military incursions and resist American-influenced global consumer culture.

Resistances to American Expansion

Few people appreciate having their lands invaded. This fundamental reality dogged the long history of American colonial and national expansion, from the seventeenth-century coastlines of eastern North America, to the twentieth-century shores of East and Southeast Asia, to the twenty-first-century banks of the Tigris and Euphrates rivers in Iraq. Emma Sky was a British Middle Eastern expert and Arabic speaker who opposed the U.S. invasion and occupation of Iraq in 2003 but volunteered to work there afterward. She hoped to help the Iraqi people rebuild their country and served first as the main political adviser to a U.S. colonel in charge of the oil-rich but volatile Kirkuk region. "When I arrived, one of the questions put to me was 'What do we need to do to be loved?'" Sky recalled in her 2015 memoir, *The Unraveling*. "I told them that people who invade other people's countries, and killed people who were no threat to them, would never be loved."[9]

While Americans might have been inclined to see their own motivations abroad as altruistic, they continually encountered people who did not appreciate their actions. Sometimes such foreigners admired the universal principles that Americans touted—liberty, equality, and justice for all—but resented their unequal application.[10] At other times such peoples simply saw Americans as invaders and paid little attention to flowery rhetoric. No one bore more fully the brunt of U.S. expansion than Native Americans, who spent centuries resisting it. Some Indian activists made this point after the attacks of September 11, 2001, by wearing T-shirts that read, "Fighting Terrorism Since 1492." Like other peoples facing invasion or occupation by the United States, indigenous North Americans wielded varying tactics of resistance, ranging from adopting white American culture, like many Cherokee, to persistent armed self-defense, like many Apache. Native American history since the 1500s can be seen as, among other things, one extended effort at resistance and adaptation.[11]

Certain patterns and themes that appeared early in Native American encounters with white settlers persisted for centuries in U.S. interactions with other peoples abroad. Cultural conflicts stood out. European and then white American culture seemed to others often subversive of their values. The Sauk Indian leader Black Hawk, for example, fought for decades against white immigrants and the U.S. Army in the lands now known as Illinois and Wisconsin, culminating in the Black Hawk War of 1832, in which he was finally captured. In later recollections, he wondered, "Why did the Great Spirit ever send the whites to . . . drive us from our homes, and introduced among us poisonous liquors, disease and death?"[12] A century later Hasan al-Banna, the Egyptian founder of the Muslim Brotherhood, echoed this dismay at the debilitating power of white outsiders. He bemoaned how European imperialists and tourists "imported their semi-naked women into these regions" along with "their liquors" and their many other "vices," all destructive of local values and morality. Americans and Europeans seemed to carry with them the prospect of moral corruption in their attitudes and behaviors regarding sex and alcohol.[13]

The nearest neighbors were the first to engage in resistance campaigns against U.S. expansion. After Native Americans, the next in line lived to the north. Those British colonies in North America that chose not to join the American revolutionaries in 1776 faced a persistent threat from a burgeoning U.S. population and its hunger for new lands. These included French-speaking Lower Canada (downstream in the St. Lawrence River valley—today's Quebec), Upper Canada (upstream around the Great Lakes—today's Ontario), and the eastern colonies of New Brunswick, Nova Scotia, Prince Edward Island, Newfoundland, and Labrador, plus the vast uncharted Rupert's Land off to the west and northwest. These British citizens, later unified as Canadians, fended off U.S. military assaults in the War of 1812 and subsequent threats of aggression. A major theme of Canadian history ever since has been containing the cultural and economic influence of a southern neighbor ten times larger in population.[14]

The neighbors who felt the heaviest weight of U.S. expansive energies lived to the south. Mexico's northern half became the southwestern quarter of the United States, after U.S. military aggression in 1846 through 1848. Similarly, Puerto Rico slipped under U.S. control in 1898, as did Cuba in a less formal and less permanent fashion. The Panama Canal Zone spent most of the twentieth century (1903–1979) as a leased U.S. territory. Washington helped overturn governments from Guatemala in 1954 to Chile in 1973 to Panama in 1989. Most of the countries in the Caribbean and Central American sphere experienced U.S. military intervention at some point. And U.S. private interests dominated the economies of the circum-Caribbean region.[15]

The very phrase "Latin America" emerged out of the regional struggle to fend off U.S. influence. In the early decades of the nineteenth century, leaders of the mainly Spanish colonies in the Western hemisphere fought their way free of Madrid's control. They saw the United States as a model of anticolonial liberation, and Americans shared a sense of camaraderie with others in the hemisphere following the path from colony to republic.[16] But the U.S. invasion and annexation of Mexican lands unsettled the region.

In response to increasingly racialized and pejorative U.S. rhetoric toward peoples south of the Rio Grande by the mid-1800s, Latin American elites began embracing the term "Latin race" rather than "Hispanic American race," as a way of identifying with a powerful Catholic France as well as including Portuguese-speaking Brazil. Then the private filibuster invasion of Nicaragua in 1856, led by William Walker, and U.S. recognition of his government, put leaders in the region on notice. In an effort to consolidate diplomatic alliances and a regional identity against the North American threat, they called themselves collectively "Latin America." Latin Americans imagined themselves as more spiritual and noble, in contrast to the northern "Anglo-Saxons," who appeared plainly aggressive and materialistic.[17]

"Poor Mexico," the late-nineteenth-century Mexican dictator Porfirio Diaz reportedly lamented. "So far from God, so close to the United States." Like Poland between Russia and Germany, or Vietnam with China, or Ireland with England, the observation underlined an inevitable challenge of geography for a smaller nation close by a more powerful and aggressive neighbor. The historian Max Paul Friedman has recently recalled the satirical article published by the Mexican economist José Iturriaga in 1951 entitled "Why I Am Anti-Soviet and Anti-Russian." At the height of the Cold War, Iturriaga sarcastically reminded readers of the real aggressor in Mexican history. "How can a good Mexican forget that in 1846 the Czar of all the Russians, James Polkov, sent Winfield Scottsky to make war on us in order to annex the province of Texas to its immense Ukrainian steppes, in which conflict we lost not only Texas but more than half our territory." Iturriaga drew a direct link to Mexican migration northward: "We cannot ignore the humiliations suffered by our wandering farmers, who, because they wanted to earn a few rubles on the other side of the Volga, are discriminated against and ill-treated because they are guilty of not being Slavs." In detailing this story, Friedman notes how one U.S. diplomat bemoaned the article's "anti-Americanism," "thereby exquisitely missing the point."[18]

History and geography required Mexicans to develop an extensive record of resisting U.S. domination. During the revolutionary upheaval of the 1910s in Mexico, some radicals hoped to retake some or all of the lands seized by the United States seven decades earlier. Others in the revolutionary regimes that followed sought to implement the 1917 Constitution's declaration that all mineral rights on the land belonged to the Mexican people. In this, they succeeded in 1938, finally nationalizing the oil-production facilities long owned and managed by foreign—particularly

American—oil companies. Still others focused on the cultural front of the struggle for full Mexican independence from the United States. The central government had long worried about the nation's northerners, far from Mexico City and close to the U.S. border. In the 1960s the Mexican government began a campaign in border cities to strengthen national identity through educational and cultural programs, including an insistence on the use of proper Spanish unadulterated by Anglicisms. This proved fruitless, as did the mirror-image English-only campaigns across the border.[19]

If neighboring Native Americans, Canadians, and Latin Americans formed the front lines of resistance to U.S. expansion, Europeans offered another salient pushing back against growing Yankee power. This was complicated. Europe is a large and diverse region, not a simple or unified one. For the first 150 years of U.S. sovereignty—that is, well more than half of American history—Europe housed the world's greatest imperial powers, its wealthiest and most technologically sophisticated societies, and some of the globe's densest populations. In the century before the restrictive 1924 U.S. immigration law, some fifty million of these people abandoned Europe for American shores. While many emigrants eventually returned, it was nonetheless a massive demonstration of voting with their feet. A vast swath of Europeans, in other words, not only failed to resist the American temptation but actually went off and became Americans. Their extensive networks of connection to family and friends back in their countries of origin gave a much larger number of Europeans direct emotional links to the United States.[20]

European emigrants came primarily from the working class, their desire to preserve their own home cultures jostling against their determination to find better economic opportunities elsewhere. More affluent Europeans had little incentive to move and often looked askance at the United States and its strange new culture; many of these elites were repelled by what they saw as the crudeness and lack of sophistication and manners among Americans. Politically liberal Europeans admired the new republic and its relatively democratic values but loathed the practice of race slavery. More conservative Europeans found American culture strikingly materialistic and even soulless, and they feared its influence. "Americanization in its widest sense," the German writer Paul Dehn noted in 1904 regarding the spread of U.S.-style department stores, "means the uninterrupted, exclusive, and relentless striving after gain, riches, and influence." A few years earlier, the prominent German philosopher Friedrich Nietzsche observed that the "breathless haste" with which Americans worked—"the distinctive vice of the new world—is already beginning ferociously to infect old Europe and is spreading a spiritual emptiness over the continent." Relentless paid labor, a characteristic widely admired by Americans then and now as a mark of ambition and discipline, could be seen as subversive of a different and more virtuous way of living.[21]

The most powerful European governments had strategic concerns about the increasingly muscular new republic across the Atlantic. Having lost the colonies in the American Revolution, Britain went to war with the Americans once more in 1812 and came close to blows again in subsequent decades. The revolutionary government in Paris edged toward war with the United States in the 1790s, and imperial French aggression in Mexico during the American Civil War risked military conflict anew with the United States. The Spanish lost most of their remaining colonies to the United States in 1898. By this time, Washington and London had developed an increasingly close relationship, and most English observers cheered the victory of their Anglophone cousins over the declining Spanish crown and enthused particularly over the liberation of Cuba from Madrid's rule. But Queen Victoria demurred: "No doubt Cuba was dreadfully governed . . . [but] they might as well say we governed Ireland badly and they ought to take possession of it and free it." The expansion of U.S. power, layered with the language of self-government, threatened the interests of older European empires.[22]

Germany, along with Japan, wound up leading the resistance to U.S. power in the first half of the twentieth century. Berlin's defeat in both world wars opened the door to a pervasive new American advance into Europe, taking at first military and political form but later even more so economic and cultural form.[23] But the close links forged through the Marshall Plan and the North Atlantic Treaty Organization (NATO) after World War II did not erase the desire of Western European governments to build their futures independent of Washington's Cold War expectations. The French were the most determined, and their attitude sometimes provoked private outrage among U.S. policy makers. French president Charles de Gaulle was, for Franklin Roosevelt, "a nut" and, for Harry Truman, a "son of a bitch." Secretary of State Dean Acheson considered the French as a whole "mentally ill"; one of his successors, George Ball, called them "psychotic." The U.S. Psychological Strategy Board suggested that the "French mind rebels at pragmatism. The Frenchman disassociates his thoughts from the facts." Later French refusal to support George W. Bush's 2003 invasion of Iraq angered conservative Americans; editorialists called the French people "cheese-eating surrender monkeys" and President Jacques Chirac "a pygmy Joan of Arc."[24]

Contemporary American concerns regarding Europe focused particularly on Russia. Moscow's relationship with the United States and with the rest of Europe had been complicated and contentious since at least the 1917 Bolshevik Revolution. Recent Russian efforts to influence elections in the United States and other parts of Europe built on the Russian authoritarian leader Vladimir Putin's efforts to position Russia as a defender of traditional Christian culture against a supposedly degenerate, secular West. For so long a threat from the secular left of communism, Russia under Putin had swung 180 degrees to oppose the United States and Western Europe from the religious and cultural right.[25]

A more fundamental difference surfaced in how Americans and Europeans viewed the relationship between individual liberty and the governing power of the state. Polling data revealed a stronger American inclination to value personal freedom against state interference, versus a European preference for the government to guarantee a minimum standard of decent living. These were not absolutes; the ranges of preference overlapped, just as the ranges among European nations varied somewhat. But a clear cultural distinction regarding individual liberty and social solidarity suggested societies that had developed differently. For all their close ties to the United States, Europeans proved unlikely to embrace fully the more libertarian ethos of American life.[26]

At the apex of American influence around the globe, the greatest resistance came from the Left. Inspired by Karl Marx's explanations of history and destiny as well as by the Bolsheviks' success in Russia, socialists and communists organized to build a future very different from the one promised by American-style democratic capitalism. The United States reached its position of global dominance in the middle decades of the twentieth century, precisely the same historical moment that the majority of the world's peoples fought their way free of primarily European imperialism. The resulting Soviet-American competition shaped the rest of the century, as the two sides offered alternative paths for developing a modern society. The Cold War ended abruptly with a Soviet withdrawal and the swift dissolution of the USSR in 1991, catching Americans and others by surprise. But along the way, communists were the fiercest opponents of American influence.[27]

They had some notable successes. Vladimir Lenin offered the strongest challenge to Woodrow Wilson's vision for a new political order after the cataclysm of World War I. The Red Army's defeat of Germany on the eastern front in World War II won respect for the Soviet Union and helped inspire communists across the emerging Third World. Mao Zedong and his comrades pulled the world's most populous nation out of the American sphere of influence with the establishment of the People's Republic of China in 1949; within a year they were fighting U.S. troops to a draw on the Korean peninsula, helping their fellow communists preserve control of North Korea. In Vietnam, communist-led revolutionaries defeated the French armed forces in 1954. They then did the same to the Americans who replaced the French. Much closer to American shores—just ninety miles away—and thus more bitter for U.S. leaders, Fidel Castro led Cuban revolutionaries to victory in 1959, overthrowing a pro-U.S. regime and replacing it with a communist government. Events in Havana marked "above all else, a declaration of independence from the United States," the journalist Robert Taber wrote. Despite the vast human rights abuses of communist regimes across the twentieth century as well as most having failed by the 1990s, it was these devoted Marxists who stood most strongly against what the prominent British newspaper editor W. T. Stead had earlier called "the Americanization of the world."[28]

Careful American observers sometimes wondered at what often seemed the superior motivation of communist versus anticommunist forces in the Third World's Cold War civil conflicts. Early in the Korean War, a U.S. colonel told the British journalist Philip Knightly, "South Koreans and North Koreans are identical. Why then do North Koreans fight like tigers and South Koreans run like sheep?" U.S. communications along the front sometimes used "HA" to signal that South Korean soldiers were "hauling ass"—that is, fleeing. During the U.S. war in Vietnam, the American-allied South Vietnamese Army of the Republic of Vietnam (ARVN) was famously riven with communist infiltrators, while ARVN had no parallel penetration of the communist-led ranks of the National Liberation Front. American disappointment with anticommunist allies dated back to the first successful communist revolution, when U.S. troops supported the anti-Bolshevik forces in the Russian civil war. "They say we are fighting for the [White] Russians," one GI told a U.S. war correspondent at the time. "Why don't they do some fighting for themselves?" Recalling the same phenomenon in the civil conflict among the Laotian people in Southeast Asia in the 1970s, the historian Kenton Clymer asked, "Why were 'their' Laos tougher than 'our' Laos?"[29]

Of course, many non-European anticommunist allies of the United States fought with great courage and some success in the civil conflicts shaping the political future of the former colonial world. South Koreans eventually built a vibrant, affluent modern democracy, while Afghan mujahedeen surprised the world by forcing the mighty Soviet armed forces to retreat. And the core problem for both Americans and Soviets during the Cold War was the determination of Third World leaders to remain independent, often playing the two superpowers off against each other. But it is true that the United States seemed to face the greater challenge. The new nations of Asia, Africa, and the Middle East had long, painful histories of being mostly exploited for their natural resources and labor by the capitalist European empires now closely allied with the United States in NATO, so they were bound to view white Western powers with particular skepticism. Only after socialism's failure became obvious in the 1980s, when China began turning to private property and market mechanisms ("Market-Leninism") and the USSR imploded, did the American style of consumer capitalism emerge as something close to a default setting for political economies around the globe—even in such countries as Vietnam, ironically, where it had been most fiercely resisted.[30]

The green challenge of Islamism soon surpassed the red challenge of communism. The brief period of seemingly unassailable American global dominance lasted only from "11/9"—the date in 1989 of the Berlin Wall's demise—to "9/11"—the date in 2001 of al-Qaeda's attacks on the United States. Revolutionary Islamists, by this time, had already been engaged with the United States for decades. The initial Muslim Brotherhood organizing since 1928 had targeted "the West" more broadly, particularly the then-most intrusive outside powers in the Middle East, Britain and France, with the more distant United States in the background. As the United States replaced the European imperialists in the region after World War II, Washington developed close ties to radical Islamists' primary "near enemies": first, the nominally Muslim but deeply authoritarian regimes in the region, and, second, the new Zionist state of Israel, carved in part out of lands seized from mostly Muslim Palestinians. The United States became the third target—the "far enemy." Iranian revolutionaries struck the first direct Islamist blow against the United States when they overthrew the U.S.-allied Shah Reza Pahlavi in 1979, kidnapped fifty-two American hostages, and held them for over a year. In 1983, Islamists in Lebanon killed hundreds of U.S. personnel in bombing attacks on the U.S. embassy and U.S. military barracks, even as the American CIA was busy funding Muslim mujahedeen fighters against the Soviet Union in Afghanistan. In 1993 Islamist radicals crossed a watershed divide by launching a direct attack on U.S. soil—the first assault on the World Trade Center in New York City.[31]

Al-Qaeda represented a new kind of challenge to the United States. A nonstate organization without citizens or territory of its own to protect, it was free from the traditional diplomatic constraints faced by actual nations. Both 9/11 and subsequent suicide attacks demonstrated the presence of large numbers of jihadists willing to give their lives to kill Americans, other Westerners, Israelis, and, above all, other Muslims who were in their way. Such zealous enthusiasm seemed greater than that of earlier communists, who had sought a secular paradise on earth and rarely engaged in suicide missions. Communism might, in principle, have offered a larger threat to the United States: it aimed at the workers of the entire world, not just believers in the Muslim lands. But the jihadists were certain they had Allah on their side. They had already helped bring down one of the world's two superpowers—the Soviets in Afghanistan in the 1980s. After U.S. soldiers ("these filthy infidel Crusaders," Osama bin Laden called them) in the 1990 run-up to the Persian Gulf War took up positions in Saudi Arabia, home to the holy cities of Mecca and Medina, bin Laden and his compatriots were determined to destroy the other superpower—the United States.[32]

Bin Laden and fellow jihadists did enormous damage to the United States. They killed almost three thousand Americans on September 11. Even better, from their point of view, they drew U.S. military forces into Afghanistan and—to their surprise and delight—even into secular Iraq, in the very heart of the Middle East. What better recruiting target could radical Islamists have imagined than over one hundred thousand non-Muslim U.S. troops occupying a majority-Muslim nation right in the center of the Islamic world? Occupations rarely age well, and complex anti-American insurgencies sprang up quickly in both Iraq and Afghanistan, killing thousands more American soldiers. U.S. Colonel Nathan Sassaman explained the situation in Iraq in late 2003: "It's like Jekyll and Hyde out here. By day, we are putting on a happy face. By night, we are hunting down and killing our enemies." After a typical raid on a home in an Iraqi village in which U.S. soldiers humiliated and terrified family members while finding no weapons, Sergeant Eric Brown acknowledged, "I feel bad for these people, I really do. It's so hard to separate the good from the bad." The reporter Dexter Filkins could only conclude, "The Americans were making enemies faster than they could kill them."[33]

Military occupation was a difficult path to winning hearts and minds. Rare success stories such as Japan and western Germany after World War II required highly unusual circumstances. In most cases civilians came to see foreign soldiers as enemies, with their propensity to violence and their common ignorance of local language and customs, not to mention their sexual interest in local women.[34] Sociological stereotyping did not help, such as one U.S. sergeant's explanation of the challenge in Iraq: "You've got to understand the Arab mind. The only thing they understand is force— force, pride, and saving face." Americans and other imperialists had been saying similar things for centuries about Native Americans, Japanese, and other opponents. Mockery of Arab cultures as backward was common. In the highest-earning film of 1981, *Raiders of the Lost Ark*, Harrison Ford's protagonist character patiently watches an Arab attacker approach him with a twirling sword, then pulls out a pistol with a tired smirk and shoots him dead. In the most popular film of 1992, Disney's *Aladdin*, a lead character declares: "I come from a land, from a faraway place, where the caravan camels roam, where they cut off your ear if they don't like your face—it's barbaric, but hey, it's home." When a U.S. reporter asked a professor at Baghdad University in 2003 how he thought the U.S. military occupation of Iraq was going, the professor responded bluntly, "You Americans know nothing about my country."[35]

The U.S. military presence in the Middle East helped move noncombatants toward resisting these heavily armed outsiders, "making enemies faster than they could kill them." That resistance, in turn, pushed back against U.S. leaders' hopes for success in the region. When al-Qaeda's successor and competitor, the so-called Islamic State, emerged from the political wreckage of the American occupation of Iraq in 2013 and seized control of a wide swath of northwestern Iraq and eastern Syria, wreaking havoc on the lives of the people under their control, neither the U.S. public nor the administration of Barack Obama was willing to wade back into another large-scale U.S. military commitment in the region.[36] Islamists since the 1920s had denounced Western culture, and the prominent Egyptian radical

Sayyid Qutb, a key inspiration for bin Laden, had registered his disgust at what he considered the materialistic, sexualized culture he encountered during six months of study in 1949 and 1950 in Greeley, Colorado—not widely known as a hotbed of the avant-garde. No doubt many socially conservative Muslims in the Middle East remained troubled by the unrestrained content of American popular culture. And radical Islamists resented the centuries-long decline of Muslim influence in a modern world dominated by the economically and politically powerful West. But the core of Islamist discontent with the United States was political rather than cultural: it was the policies more than movies, weapons rather than bathing suits, particularly the support of repressive regimes in Saudi Arabia and Egypt and for Israel's occupation of Palestinian territories.[37]

Resurgent Xenophobia at Home

Just as various peoples around the world resisted the rising current of U.S. influence, particularly once it reached flood tide after 1945, so too did many Americans at home continue to distrust and oppose new foreigners arriving on American shores. Like their communist and Islamist opponents abroad, anti-immigrant activists at home sought to keep Americans and others apart. It was a familiar story, newly visible in the 2016 election and its aftermath.

Expanding formal equality and increasing multiculturalism formed a central current of late-twentieth- and early-twenty-first-century U.S. history. The dramatic arc of racial and religious inclusion brought the nation much closer to the promise of the Declaration of Independence by 2000 than it had been in 1900. At least as impressive was the post-1960 reduction of sex discrimination, opening up a period of female opportunity unprecedented in recorded human history. The public mainstreaming of gay and lesbian Americans in the twenty-first century also had no precedent. Americans born after 2005 were growing up knowing only a black president. These were extraordinary changes that had been nearly unimaginable just a few decades earlier. They lulled many observers into thinking that old-fashioned racially tinged xenophobia had lost its traction among white American voters.

Then came Donald Trump. The election as president of a man with such a remarkable public record as a celebrity-obsessed charlatan stunned nearly everyone, including Trump and his closest advisers. A New Yorker through and through, he was a highly affluent product of one of the world's most cosmopolitan cities. But he had a long history of discriminatory behavior toward potential African American customers as a landlord and real estate investor. He entered national politics most prominently as a promoter of the fraudulent "birther" claim that Barack Obama, the nation's first black president, had not been born in the United States and was thus an illegitimate occupant of the White House. And he centered his 2016 campaign on the supposed threat to the nation from dangerous immigrants, specifically Mexicans and Muslims. He identified the former as criminals and rapists, calling for a "beautiful wall" on the southern border, and he cast the latter as terrorists, issuing travel bans for several majority-Muslim countries. His supporters during the campaign and his presidency were most stirred by his calls for limiting immigration from what he identified as "shithole" countries. Lest anyone miss the racial coding of such African, Caribbean, Latin American, and Middle Eastern countries, he appealed for more immigrants from places such as Norway—although a few days later his secretary of homeland security, Kirstjen Nielsen, a blond Scandinavian American, told a Senate hearing, with a straight face, that she did not know Norway's racial makeup.[38]

Even the most casual observer of American politics in 2016 and after could not miss the dramatic reappearance of an open, at least rhetorical hostility to people of color, particularly those born elsewhere.[39] But other factors also shaped the electoral outcome that year, perhaps even more powerfully.[40] One was Trump's opponent Hillary Clinton, who alienated many voters and also ran an undistinguished campaign. Another was the Russian propaganda campaign to exacerbate political divisions in the United States and nudge the election away from the Russia-hawk Clinton to the Russophilic Trump. A third factor was the FBI decision to announce, just days before the election, a reopening of an investigation into Clinton's use of a private email server during her term years earlier as secretary of state. Perhaps most important was the deep sense of economic insecurity and cultural resentment that Trump tapped into. Conservative white voters, particularly older and less-educated ones, were worried (like other voters) about sharply rising economic inequality and dimming economic prospects for their children, while also continuing to be concerned about ongoing cultural shifts regarding homosexuality, secularization, gun rights, and abortion rights.[41] They disdained what often seemed like a deadlocked, incompetent U.S. Congress. Pulling the lever for the louche, deceitful Trump for some was simply a matter of voting Republican, but for others it served also as a kind of raised middle finger to Washington, "the system," and elites. It was a roar of anger.[42]

The issue of immigration restriction emerged as a fully partisan one during the 2016 campaign. The Democratic Party had been identified with its immigrant supporters since the nineteenth century, and it remained a strongly pro-immigrant voice in the twenty-first. Republicans had been more divided on immigration over time. They had been primarily responsible for the 1924 Johnson-Reed Act that created the highly restrictive, ethnoracially determined national-origins system. But the Republican Party had also been founded on supporting entrepreneurship, and businesses generally preferred large, competitive labor forces that allowed them to hire competent workers at relatively low wages. Certain challenging but vital industries absolutely depended on inexpensive immigrant labor, such as commercial agriculture and meatpacking. Many Republicans thus had long promoted relatively open immigration. This was still evident in the Republican administration of George W. Bush up through 2009, and it remained true with many others in the party in the late 2010s.

Regardless of this split among party elites, however, the popular base of the Republican Party moved steadily into the immigration-restrictionist wing as the twenty-first century progressed.[43] Partly this derived from the September 11 attacks and the subsequent wars in Afghanistan and Iraq, which convinced many conservative Americans that Muslims were potentially dangerous. Islamists and Islamophobic Americans fed off each other. This shift in the Republican base also derived from the steep economic recession that began in 2008 and resulting anxieties about competition for jobs. And a third significant factor in the GOP's recent consolidation as an anti-immigrant party was the combination of post-1965 immigration being primarily nonwhite and the Republican Party's steady accommodation of white racism during the same period. Rising partisan polarization suggested that the GOP's coalescing unity against immigrants might well become its new norm.[44]

This is not an argument that all white Republicans are racist—hardly. Rather, the party of Lincoln (and the Union Army) as a whole had made a series of decisions since the mid-1960s to woo white Southerners to its ranks and to make room for the voices in American politics most opposed to the interests of people of color. From Richard Nixon's "Southern strategy" in 1968 to Donald Trump's close identification with "white nationalists" in 2016, Republicans marched persistently down the road to becoming nearly an all-white institution, even as the nation as a whole was growing more racially diverse.[45] Even Michael Steele, the African American selected to head the Republican National Committee in 2009 in the aftermath of black Democrat Barack Obama's election, answered a question about whether his party still had a problem with racism in 2018, "Yes, they do. And I think we need to be honest and acknowledge it."[46] The year 2016 marked a kind of coming-out party for white racial pride, including a sharp escalation in violent attacks on people of color and their white supporters.[47] Just eight months into Trump's presidency, white nationalists and neo-Nazis staged a rally in Charlottesville, Virginia, during which they assaulted antiracist counterprotesters, killing one and seriously injuring several more. Trump startled the nation and his own party by morally equating the two sides and declaring that "some very fine people" had been marching with the neo-Nazis.[48]

Trump put an exclamation point on the GOP's racial trajectory by appointing as one of his closest initial White House advisers Steve Bannon, the former head of the white nationalist or "alt-right" media outlet Breitbart News.[49] The president's most influential adviser on immigration issues remained Stephen Miller, a young hardliner who publicly supported a bill that would penalize immigrants who did not speak English. In 2018 the U.S. Citizenship and Immigration Services informed its employees that the agency's mission statement was eliminating a reference to the United States as a "nation of immigrants."[50] Trump remained famously nonideological, however. He dumped Bannon after just seven months. For all his sound and fury, Trump had long imagined himself as a "deal maker," and he lacked evidence of principled commitment to any standard other than the accumulation of fame and fortune. He loved to surprise both opponents and supporters with unpredictable declarations, even as he pursued policies to restrict nonwhite immigration.

Certain hypocrisies and ironies of the administration stood out regarding immigration. The freelance writer and researcher Jennifer Mendelsohn noted that presidential aide Miller "favors immigrants who speak English. But the 1910 census shows his own great-grandmother couldn't." Mendelsohn published a photograph of a census document showing that Miller's ancestor spoke only Yiddish. When White House official Dan Scavino claimed that familial chain migration was "choking" the United States—an opinion also expressed by the president—Mendelsohn dug up census records showing more than a half-dozen close Scavino relatives arriving in the United States within a few years of one another, and she wondered if this might not also be considered chain migration. The logic of "that was then—this is now" seemed precarious.[51]

Trump's own paternal grandfather Friedrich Trump had emigrated from southwestern Germany, where his family's surname had once been "Drumpf" (provoking the comedian John Oliver to promote the slogan, "Make Donald Drumpf Again"). But German heritage during World War I was not well regarded by many other Americans—at the time, some might even have considered Germany a "shithole" country and wondered why the United States needed any more people from there. So Trump's father at times presented his lineage as Swedish rather than German. Trump also claimed Swedish heritage as late as 1990, despite growing up with his German immigrant grandmother Elizabeth living across the street from the family until her death in the 1960s. The president's mother, meanwhile, had emigrated from Scotland, where she had spoken Gaelic as her first language on the island of Lewis in the Outer Hebrides.[52]

Perhaps the most telling aspect of the story of Donald Trump and immigration is the most intimate. As a young, handsome, and unusually wealthy New Yorker, he built an early reputation as a playboy and socialite. He managed to gain five draft deferments during the Vietnam War, four for education and one for a medical condition of "bone spurs" in his heels, despite active athletic engagement during his college years. He claimed that the condition later resolved itself gradually and without surgical intervention. Years later, he bantered with his friend the radio host Howard Stern about how avoiding sexually transmitted diseases during his active bachelor's dating life was his "personal Vietnam." "I feel like a great and very brave soldier," he joked.[53]

This immigrant's son eventually married, three different times. Reported extramarital affairs with at least one adult-film star and one former Playboy "Playmate of the Year" required interventions by intermediaries to pay the women involved handsomely for their silence.[54] Most interesting of all was Trump's choice, from among the scores or hundreds of women he had dated, to have two of his three wives be immigrants. Better yet, they came from regions—the Czech lands and Slovenia—that had once been considered only marginally "white" and from which newcomers had once been tightly restricted. (This was also true of Russia, a country for which he expressed great admiration.) For a symbolic leader of immigration restriction, Trump was intensely drawn at least to individual female immigrants.

Americans, like their president, tended to have complicated rather than simple feelings about immigrants, ranging from anxious fear to warm admiration. In comparison to most other countries and all other great powers, the United States had long defined itself as a nation of immigrants. In practice, official policies toward newcomers had alternated between periods of relative welcome and eras of exclusion. The 2016 election certainly marked a resurgence of fearful hostility on the conservative end of the American political spectrum, one that gained real traction through the Trump administration's policies and procedures. The turn of sentiment against outsiders was not unique to the United States in this period, however. European nations experienced a similar burst of right-wing, anti-immigrant populism in the 2010s, with parties expressing such views even coming to power in Hungary and Poland, partly in response to a large influx of non-European refugees from war-torn Syria and drought-stricken West and Central Africa. Anxieties about immigration also underpinned Brexit, the 2016 British referendum on leaving the European Union. Fearful of the effects of globalization, distrustful of governing elites in their own countries, and worried about immigrants and refugees, the white working classes of the wealthy West made their political voice heard.[55]

It is unclear how long this latest xenophobic reaction will last in the United States or how great an effect it will have. There was certainly no escaping the broad cultural message to the rest of the world that many older white Americans, particularly those with less education, did not welcome more foreign arrivals. Fewer immigrants and refugees were allowed in under Trump administration policies. But the American political spectrum was broad and anti-Trump resistance powerful, as demonstrated in the 2018 congressional elections. For all the growing consolidation of immigration restrictionism in the Republican Party, the Democrats embodied an opposite, welcoming position. Demographic trends favored the latter, as the nation continued to become increasingly diverse and multiracial, particularly among younger citizens. Trends in such media as film and television pointed in the same direction. If the past proved to be any guide, the xenophobic tide of the middle and late 2010s seems likely to ebb, sooner or later.[56]

Does Globalization Reduce Foreignness?

"Without the Cold War, what's the point of being an American?" asked Harry "Rabbit" Angstrom, the everyman protagonist of John Updike's popular 1990 novel *Rabbit at Rest*. Forty-five years of nuclear-armed, seemingly permanent emergency spent facing down the Soviet Union left Americans disoriented by its disappearance. What followed was the period associated ever since with globalization. Before the late 1980s, the term "globalization" appeared hardly at all in the titles of new books published in English; by the 1990s, it was commonplace. It recast the foreign as familiar.[57]

The forces of global integration had been hard at work long before the end of the Cold War. Meshing the former communist sphere into the capitalist world economy marked merely an acceleration of an ongoing process. It had begun as early as 1000 CE with the Viking expeditions to North America, beginning a reuniting of human cultures that had previously been diversifying for at least tens of thousands of years, ever since the first *Homo sapiens* walked out of Africa. Columbus's voyages kicked this process of globalization into high gear. The next five hundred years witnessed many moments of greater speed toward connectedness, particularly the onset of the Industrial Revolution and the peaking of imperialism.[58]

Following the disaggregating caesura of 1914 through 1945, in which two world wars and the Great Depression divided nations from one another, the pace of globalization picked up anew. This time the United States led the forces of integration and benefited dramatically from its results. Determined not to return to the prewar economic slump and facing a worldwide socialist challenge, the United States made a historic shift into active global leadership in peacetime. It built alliances around the world and facilitated the expansion of international trade, finance, travel, and communication. Seizing the role of organizer and sending its people all around the world, the United States encountered more foreigners than ever before. It got used to them.

The international system that the United States sought to shape seemed smaller and smaller to Americans after 1945. Part of this was thanks to innovations in transportation and communication that brought foreign places functionally closer. Part of it derived from a U.S. determination to contain Soviet and communist influence everywhere, including waging war in places relatively few Americans had even heard of beforehand, such as Korea and Vietnam. Partly, too, the world felt smaller because its population had doubled from 1900 to 1950 and doubled again by 2000. It was simply more crowded. Population flows also increased, particularly from poorer to richer lands. From the utter devastation of World War II, Germany was rebuilt into a modern economic powerhouse, in part because of a million guest workers welcomed from abroad by 1964. "Without the additional work of foreigners," the German Employers' Association announced that year, "our economic development in recent years would be unthinkable." A parallel "Bracero" program in the United States in the same years funneled much-needed Mexican workers into the booming U.S. economy.[59]

Tourism provided an avenue for more affluent Americans than ever before to see more of the outside world. Here the technological innovations of air travel were crucial, particularly jet airliners. *Fortune* magazine in 1943 declared that with all the world's cities now within twenty-four hours' reach of one another, "the traditional boundaries of political sovereignties seem to be on the verge of extinction." The historian Jenifer Van Vleck observes that between 1945 and 1960, "mass air travel developed in tandem with the national security state." The leading U.S. international airline, Pan American, launched a 1957 advertising campaign to render foreign places alluring and nonthreatening. "Do you collect ancient ruins?" it asked. "Do you collect foreign golf courses? Do you collect exotic islands?" This meant collecting experiences at such places, not actually owning foreign golf courses, a rare experience familiar only to people such as Donald Trump. Americans were showing up overseas in great new numbers. Shopping in this fashion for experiences in previously exotic places reduced the distance between the foreign and the familiar, just as eating "ethnic" food intrigued American consumers.[60]

The line between national and international grew less stark. Pan American began printing its routes and the cities it served on world maps depicting a globe without national borders.[61] For businesses, no place was truly foreign; everywhere was a potential market or source of goods and materials. American consumers felt the same way, whether abroad or at home. Since the 1910s, U.S. companies had dominated the domestic market for automobiles, the most expensive item for buyers other than a house. In the 1970s, however, Americans began purchasing on a mass scale cars manufactured in Japan and West Germany. Honda and Volkswagen competed fiercely with Ford and General Motors. At first this development was countered by some "buy American" consumer sentiment, rooted in both nationalism and loyalty to an earlier tradition of skilled workmanship.[62] By the 1990s, however, xenophobic bumper stickers such as "Toyota—The Same People Who Brought You Pearl Harbor" had largely disappeared, and owners of Japanese cars in the United States could be seen sporting even very conservative political bumper stickers. U.S. and Japanese cars also increasingly resembled each other in design and were often assembled in each other's territory. In yet another realm, the foreign and the American were becoming less distinguishable.[63]

The digital revolution epitomized globalization and the sense of immediate connectivity to everywhere. The World Wide Web emerged in the 1990s and reshaped human communication in the early twenty-first century. The physical location of a person or a company no longer seemed to matter as much. Labels on products increasingly used internet rather than geographical addresses (and an 800 number instead of a specific area code). The earlier specificity of Atlanta as a Coca-Cola town or Pittsburgh as a steel town declined. In some ways, this made everything more foreign, since less and less was local and located; this awareness powered much of the antiglobalist reaction that ranged all the way from "buy local" campaigns to al-Qaeda terrorism. But it also made the entire globe seem accessible and therefore no longer really foreign. In the earlier era of landline telephones, pundits had joked about how Manhattan residents who moved elsewhere yearned to keep their "212" area code as a signifier of their New York City identity. Now, in the era of mobile phones, they could actually do so. The "area" in "area code" was losing its precise meaning. Just as the Channel Tunnel after 1993 did for the island of Great Britain, the internet served as a kind of "Chunnel" for Americans, linking them directly to foreigners in previously unimagined ways.

Increasing contact and growing familiarity with foreigners in the age of globalization did not always mean that Americans understood them. U.S. residents had long been known for a tendency to combine personal friendliness with limited sophistication, as a recent example indicated. In the spring of 2016, a thirty-something blond American boarded her American Airlines flight in Philadelphia, bound for Syracuse. She quickly became suspicious of the nicely dressed man of similar age seated beside her. With dark curly hair and olive complexion, he did not seem friendly enough to her, giving only brief replies to her curious questions. Instead, he appeared overly focused on what he was writing on a pad in some language other than English. She suspected it might be Arabic. She shared her concern by note with a flight attendant, and the plane wound up delayed for two hours as first she deplaned and then he was taken off and questioned. He turned out to be Guido Menzio, a tenured Ivy League professor at the University of Pennsylvania. Rather than of Arab heritage, he was Italian by origin. Rather than scribbling in Arabic, he had been writing a differential equation. Perhaps not surprisingly in an era of relative American educational decline, the indecipherable language was mathematics.[64]

Failing to comprehend other peoples and places was not a new problem. One American wrote home about arriving in Paris in the 1920s: "It was a bit terrifying at first, plunking down in a strange city, with strange money to handle, and a strange language in my ears. God is it foreign. I had no idea Europe could be so European." The historian Brooke Blower quotes a writer for an American magazine in 1926 capturing the broader phenomenon: "Real life, we seem to think, goes on in the United States; the rest of the world is a funny show."[65] After World War II, Americans in their new affluence and power emerged as the quintessential international tourists, often insensitive to local customs, particularly in a country such as France, where they dressed less formally and spoke more loudly than the French. When Dwight Eisenhower in 1956 launched the People-to-People Foundation to encourage exchanges between Americans and citizens of other countries, the writer William Faulkner joked that if the president really wanted to win the Cold War, he should suspend all passports for a year.[66] A few years later, *U.S. Lady* magazine reminded the wives of U.S. military personnel living overseas: "When you're in a foreign country—you're the foreigner."[67]

In the twenty-first century, Americans continued to vary widely in their curiosity about the rest of the world, but their average knowledge in this regard remained limited. Where things actually *were* remained mysterious to most. A 2006 survey showed that nearly half of college-age Americans could not find the Indian subcontinent on a map of Asia, and three-quarters could not locate Israel—the most important U.S. ally in the region—on a map of the Middle East. How the United States was engaging with the outside world was similarly murky. To pollsters asking in 2010 what percentage of the U.S. federal budget went to foreign aid, the mean reply was 27 percent, while the mean preferred percentage was 13 percent. The actual figure was less than 1 percent.[68] Some observers took comfort in dark humor about such widespread ignorance of the world beyond U.S.

borders. The comedian Seth Meyers used Russia's aggression toward its western neighbor in 2014: "Despite the fact that the Ukraine has been all over the news for the past few weeks, a survey found that 64 percent of U.S. students still couldn't find Ukraine on a map. Said Vladimir Putin, 'Soon nobody will.'"[69]

Part of the difficulty for Americans in understanding non-Americans was linguistic. A large majority could communicate only with those foreigners who spoke English. In 2002, less than half of American high-schoolers were studying another language, as were only 8 percent of American college students. As a result, just one-quarter of Americans could converse in a second tongue, and more than half of those did so in Spanish, reflecting in part the recent immigrant background of many residents. By contrast, 54 percent of Europeans could hold a conversation in a second language.[70] Most educated Europeans spoke at least a modicum of English. The writer Cullen Murphy noted that in the ancient Roman Empire educated people spoke at least two languages, as did ambitious immigrants: "Americans have their priorities backward. They worry needlessly about the second part: whether the immigrants will ever learn English. They should be worrying about the first part: whether the elites will ever speak anything else."[71]

For all of Americans' provincialism and sometimes reactionary national politics, the United States in the early twenty-first century continued to grow more diverse and more familiar with cultures and peoples who had previously seemed quite strange. Americans still did not use the metric system like the rest of the world, and they still tended to prefer football to the far more widely watched soccer. But popular culture became more globalized all the time in the internet era. Just as American jeans and sneakers and American hip-hop music circulated out across U.S. borders, Italian design and South Korean K-Pop songs and styles flowed in. Just as McDonald's and other American fast-food restaurants took hold around the globe, once-exotic foods such as sushi and fish sauce became staples in the United States. Half of the fresh fruit and a third of the fresh vegetables that Americans consumed came from abroad. For younger Americans in particular, the foreign was not so foreign. The television critic Jeff Yang pointed in 2015 to "a deluge of new shows that push the definition of American further. . . . Today's millennial viewers are fascinated by difference, not repelled by it." The backward-looking orientation of Trump voters expressed a reaction, at least in part, to the clear trend of younger Americans—the nation's future—toward accepting and even embracing new forms of diversity.[72]

The Lure of American Individualism

The influence of the United States in the world defied precise measurement. With the largest economy and most powerful military for the last seventy-five years, the nation clearly carried global weight. But its recent military ventures had not gone well, leading to open-ended conflicts in unstable Afghanistan and Iraq. Its economic might was increasingly challenged by a rising China abroad and by growing indebtedness, inequality, and insecurity at home. American political significance was undercut by the decline of liberal democracy and the sharp uptick in authoritarian rule in important states such as Turkey, Russia, and China as well as in Poland and Hungary, with similar inclinations visible across Europe and in the United States.

If the democratic moment ushered in by the extraordinary events of 1989 through 1991 had not turned out to be exactly "the end of history," nothing since had replaced the dominant models of self-governance, individual rights, and market-driven consumer capitalism. The fall of the Soviet Union and the liberation of Eastern Europe marked the demise of socialist economics, while the dismantling of apartheid and the liberation of southern Africa brought an end to a half-millennium of official racism and colonialism. Where Communist Party rule survived, such as in China and Vietnam, it did so by managing a shift to private property and market mechanisms—that is, precisely by no longer actually being communist. Marx, Mao, and Ho would have rolled over in their graves. Racism survived in less formal ways, reemerging in the blood-and-soil nationalisms visible in the United States and Europe by 2016, but they were still primarily minority movements. The backward-facing aspirations of Islamist radicals continued to roil majority-Muslim lands, but they offered no globally attractive model to contest the predominance of free-market capitalism, which critics often called neoliberalism. The model nation for this kind of political economy and its highly individualistic and inclusive culture remained the United States.[73]

Throughout their history, Americans had expected to be that model nation, that city upon a hill. Near his death, Thomas Jefferson wrote of the establishment of the United States: "May it be to the world, what I believe it will be, (to some parts sooner, to others later, but finally to all,) the signal of arousing men to burst the chains under which monkish ignorance and superstition had persuaded them to bind themselves, and to assume the blessings and security of self-government." Jefferson believed that "all eyes are opened, or opening, to the rights of man." Individual human rights indeed became a watchword in international politics precisely in the era of U.S. dominance, from the 1940s onward and particularly in the 1970s, not coincidentally when the rights-abusing USSR tipped into decline. Jefferson considered that peoples everywhere would come to see "the palpable truth, that the mass of mankind has not been born with saddles on their backs, nor a favored few booted and spurred, ready to ride them legitimately, by the grace of God."[74]

Such a perspective was still, well, revolutionary at the time of the American and French revolutions in the late eighteenth century. More common was the view embodied in Jefferson's own enslavement of people of African heritage, which cut like a buzz saw against his inspirational, egalitarian pronouncements. Human societies all the way back to the beginning of recorded history had been built on an assumed inequality of persons. The ancient Greeks and Romans certainly saw nothing resembling an even playing field, but rather a natural hierarchy or social pyramid. Against this assumption, Paul of Tarsus, the great Christian evangelist, posited instead the revolutionary idea of the moral equality of all human beings. "There is neither Jew nor Greek," he wrote in his letter to the Galatians: "there is neither slave nor free, there is no male or female, for you are all one in Christ Jesus." On this foundation of Christian theology developed later, through the Protestant Reformation and the Enlightenment, the modern conception of equal rights for all individuals—even if recognized in the breach as often as in practice—and a greater sense of justice and human agency. The United States, as a society born out of Enlightenment Europe and Protestant England, with the latter's concern for private property and personal liberty, leaned to individualism from its origins.[75]

In the late twentieth century, the traditional American emphasis on individual rights and opportunities grew yet more powerful. The do-your-own-thing style of the 1960s counterculture merged with the small-government emphasis of the rising conservative movement to promote a new kind of commonsense libertarianism in the American mainstream, spanning from gun ownership to gay marriage to corporate deregulation. The resulting culture of hyperindividualism was the opposite of conservative. It did not try to maintain traditional social practices and relationships. Rather, it promised people freedom from precisely such constraints. The

United States had long been one of the world's most mobile societies in terms of people moving away from their families of origin and across county and state lines in pursuit of economic opportunities. With its emphasis on entrepreneurship and profit making, American culture valued novelty, change, risk taking, and individual achievement. It aimed to give people what they wanted and to make money doing so. Markets seemed the surest path to providing human happiness.[76]

Perhaps more than other societies encountering foreignness, the United States operated, once again, like an amoeba. Confronted with new ideas and new peoples, American culture proved persistently adept at bumping up against and then incorporating and absorbing these, whether internal dissenters or external newcomers. Immigrants founded a dramatically disproportionate number of the nation's largest companies, while once countercultural phenomena such as rock 'n' roll music, marijuana, and gay weddings gradually morphed into sprawling, legitimate businesses. The very diversity that troubled some voters in 2016 represented a nearly infinite number of entrepreneurial opportunities. Since the 1960s increasingly skeptical of their political system, contemporary Americans experienced their connections to one another primarily as fellow consumers rather than fellow citizens. American-style freedom might have once focused more on the political realm of voting and self-government. Now it meant primarily being able to buy what one wanted. By the 2010s, in the online shopping culture of Amazon, it required just the click of a mouse.[77]

Americans assumed that other peoples also wanted to benefit from the efficiencies and conveniences as well as styles of consumer capitalist culture that the United States had developed more fully than anywhere else. American assembly lines and innovations had long been admired around the world. In a debate among Soviet officials in 1928 about how fast they should expect to be able to build a vast new steel plant in the city of Magnitogorsk, one participant had argued for a six-year timeframe rather than a shorter one: "Even if we were Americans, we could not build the factory in four years." As the British writer Francis Spufford imagined Soviet leader Nikita Khrushchev thinking in 1959, Americans "had a kind of genius for lining up the fruitfulness of mass production with people's desires." The New York Times columnist Nick Kristof recalled financing a visit to the USSR, when he was a student in the early 1980s, by smuggling in some blue jeans and Walkmans and selling them on the black market. By the early twenty-first century, with the Iron Curtain long gone, Apple, Walmart, and Amazon rapidly expanded sales around the world, evidence of the appeal of providing people with products they believed would improve their lives.[78]

Nothing revealed the absorptive character of American society more than the ongoing incorporation of newcomers. One-quarter of the U.S. population in 2015—nearly 80 million people—consisted of immigrants and their children. This included, of course, First Lady Melania Trump and her son Barron, as well as the president. Regardless of xenophobic sentiments among some members of President Trump's own party, a comprehensive study of assimilation by the National Academies of Sciences, Engineering, and Medicine found that contemporary immigrants and their offspring were learning English at least as rapidly as earlier generations of newcomers had. In comparison with native-born Americans, immigrants also turned out to rate more highly, on average, in terms of individual and community well-being. They had longer life expectancies and fewer chronic health conditions. Immigrant divorce rates and out-of-wedlock birth rates were much lower. Neighborhoods with high concentrations of immigrants had significantly lower rates of crime and violence than comparable nonimmigrant neighborhoods. Foreign-born men in their twenties and thirties were incarcerated at one-fourth the rate of their native-born age peers. Immigrants had a measurably positive influence on American society.[79]

Unfortunately, the same could not be said about the impact on foreigners of living in the United States. Over time they became a lot less foreign, doing well on average in employment, education, and cultural acclimatization, and most of them benefited from greater personal liberty than they had enjoyed in their lands of origins. But the newcomers also became a lot more American in other, less helpful ways. Their health outcomes declined on average, as they took up American lifestyles and diets, which had led the United States to the highest rates of obesity in the world (the satirical *Onion* described Americans as now eating "one continuous meal," known no longer as lunch or dinner but simply as "Meal"). Immigrants' rates of divorce and bearing children outside of marriage, which correlated with higher poverty rates, converged over time with those of other Americans. Their associations with crime, violence, and incarceration became more typical of all U.S. residents. For better and worse, American society continued to pull in newcomers by the tens of millions and make them fully American.[80]

In this regard the United States seemed unusual. Plenty of other nations welcomed immigrants and refugees, some, like Canada, making them an even larger fraction of their society. But no country close to the United States in size, power, and influence operated as the United States did. One close observer of this phenomenon was Zainab Ahmad, a native Long Islander, a Cornell alumnus, a child of immigrant Pakistani parents, and assistant U.S. attorney for the Eastern District of New York, who specialized in counterterrorism and had extensive experience interviewing apprehended al-Qaeda operatives. "Immigrant communities in Europe," Ahmad observed, "are much more ghettoized, much less warmly accepted." By contrast, "America is the most successful country in the world at integrating immigrants, and that helps keep us safe." Like Canada but in contrast to Western European nations, the United States granted unqualified birthright citizenship, and religion, particularly Islam, remained a much less significant barrier to integration and source of conflict.[81]

The contrasting experiences of Muslim immigrants in France and the United States struck Walied Shater, a Secret Service agent and Muslim American, when he accompanied President George W. Bush on a visit to Paris in 2004. Shater was responsible for arranging hotel rooms, cell phones, translators, and transportation for "a small army" of fellow Secret Service agents as the presidential advance team. Twenty cars and twenty French drivers, all dressed in suits, lined up outside the five-star hotel each day. And each day French police stopped and questioned only one driver, a clean-shaven French-born citizen of Moroccan heritage named Ahmad, calling Shater to the front desk to verify Ahmad's credentials. One day Shater drove around the city with Ahmad and was surprised to see him stopped for identification checks three times by police at roundabouts and traffic lights. To Shater's questions, he replied simply, "You cannot change French society." Ahmad referred to the French as "them" rather than "us," while Shater, by contrast, used "we" to speak of his U.S. countrymen. "America is different," Ahmad said.[82]

A comparison with the nation's strongest economic competitor was similarly revealing. "It started as a thought experiment: I wondered what it would take for me, the son of Chinese immigrants, to become a citizen of China," wrote Eric Liu, a former White House aide. The nearest Chinese consulate proved no help, nor did other research efforts. In pursuing this idea, Liu came to realize that the Beijing government simply did not expect such requests and had no interest in accommodating them. "Try as I might, I just can't become Chinese," he concluded. Liu pointed out that regardless of the size of China's economy, "the U.S. retains a deep, enduring competitive advantage: America makes Chinese Americans. China doesn't make American Chinese." China lagged far behind the United States in the twenty-first-century strength of "embracing diversity and making something great from many multicultural parts." Lee Kuan Yew, the founding prime minister of Singapore, was another descendant of Chinese émigrés who observed the same dynamic. Lee noted that while China could draw on a talent pool of its own 1.3 billion people, the United States could tap the world's seven billion people, recombining them in a more diverse and thus more creative culture than could ethnic Han nationalism.[83]

The Yale University historian Valerie Hansen titled her survey of Chinese history before 1600 *The Open Empire*. The same title would fit well for U.S. history since that time. Like premodern China, the modern United States grew in reach and significance in large part through a marked openness to outside cultural and economic influences. One indicator was the nation's emergence by the mid-twentieth century as the top recipient of internationally adopted children. Between 1971 and 2001, U.S. citizens adopted some 265,000 youngsters from other countries, the majority from Asia. Iftekhar Aslam, a twenty-three-year old U.S. citizen originally from Pakistan, reflected a similar experience when interviewed in 2012 in a Manhattan hospital. His wife had just given birth to their first child, and he spoke of the kindness of a night nurse who had shown him how to open his chair into a bed so he could get some sleep: "They treated us like family." Aslam added that he had not minded sharing the room, divided by a curtain, with another pair of new parents, "Israel people." He added joyfully, "That's New York—it's freedom here!"[84]

Despite Americans' enduring concerns about the effect of outside influences on their society, the United States turned out to have an even more powerful effect on foreigners both at home and abroad. In its earliest days, leaders of the new North American republic feared the corrupting ways of powerful European societies. Europe seemed simultaneously an admirable landscape of high culture and a troubling terrain of cynical moral laxity. Thomas Jefferson warned that "no American should come to Europe under thirty years of age" because of its social and moral temptations. In the same spirit a century later, an American YMCA leader in 1918 warned a U.S.

official that "America has as much to fear from the French women of Paris" as from the German enemy.[85] As the twentieth century proceeded, however, such concerns paled in comparison to the allure of what the United States embodied and offered to others. The twin sirens of individual freedom and material acquisition gave the increasingly powerful United States a unique attractiveness in the eyes of many outsiders.

American films spread images and ideas of American culture around the world, dominating the silver screens on all continents and helping shape the visual imaginary of a global audience. The novelist Viet Thanh Nguyen, a recent Pulitzer Prize winner and immigrant from Vietnam, referred to "Hollywood's function as the launcher of the intercontinental ballistic missile of Americanization." Those ICBMs first fired off in the 1920s and have not stopped launching since. The mass-circulation British newspaper *Daily Express* observed in 1927 the transformation of British filmgoers into people who "talk America, think America, and dream America. . . . We have several million people . . . who, to all intent and purpose are temporary American citizens." A similar story unfolded with American popular music, from jazz to rock and roll to hip-hop, carried worldwide by radio from the 1920s onward, and with American television shows and later predominantly English-language websites and postings on the internet. Communist governments from the Soviet Union to Cuba had long banned rock and roll as a degrading, antisocialist art form that carried the seeds of capitalist individualism. But the decline of communism opened the floodgates to the Rolling Stones and others performing from Moscow to Havana. Globalization did not mean simply Americanization, but American voices and styles were the most prominent in the emerging global popular culture of the twenty-first century.[86]

"In America," the Indian British writer Aatish Taseer notes, "one rarely hears about what the transmission of global culture—which is in fact American culture—feels like on the receiving end." Rather than a neutral process, he argues, "this transmission creates a profound disturbance. It reconfigures a society—its mores, its values, its relationships." Taseer underlines "the trauma an old society undergoes as it tries to absorb the appeal of a foreign culture, while at the same time trying to remain true to itself and its genius." He was referring to this "profound disturbance" in India, but it was felt similarly across the world. Even in the powerful People's Republic of China, with its vigorous censorship and anxiety about outside influences, the journalist Chris Buckley observed that American movies, television, music, and technology "are widely and avidly consumed." In 2010 China's authoritarian leader Xi Jinping, managing a complicated relationship with the United States, sent his only daughter out of the country for college—to Harvard. The days were long gone when Mao Zedong and other communist leaders had little connection to American life and when only defeated anticommunists were closely associated with the United States, such as Madame Chiang Kai-shek, the Wellesley College graduate and English-speaking Christian.[87]

In the early twenty-first century, perhaps no feature of contemporary American life was more readily visible than the sheer size of its individual citizens. They were, as a cohort, exceptionally overweight, like their president after 2016. They also seemed to be successfully exporting a diet that contributed to that tendency toward obesity. A recent study of 190 nations revealed that while vegetables, fruits, and other healthy eating options might have been more widely available around the globe than ever before, "the world is mostly hungry for junk food." Mass-produced snack foods, rich in fat, carbohydrates, and salt, remained an industry created and dominated by U.S. corporations. Americans recognized their typically large size as part of their identity: a recent study found that Americans identified overweight Asian Americans as significantly more "American"—and thus less likely to be undocumented immigrants—than Asian Americans of normal weight. Asian Americans could pass the eye test for familiarity rather than foreignness by taking on mainstream American behaviors, however deleterious to their health. Ultimately it seemed not that Americans were being corrupted by morally suspect outsiders but that immigrants and foreigners were being corrupted by the subversive indulgences of American life.[88]

They were also being undercut by American informality. Fast food and other forms of rapid dining spread abroad after their emergence in the 1950s, displacing traditional meals taken in family settings. Meanwhile, sneakers and jeans swept across much of the world, to the dismay of sartorial traditionalists in other countries. And in the contemporary United States, the use of first names abounded, to the surprise of many newcomers. This marker of informality was common even with people one had never met before and with much older people, as was the typical presumption of a nickname—addressing a sixty-something "Thomas Smith" checking into a hotel, for example, as neither "Mr. Smith" nor "Thomas" but simply "Tom." Javad Zarif moved to the United States from Iran at age seventeen to attend boarding school and wound up staying for the next twenty years. When Zarif later became Iran's foreign minister, he negotiated closely with U.S. Secretary of State John Kerry in 2014 on a pathbreaking nuclear arms development agreement. They called each other John and Javad. "That's one of the first things you Americans do," Zarif told a reporter. "Had I not been in the U.S. for such a long time, I would have been astonished for the Secretary of State of the adversary to start calling me by my first name." Even in an era of rising economic inequality, the United States retained its strong socially egalitarian sensibility.[89]

Every society balances the interests of its individual members with the needs of the broader community. The manner of that balancing helps define a culture. No perfect recipe mixes just the right degree of personal liberty with social cohesion, though chauvinists in every land assume theirs is the best blend. Arranging cultures along an axis from more communal to more libertarian yields a range stretching from a society such as Japan, histori-cally devoted to the collective good, to a culture like that of the United States, rooted in a near-obsession with individual autonomy reflected in the Bill of Rights. Those first ten amendments to the Constitution high-lighted a determination to preserve citizens' liberty from governmental encroachment. Americans, of course, denied such liberties to enslaved and indigenous peoples early on and limit them for others—the incarcerated, those with felony records, the mentally ill, immigrants without legal status—still today. In comparison to other nations, however, the United States stood out for its emphasis on citizens' rights rather than responsi-bilities, for the individual rather than the collective.

To modern Americans, such an approach seems like common sense. Polls had measured declining American faith since the 1960s in all kinds of insti-tutions and authorities, most notably government, along with a diminish-ing sense of community connection. Even more than in earlier generations, Americans felt that they were on their own. Compared to residents of other countries, Americans revealed to pollsters a significantly stronger commit-ment to individual rights and a greater optimism about their ability to control events and determine their own future. They also acknowledged more feelings of loneliness than in previous generations. Thomas Jefferson's

"Empire for Liberty" and Harry Truman's "Defending the Free World" had evolved after the 1970s into a culture of declining restraint on individual choice and behavior. From the launching of a new magazine, *Self*, in the 1970s to the ubiquitous taking of photo "selfies" in the 2010s, American society encouraged individual self-absorption to the point, for some, of narcissistic preoccupation.[90]

The contrast to more communal, traditional cultures could be stark and apparent in language alone. Americans might use first-person pronouns more than any other people. This is a nation of "I," "me," and "mine." Native American cultures, by contrast, tended to emphasize relationships and social connections. "In the ethos of Mohawk culture, as in its language, 'I' cannot stand on its own," the writer Judith Thurman explains. "The first-person singular is always part of a relationship. So you don't say, 'I am sick.' 'The sickness,' in Mohawk, 'has come to me.'" Half a world away, traditional Vietnamese thought in similar ways. "Traditional Vietnamese law rested not upon the notion of individual rights, but the notion of duties," Frances FitzGerald writes in her Pulitzer Prize–winning history *Fire in the Lake*. "In the Vietnamese language there is no word that exactly corresponds to the Western personal pronoun I, je, ich." People spoke of themselves in terms of "a system or relationships" with those around them rather than as fully autonomous individuals as Americans might.[91]

American-style individualism appealed to people seeking greater personal freedoms and economic opportunities. Whether coming to the United States or living elsewhere, non–Americans felt the gravitational force of American culture in the decades following World War II. Critics both at home and abroad might see it as a corrupting influence, cutting against ties of social solidarity and responsibility. Those of a critical Christian perspective might view American individualism as catering to humans' basest instincts of materialistic greed and self-centeredness—"sin," some might say. Indeed, resistance to the influence of mainstream American cultural values formed an important theme of modern international history. However, others, both within and beyond the United States, saw not a corrupting culture but a path to greater liberty and opportunity. They found a culture of robust diversity and creativity, a place that seemed different and perhaps more welcoming. They were drawn either to the United States or to aspects of its society that could be absorbed or replicated elsewhere. Americanness, in all its individualistic, materialist, egalitarian energy, turned out to be an engine of subversion, the cutting edge of globalization that alienated conservatives everywhere, from Islamists to aristocrats, while intriguing and delighting more liberal cosmopolitan people, particularly the young. American values of greater inclusiveness, individual expressiveness, and competitive ambitiousness undercut older communal, collective, and spiritual traditions and behaviors.[92]

Conclusion

Not So Foreign After All

I never thought my country would be the one people had to run from."
Mariah Walker was a staff member at Vive, a refugee shelter in Buf-
falo, New York, for people seeking to get across the Niagara River to
asylum in Canada. She was explaining the disorientation she felt in the early
months of 2017, after U.S. voters elected Donald Trump as president and
his administration ratcheted up the deportation of migrants and refugees
who lacked documentation. Hundreds or even thousands of desperate people moved north to the border, where they slipped across into Canada, the
country they now saw as the greater place of freedom.[1]

How low the mighty seemed to have fallen. From 1776 to the Statue of
Liberty to World War II and the Cold War, Americans had long understood themselves as the freest people on the earth. The United States was
supposed to be the land people tried to get *into*, not out of. Of course, the
vigorous assertion of American liberty had long been contradicted, in part,
by the sustained rejection of full freedom for people of color, from Indian
land dispossession and African slavery to contemporary racialized economic
inequality. The same was true with gender and sex and the limits on women
and gay and trans people over time. At times there seemed almost a direct
correlation between the volume of proclamations of liberty and the fierce-
ness of suppression of certain groups, an example of what psychologists call
denial; few people like to be reminded of their hypocrisies. As any student
of American slavery and the Underground Railroad knows, the year 2017

was hardly the first time people had harbored in upstate New York on a flight north to Canadian freedom. Young men seeking to evade the military draft during the Vietnam War had traced a similar path.[2]

Race and ethnicity remained scalpel-sharp tools for some citizens to try to exclude others they viewed as foreign. The nine justices of the U.S. Supreme Court, with their lifetime tenure, might hold the most elite, respected position in the United States. While some of them discounted the enduring significance of race in American life, Justice Sonia Sotomayor understood the way evidence of non-European heritage continued to cast uncertainty on a person's status in the modern United States. She recalled, as a young woman of Puerto Rican descent born and raised in New York City, how, after telling a new acquaintance her hometown, "then is pressed, 'No, where are you really from?' regardless of how many generations her family has been in the country." Americans across the political spectrum continued to refer commonly to other residents, usually without ill intent, as "Asians" and "Mexicans," without any awareness of whether they were foreign nationals or immigrants—or just native-born U.S. citizens. Such emphasis on ethnoracial heritage as still the key marker of identity recalled, revealingly if unintentionally, the "once a Jap, always a Jap" logic of World War II–era incarceration camps.[3]

The enduring force of racial essentialism continued to shape the nation's southern border in startling fashion in 2019. While migration from Mexico had slowed dramatically over the previous decade, a growing number of refugees fleeing violence and poverty in Central America, most of them families, challenged U.S. border authorities. Inadequate border processing facilities were overwhelmed. Part of the Trump administration's response was to discourage refugees by separating children from their parents, sometimes for months and without clear plans for reuniting them. Reports of very young, unaccompanied children incarcerated in stark concrete cells without adequate care or supervision shocked Americans across the political spectrum. The president's hostility to Hispanic newcomers then found a horrifying echo in the slaughter of twenty-two people in a Walmart store in El Paso, Texas, by a young white gunman who had driven to that city to target Latinos—after posting an online screed about a "Hispanic invasion," using language very similar to Trump's. The massacre recalled recent mass shootings of Jews in a Pittsburgh synagogue in 2018 and of African Americans in a church in Charleston in 2015. Violence by some white men against people of color and ethnic minorities remained a grim American practice.[4]

Like the citizens of other nations, Americans were variously curious about, attracted to, and repelled by things and people that were new to them. The key word "alien" captured this ambiguity. As a noun, it could refer both to a foreigner who was not a naturalized citizen and to a hypothetical being from another planet or galaxy. In other words, an alien could be either quite familiar (an undocumented immigrant working in one's town or one's home) or radically bizarre (a Martian). Even the science-fiction kind of alien from another solar system—the most alien—could appear in American culture in both positive and negative lights. In popular American films, such creatures horrified audiences in *Alien* (1979), instructed them in *E.T.: The Extra-Terrestrial* (1982), and amused them in *Star Wars* (1977) and *Men in Black* (1997). Similar fascination with human outsiders could be seen in the popularity of migrant-themed movies from *West Side Story* (1961) and *The Godfather* (1972) to *My Big Fat Greek Wedding* (2002) and *Spanglish* (2004). Different cultures jostling together underpinned innumerable television shows and novels, both tragic and comic. That jostling fascinated viewers and readers, as it did artists and scholars.

Even the Republican Party remained ambivalent about outsiders. At the height of the Syrian refugee crisis in 2015, Mike Huckabee, the former Arkansas governor and an ordained Baptist minister, denounced the idea that "we could be inviting some of the most violent and vicious people on Earth to come right in here and live among our families." By contrast, Senator Lindsey Graham of South Carolina and former Florida governor Jeb Bush advocated following Pope Francis's admonition to accept "the stranger in our midst" and be "not fearful of foreigners." Grounded in their own history of persecution for unorthodox religious beliefs, Mormon Republicans in deep-red Utah resisted condemnation of contemporary Muslims as outsiders. The 2016 election revealed the party's nurturance of anti-immigrant sentiments but also some underlying attachment to newcomers. Donald Trump may have railed against Muslims and Mexicans, but he was the son of a Scottish immigrant and two of his three marriages had been to immigrants, giving the nation the first foreign-born First Lady with no previous American ties.[5]

The previous Republican president, George W. Bush, had a Mexican sister-in-law, spoke some Spanish, and pursued close ties with Mexico. A week after the September 11 attacks, Bush had told the nation and the world that Islam "is practiced freely by many millions of Americans and by millions more in countries that America counts as friends. Its teachings are good and peaceful, and those who commit evil in the name of Allah blaspheme the name of Allah." In the months leading up to the 2016 election, reporters found conservative Republican voters in Iowa uncertain about newcomers. "I'm as prejudiced as the day is long. It's a bad thing that all these illegal Mexicans are here," one small-business owner said. He paused and added: "But they're hard workers. They're doing jobs that lazy Americans won't do." Here was the rub: undocumented immigrants might prove more admirable than native-born citizens. The prominent Republican former secretary of state, General Colin Powell, whose parents had come from Jamaica, reminded Americans in 2016 of the importance of one-quarter of Americans being either immigrants or the children of immigrants.[6]

In a fashion parallel to how they thought about immigrants coming to the United States, Americans in the early twenty-first century felt ambivalent about how their nation should engage other peoples abroad. Even if other peoples turned out to be similar to Americans, at least on the inside, and even if they desired to live more like Americans, as Americans tended to believe, it was not clear how best to encourage that process. In the imperial age that came to an end after World War II but that had shaped most of U.S. history along the way, the United States had expanded its geographical territory, trade relations, and cultural influence by any means necessary. The historian Tyler Dennett observed in 1922, for example, that "Christianity was, in a measure, like opium, being imposed upon China without the consent of the people," primarily at the hands of Americans and British. Similar kinds of U.S. impositions altered governments from Iran to Guatemala during the Cold War. An updated, more multicultural kind of imposition reshaped the modern Middle East with the U.S. invasion of Iraq in 2003, when the Bush administration declared that "America's experience as a great multi-ethnic democracy affirms our conviction that people of many heritages and faiths can live and prosper in peace."[7]

This tendency to see its own past as inclusive and successful and to assume that other nations should follow its lead left the United States exposed when its actions abroad did not work out as expected. In the greater Middle East, the Bush administration's wars in Iraq and Afghanistan failed to stabilize the region or remake it in America's image. Imposing on others did not seem a successful strategy. At home the unfulfilled hope of these military ventures disillusioned the American public and subsequent administrations. Traditional aspirations to win over the loyalties—the hearts and minds—of other peoples declined. As one marine tells a reporter immediately after a surprise firefight with Afghan Taliban forces in the film *Whiskey Tango Foxtrot* (2016), "It's all about hearts and minds—the two best places to shoot people." After taking office in 2009, Barack Obama temporarily boosted the number of U.S. troops in Afghanistan, oversaw the pursuit and killing of Osama bin Laden, and increased the use of drone strikes, but reduced the overall scope of U.S. military operations. Then the Trump administration's official National Security Strategy in 2017 declared it was "confident of the positive example the United States offers to the world. We are also realistic and understand that the American way of life cannot be imposed upon others, nor is it the inevitable culmination of progress." "America First" was in. At least formally, imposing American ways upon others was out.[8]

At the same time, the American model was under pressure. While U.S. leaders in the early twenty-first century wrestled with the challenge of continued resistance abroad to their influence, accumulating evidence of changes in Earth's climate simultaneously raised questions about the long-term viability of the American way of life. The United States in the twentieth century had pioneered mass consumption in a large, fossil fuel–powered, industrial society. It created the world's largest middle class by the 1950s, an unprecedented achievement of widespread economic opportunity, security, and good health. The costs of the project, however, accumulated over time. Observers decried the widespread pollution of the nation's waters, land, and air. Environmental damage did not respect national boundaries, and the United States, in its sheer size and density of economic development, became the world's largest producer of greenhouse gases and by far its largest per capita contributor to global warming. With the "frenzy of getting and spending that started in the United States, spread to a recovered Europe, and has since caught on in China and India," the writer Rebecca Solnit noted, Earth's climate was spiraling into an unpredictable and perilous future. Solnit wondered if "future generations will curse this turning point in our history and look back on the world as it was in 1980 or 1940 or 1750 as an almost unimaginable paradise of stability and abundance."[9]

Even by economic measurements, the story Americans had long told themselves and the world about the success of their distinctive society no longer seemed quite so persuasive. A sense of this decline explained part of the appeal of Donald Trump's 2016 election slogan, "Make America Great Again," however misleading it may have been in other ways. By 2014, middle-class incomes in Canada for the first time surpassed those in the United States. Metrics of overall social well-being revealed the United States lagging well behind other Western nations in the prevention of child poverty and in female life expectancy. Compared to its peers, the United States emphasized individual freedom from constraint more than social stability and support. As economic inequality increased after the 1970s, the United States remained an alluring place to be rich: a society where wealth was widely admired and the tax burden on the top tier was low, at least in comparison to other affluent nations. Did this make Americans satisfied? Perhaps. But the 2018 update of the annual World Happiness Report, produced by three leading economists using Gallup Poll data, ranked the United States eighteenth among all nations in average citizen satisfaction and well-being, well behind the leading northern European countries with their more robust sense of social solidarity.[10]

How Americans would think about themselves and about foreigners in the future remained unclear at the opening of the third decade of the new millennium. Successful leadership of a supposed free world during the Cold War decades from the 1940s to the 1990s required the United States to embrace formally its own diversity and global diversity, despite lingering resistance. The nation was now inclusive and egalitarian in ways that had been almost unimaginable two generations earlier, in terms of race, ethnicity, religion, gender, and sexual orientation, even as persistent racism and xenophobia helped put a person into the presidency who would also have been difficult to imagine fifty years before. California in the past had often proved a harbinger of where the nation was headed, and it might again in its demographic arc. The sharply increasing diversity there in the late twentieth century stimulated a period of anti-immigrant backlash in the 1990s, before the Golden State adjusted to its majority-minority present and future and emerged as the country's stoutest bulwark of political and cultural support for diversity as well as its most robust economy. Something similar might unfold elsewhere over time.[11]

I grew up in North Carolina in the 1960s, where political leaders scored a lot of points by stoking fear among voters. They warned frequently of the supposed threats of subversion that came from communists, as well as from racial integrationists, from gays and lesbians, from countercultural hippies, from insubordinate women, and the like. I spent much of my youth trying to grasp the full range of the ignorance and ill will of powerful people such as Jesse Helms, who represented the state for thirty years in the U.S. Senate. They were wrong about a lot of things. They were certainly wrong about subversion.[12]

If there was, in fact, a subversive force loose in the world of the late twentieth and early twenty-first centuries, it might best be seen as coming not from the usual outsider suspects but from America's own democratic ideals, combined with America's own absorptive popular culture and seemingly infinite consumer pleasures. That culture and its products encouraged the spread of the viruses of individualism, of headlong material consumption, of perpetual innovation, and of the relentless quest for wealth, which tended to disrupt other more traditional cultures. "What is the process of civilizing," the prominent U.S. clergyman Josiah Strong had asked in 1885, "but the creating of more and higher wants?" Americans have been at the front edge of that "process of civilizing" ever since.[13]

The pursuit of profits and opportunities overturned the old and brought in the new. This "process of Creative Destruction," the free-market economist Joseph Schumpeter observed, was "the essential fact about capitalism."[14] With the United States and its freewheeling culture at the forefront, capitalism proved the greatest force for change over the last half-millennium. A wide swath of Americans might have imagined themselves to be what they called "conservatives," but their way of life brought persistent pressure for reordering everywhere it flowed.[15] There was nothing conservative about it. Americans, instead, turned out to be the real subversives of the modern world, confident and determined, at home and abroad, that other peoples would, if given the chance, choose to live just like them.

Notes

Preface

1. Important recent work in this field includes Thomas Bender, *A Nation Among Nations: America's Place in World History* (New York: Hill and Wang, 2006); Matthew Frye Jacobson, *Barbarian Virtues: The United States Encounters Foreign Peoples at Home and Abroad, 1876–1917* (New York: Hill and Wang, 2000); Jefferson Cowie, *The Great Exception: The New Deal and the Limits of American Politics* (Princeton, NJ: Princeton University Press, 2016); Paul A. Kramer, "The Geopolitics of Mobility: Immigration Policy and American Global Power in the Long Twentieth Century," *American Historical Review* 123, no. 2 (April 2018): 393–438; Donna R. Gabaccia, *Foreign Relations: American Immigration in Global Perspective* (Princeton, NJ: Princeton University Press, 2012); Gary Gerstle, *American Crucible: Race and Nation in the Twentieth Century* (Princeton, NJ: Princeton University Press, 2001); Madeline Y. Hsu, *The Good Immigrants: How the Yellow Peril Became the Model Minority* (Princeton, NJ: Princeton University Press, 2015); Daniel Immerwahr, *How to Hide An Empire: A History of the Greater United States* (New York: Farrar, Straus and Giroux, 2019).
2. George Saunders, "Trump Days," *New Yorker,* July 11 & 18, 2016, 61.
3. Thomas Borstelmann, *The 1970s: A New Global History from Civil Rights to Economic Inequality* (Princeton, NJ: Princeton University Press, 2012), 73–121; Mary L. Dudziak, *Cold War Civil Rights: Race and the Image of American Democracy* (Princeton, NJ: Princeton University Press, 2000); Thomas Borstelmann, *The*

Cold War and the Color Line: American Race Relations in the Global Arena (Cambridge, MA: Harvard University Press, 2001).

1. The Challenge of Contact with Foreigners

1. The colonel in the film uses an epithet for Asians, but he clearly means all foreigners. *Full Metal Jacket*, dir. Stanley Kubrick (Warner Brothers, 1987); George Packer, *The Assassins' Gate: America in Iraq* (New York: Farrar, Straus and Giroux, 2005), 331.

2. Cullen Murphy has made a similar point in *Are We Rome? The Fall of an Empire and the Fate of America* (Boston: Houghton Mifflin, 2007), 145–46. On American universalism, see Odd Arne Westad, *The Global Cold War: Third World Interventions and the Making of Our Times* (New York: Cambridge University Press, 2005), 1–38. For American exceptionalist thinking, see Godfrey Hodgson, *The Myth of American Exceptionalism* (New Haven, CT: Yale University Press, 2009).

3. Eliot A. Cohen, *Conquered Into Liberty: Two Centuries of Battles Along the Great Warpath That Made the American Way of War* (New York: Free Press, 2011), 134.

4. Matthew Frye Jacobson, *Barbarian Virtues: The United States Encounters Foreign Peoples at Home and Abroad, 1876–1917* (New York: Hill and Wang, 2000); Thomas Borstelmann, *The Cold War and the Color Line: American Race Relations in the Global Arena* (Cambridge, MA: Harvard University Press, 2001), 10–44; Harvey Levenstein, *Seductive Journey: American Tourists in France from Jefferson to the Jazz Age* (Chicago: University of Chicago Press, 1998); Paul Kennedy, *The Rise and Fall of the Great Powers: Economic Change and Military Conflict from 1500 to 2000* (New York: Random House, 1987), 275–332.

5. U.S. Department of State, *Our Foreign Policy*, Department of State Publication 3972, General Foreign Policy Series 26 (Washington, DC: U.S. Government Printing Office, 1950).

6. For a recent overview of changing conceptions of "race" in this era, see Michael Yudell, *Race Unmasked: Biology and Race in the Twentieth Century* (New York: Columbia University Press, 2014). Similar universalist assumptions underpinned much of modernization theory and U.S. policies for economic development in nonindustrialized nations. "Development," the leading historian Nick Cullather notes, asserted that "all nations followed a common historical path and that those in the lead had a moral duty to aid those who followed." Cullather, *The Hungry World: America's Cold War Battle Against Poverty in Asia* (Cambridge, MA: Harvard University Press, 2010), 75.

7. Alan Taylor, *Colonial America: A Very Short Introduction* (New York: Oxford University Press, 2013), 7.

8. Amy S. Greenberg, *Manifest Destiny and American Territorial Expansion* (Boston: Bedford/St. Martin's, 2012).

9. Kristin L. Hoganson, *American Empire at the Turn of the Twentieth Century* (Boston: Bedford/St. Martin's, 2016); Jacobson, *Barbarian Virtues*; George C. Herring, *From Colony to Superpower: U.S. Foreign Relations Since 1776*, 2nd ed. (New York: Oxford University Press, 2017).

10. Thomas Bender, *A Nation Among Nations: America's Place in World History* (New York: Hill and Wang, 2006), 192.

11. Michael F. Robinson, "Science and Exploration," in *Reinterpreting Exploration: The West in the World*, ed. Dane Kennedy (New York: Oxford University Press, 2014), 30.

12. Brooke L. Blower, *Becoming Americans in Paris: Transatlantic Politics and Culture Between the World Wars* (New York: Oxford University Press, 2011), 34 (quotation); Murphy, *Are We Rome?*, 31.

13. Thomas G. Andrews, *Coyote Valley: Deep History in the High Rockies* (Cambridge, MA: Harvard University Press, 2015), 5.

14. Jonathan Haidt and Lee Jussim, "Hard Truths About Race on Campus," *Wall Street Journal*, May 7–8, 2016; Joshua Greene, *Moral Tribes: Emotion, Reason, and the Gap Between Us and Them* (New York: Penguin, 2013).

15. Juliet B. Schor, *The Overworked American: The Unexpected Decline of Leisure* (New York: Basic Books, 1991).

16. Charles S. Maier, *Once Within Borders: Territories of Power, Wealth, and Belonging Since 1500* (Cambridge, MA: Harvard University Press, 2016).

17. Murphy, *Are We Rome?*, 16; Benedict Anderson, *Imagined Communities: Reflections on the Origin and Spread of Nationalism* (London: Verso, 1983).

18. Eliga Gould, *Among the Powers of the Earth: The American Revolution and the Making of a New World Empire* (Cambridge, MA: Harvard University Press, 2012), 1–2 (John Adams); Bender, *A Nation Among Nations*, 112 (John Quincy Adams). Canadians seemed to remain the least foreign of foreigners, as 76 percent of Americans in a 1942 poll considered their northern neighbors "as good as we are in all important respects"—higher than the second-place English at 72 percent or the third-place Dutch at 62 percent. Michaela Hönicke Moore, *Know Your Enemy: The American Debate on Nazism, 1933–1945* (New York: Cambridge University Press, 2010), 147.

19. Deborah Sontag, "Once a Pariah, Now a Judge," *New York Times*, August 30, 2015.

20. Toni Morrison, *Beloved: A Novel* (New York: Knopf, 1987).

21. Francis Fukuyama, *The End of History and the Last Man* (New York: Free Press, 1992); David Northup, "Globalization and the Great Convergence: Rethinking World History in the Long Term," *Journal of World History* 16, no. 3 (September 2005): 249–67; Taylor, *Colonial America*, 11.

22. Nicholas Wade, "When Britain Split from Europe, in a Big Way," *New York Times*, April 4, 2017.

23. Such admiration has not disappeared. American popular culture continues to pay close attention to the British royal family, in particular, recent younger female members from Princess Diana to the duchess of Cambridge, Kate Middleton, and the (American) duchess of Sussex, Meghan Markle.

24. Under other regimes of citizenship and descent, such as racial identity in the slavery-era United States or traditional Jewish religious law, the inheritance of one's mother's identity would have rendered Churchill an American.

25. Tara Zahra, *The Great Departure: Mass Migration from Eastern Europe and the Making of the Free World* (New York: Norton, 2016); Linda Colley, *Captives* (New York: Pantheon, 2002), 19 (Hamilton); Stephen Castles and Mark J. Miller, *The Age of Migration: International Population Movements in the Modern World*, 4th ed. (New York: Guilford, 2009); Dirk Hoerder, *Cultures in Contact: World Migrations in the Second Millennium* (Durham, NC: Duke University Press, 2002).

26. Rachel St. John, *Line in the Sand: A History of the Western U.S.-Mexico Border* (Princeton, NJ: Princeton University Press, 2011); Tony Rees, *Arc of the Medicine Line: Mapping the World's Longest Undefended Border Across the Western Plains* (Lincoln: University of Nebraska Press, 2008). For a penetrating exploration of geography and changing views of related cultural essences, see Martin W. Lewis and Kären E. Wigen, *The Myth of Continents: A Critique of Metageography* (Berkeley: University of California Press, 1997).

27. U.S. Department of State, Bureau of Consular Affairs, "Who We Are and What We Do: Consular Affairs by the Numbers," May 2014, http://travel.state .gov/content/dam/travel/CA%20Fact%20Sheet%202014.pdf.

28. Victoria Hattam, *In the Shadow of Race: Jews, Latinos, and Immigrant Politics in the United States* (Chicago: University of Chicago Press, 2007), 111–12; Kenneth Prewitt, *What Is Your Race? The Census and Our Flawed Efforts to Classify Americans* (Princeton, NJ: Princeton University Press, 2013).

29. Yudell, *Race Unmasked*; Allyson Hobbs, *A Chosen Exile: A History of Racial Passing in American Life* (Cambridge, MA: Harvard University Press, 2014).

30. Invisible evidence began to emerge more abundantly with the spread of individual genetic testing in the early twenty-first century. A number of surprised "white" people discovered that they had some percentage of African heritage rather than the 100 percent European descent that they had previously assumed. See, for example, "DNA Testing: A Clash of Science and Racial Identity," *Omaha World-Herald*, February 26, 2018.

31. Spencie Love, *One Blood: The Death and Resurrection of Charles R. Drew* (Chapel Hill: University of North Carolina Press, 1996); Thomas A. Guglielmo,

"Red Cross, Double Cross: Race and America's World War II–Era Blood Donor Service," *Journal of American History* 97, no. 1 (June 2010): 63–90.

32. Terry H. Anderson, *The Pursuit of Fairness: A History of Affirmative Action* (New York: Oxford University Press, 2004).

33. On the significance of colonization efforts for shaping racial inequality in the United States, see Nicholas Guyatt, *Bind Us Apart: How Enlightened Americans Invented Racial Segregation* (New York: Basic, 2016).

34. Cordelia Fine, *Testosterone Rex: Myths of Sex, Science, and Society* (New York: Norton, 2017).

35. William Faulkner, address to the Southern Historical Association, Memphis, November 10, 1955, in *Essays, Speeches, and Public Letters*, ed. James B. Meriwether (New York: Modern Library, 2004), 146; Mary L. Dudziak, "Desegregation as a Cold War Imperative," *Stanford Law Review* 41, no. 1 (November 1988): 61–120; Dudziak, *Cold War Civil Rights: Race and the Image of American Democracy* (Princeton, NJ: Princeton University Press, 2000); Borstelmann, *The Cold War and the Color Line*.

36. Peggy Pascoe, *What Comes Naturally: Miscegenation Law and the Making of Race in America* (New York: Oxford University Press, 2009), 296; Laura Meckler, "Interracial Marriages on the Rise in the U.S.," *Wall Street Journal*, May 19, 2017; Brooke Lea Foster, "For Interracial Couples, Growing Acceptance, with Some Exceptions," *New York Times*, November 26, 2016; Miriam Jordan, "Asians to Represent Largest Foreign-Born Group in U.S. by 2055," *Wall Street Journal*, September 28, 2015; Robert Kurzban et al., "Can Race Be Erased? Coalitional Computation and Social Categorization," *Proceedings of the National Academy of Sciences*, 98, no. 26 (December 2001): 15387–92.

37. Andrew Keh, "No Time but the Present for Heat and James," *New York Times*, May 25, 2014; Kelefa Sanneh, "Don't Be Like That," *New Yorker*, February 9, 2015, 68 (Patterson); Ta-Nehisi Coates, *Between the World and Me* (New York: Spiegel & Grau, 2015). On Trump's "white nationalist" support, see Daniel Geary, Camilla Schofield, and Jennifer Sutton, eds., *The Global History of White Nationalism: From Apartheid to Donald Trump* (Manchester: Manchester University Press, 2020).

38. Edmund S. Morgan, *American Slavery, American Freedom: The Ordeal of Colonial Virginia* (New York: Norton, 1975); Guyatt, *Bind Us Apart*, 201 (Johnson); Matthew Karp, *This Vast Southern Empire: Slaveholders at the Helm of American Foreign Policy* (Cambridge, MA: Harvard University Press, 2016).

39. Steven Hahn, *A Nation Under Our Feet: Black Political Struggles in the Rural South from Slavery to the Great Migration* (Cambridge, MA: Harvard University Press, 2003), 484 (Holland); Alan Taylor, *The Internal Enemy: Slavery and War in Virginia, 1772–1832* (New York: Norton, 2013); Manisha Sinha, *The*

Slave's Cause: A History of Abolition (New Haven, CT: Yale University Press, 2016).

40. See Morgan, *American Slavery, American Freedom* on this point.

41. Scott Weidensaul, *The First Frontier: The Forgotten History of Struggle, Savagery, and Endurance in Early America* (Boston: Houghton Mifflin Harcourt, 2012), 154–55; Richard White, *The Middle Ground: Indians, Empires, and Republics in the Great Lakes Region, 1650–1815* (New York: Cambridge University Press, 1991); Jill Lepore, *The Name of War: King Philip's War and the Origins of American Identity* (New York: Knopf, 1998); Fred Anderson, review of Ian K. Steele, *Setting All the Captives Free: Capture, Adjustment, and Recollection in Allegheny Country*, in *Journal of American History* 101, no. 3 (December 2014): 884–86.

42. Lawrence A. Peskin, *Captives and Countrymen: Barbary Slavery and the American Public, 1785–1816* (Baltimore, MD: Johns Hopkins University Press, 2009), 190 (quotations); Alan Taylor, *The Civil War of 1812: American Citizens, British Subjects, Irish Rebels, and Indian Allies* (New York: Knopf, 2010).

43. Robert Bothwell, *Your Country, My Country: A Unified History of the United States and Canada* (New York: Oxford University Press, 2015), 54–60.

44. Thomas Jefferson, *Notes on the State of Virginia*, query 8, "The Number of Its Inhabitants" (Paris, 1785), http://avalon.law.yale.edu/18th_century/jeffvir.asp.

45. Taylor, *Colonial America*, 55; John Demos, *The Unredeemed Captive: A Family Story from Early America* (New York: Knopf, 1994).

46. Peskin, *Captives and Countrymen*, 1–2.

47. Peskin, *Captives and Countrymen*, 164–65.

48. Paul Baepler, ed., *White Slaves, African Masters: An Anthology of American Barbary Captivity Narratives* (Chicago: University of Chicago Press, 1999), 1–6 (quotation at 1; emphasis in original); Mrs. Mary Rowlandson, *Narrative of the Captivity and Restoration of Mrs. Mary Rowlandson* (Cambridge, MA, 1682), http://www.gutenberg.org/files/851/851.txt.

49. Robert J. Allison, *The Crescent Obscured: The United States and the Muslim World. 1776–1815* (New York: Oxford University Press, 1995), 110; Peskin, *Captives and Countrymen*, 100–1, 110; Kathleen Duval, "When We Opened Our Doors," *Wall Street Journal*, February 18–19, 2017 (Virginian).

50. Baepler, ed., *White Slaves, African Masters*, 24; Peskin, *Captives and Countrymen*, 164–65; Edward E. Baptist, *The Half Has Never Been Told: Slavery and the Making of American Capitalism* (New York: Basic, 2014).

51. Allison, *The Crescent Obscured*, 107; Peskin, *Captives and Countrymen*, 24; Baepler, ed., *White Slaves, African Masters*, 6.

52. Allison, *The Crescent Obscured*, 45–46, 50–51, 61–62, 118.

53. Thomas Frank, *What's the Matter with Kansas? How Conservatives Won the Heart of America* (New York: Metropolitan, 2004); Larry M. Bartels, "What's the

Matter with *What's the Matter with Kansas?,*" *Quarterly Journal of Political Science* 1 (2006): 201–26.

2. Freedom: American Culture as Human Nature

1. Joan Givner, *Katherine Anne Porter: A Life,* rev. ed. (Athens: University of Georgia Press, 1991), 386.
2. Odd Arne Westad, *The Global Cold War: Third World Interventions and the Making of Our Times* (New York: Cambridge University Press, 2005), 9 (first Jefferson); Kariann Akemi Yokota, *Unbecoming British: How Revolutionary America Became a Postcolonial Nation* (New York: Oxford University Press, 2011), 63–65 (second Jefferson); Thomas Bender, *A Nation Among Nations: America's Place in World History* (New York: Hill and Wang, 2006), 205–6; Benjamin C. Waterhouse, *The Land of Enterprise: A Business History of the United States* (New York: Simon & Schuster, 2017).
3. Daniel T. Rodgers, *As a City on a Hill: The Story of America's Most Famous Lay Sermon* (Princeton, NJ: Princeton University Press, 2018), tracks the changing manner in which Americans have understood over time John Winthrop's originally obscure 1630 sermon.
4. Colin Woodward, *American Character: A History of the Epic Struggle Between Individual Liberty and the Common Good* (New York: Viking, 2016), 20–22.
5. Daniel Hannan, "Keep Free and Carry On," *Wall Street Journal,* November 6–17, 2013, C2 (Tocqueville); Malcolm Gaskill, *Between Two Worlds: How the English Became Americans* (New York: Basic Books, 2014); Yokota, *Unbecoming British,* 218–19.
6. Linda Colley, *Captives* (New York: Pantheon, 2002), 218.
7. Daniel Kilbride, *Being American in Europe, 1750–1860* (Baltimore, MD: Johns Hopkins University Press, 2013), 50; Yokota, *Unbecoming British,* 11–12.
8. Yokota, *Unbecoming British,* 231; Gordon H. Chang, *Fateful Ties: A History of America's Preoccupation with China* (Cambridge, MA: Harvard University Press, 2015), 23.
9. Eliga H. Gould, *Among the Powers of the Earth: The American Revolution and the Making of a New World Empire* (Cambridge, MA: Harvard University Press, 2012), 127.
10. Kilbride, *Becoming American in Europe,* 76, 101, 106–7, 114–15, 128.
11. Gould, *Among the Powers of the Earth,* 110; Max Paul Friedman, *Rethinking Anti-Americanism: The History of an Exceptional Concept in American Foreign Relations* (New York: Cambridge University Press, 2012), 26 (first Talleyrand), 28 (Ruskin), 37–38 (second Talleyrand, Kipling, Wilde).

12. Friedman, *Rethinking Anti-Americanism*, 34.

13. Friedman, *Rethinking Anti-Americanism*, 28–30.

14. Edward L. Ayers et al., eds., *All Over the Map: Rethinking American Regions* (Baltimore, MD: Johns Hopkins University Press, 1996); Colin Woodard, *American Nations: A History of the Eleven Rival Regional Cultures of North America* (New York: Viking, 2011); Joel Garreau, *The Nine Nations of North America* (Boston: Houghton Mifflin, 1981); Charles Postel, "Murder on the Brazos: The Religious Context of the Populist Revolt," *Journal of the Gilded Age and Progressive Era* 15, no. 2 (April 2016): 197–219; R. G. Ratcliffe, "Perry Says Texas Can Leave the Union If It Wants To," *Houston Chronicle*, April 15, 2009; Gail Collins, "My State's Prettier Than Yours," *New York Times*, May 14, 2014; Robert Wuthnow, *Rough Country: How Texas Became America's Most Powerful Bible-Belt State* (Princeton, NJ: Princeton University Press, 2014).

15. Barry Rubin and Judith Colp Rubin, *Hating America: A History* (New York: Oxford University Press, 2004), 27.

16. Edward McClelland, *How to Speak Midwestern* (Cleveland, OH: Belt, 2016); Jennifer Schuessler, "'How to Speak Midwestern': A Heartland Dialect Guide," *New York Times*, December 4, 2016; Emily Badger and Kevin Quealy, "Where Is America's Heartland? Pick Your Map," *New York Times*, January 3, 2017, https://www.nytimes.com/interactive/2017/01/03/upshot/where-is-americas-heartland-pick-your-map.html.

17. Bender, *A Nation Among Nations*, 153.

18. Jenifer Van Vleck, *Empire of the Air: Aviation and the American Ascendancy* (Cambridge, MA: Harvard University Press, 2013), 109.

19. James Truslow Adams, *The Epic of America* (New York: Blue Ribbon, 1931). For a different angle of analysis on the idea of the American dream, see Sarah Churchwell, *Behold, America: The Entangled History of "America First" and the "American Dream"* (New York: Basic Books, 2018).

20. Brooke L. Blower, *Becoming Americans in Paris: Transatlantic Politics and Culture Between the World Wars* (New York: Oxford University Press, 2011), 2–3.

21. David Reynolds, *Rich Relations: The American "Occupation" of Britain, 1942–1945* (New York: Random House, 1995); Studs Terkel, *"The Good War": An Oral History of World War II* (New York: Pantheon, 1984), 229.

22. "What Is the American Look?" *Life*, May 21, 1945, 87; Emily S. Rosenberg, "The American Look: The Nation in the Shape of a Woman," in Emily S. Rosenberg and Shanon Fitzpatrick, *Body and Nation: The Global Realm of U.S. Body Politics in the Twentieth Century* (Durham, NC: Duke University Press, 2014), 191–92.

23. K. Healan Gaston, "Interpreting Judeo-Christianity in America," *Relegere: Studies in Religion and Reception* 2, no. 2 (2012): 291–304; Mark Silk, "Notes on the Judeo-Christian Tradition in America," *American Quarterly* 36, no. 1 (1984):

65–85; Andrew Preston, "Monsters Everywhere: A Genealogy of National Security," *Diplomatic History* 38, no. 3 (June 2014): 497.

24. James J. Sheehan, *Where Have All the Soldiers Gone? The Transformation of Modern Europe* (Boston: Houghton Mifflin, 2008), 176; John Fousek, *To Lead the Free World: American Nationalism and the Cultural Roots of the Cold War* (Chapel Hill: University of North Carolina Press, 2000).

25. Gary Gerstle, *American Crucible: Race and Nation in the Twentieth Century* (Princeton, NJ: Princeton University Press, 2001); Leonard Dinnerstein, *Antisemitism in America* (New York: Oxford University Press, 1994); Otis L. Graham, "The Unfinished Reform: Regulating Immigration in the National Interest," in *Debating American Immigration, 1882–Present*, ed. Roger Daniels and Otis L. Graham (Lanham, MD: Rowman & Littlefield, 2001), 129–31; Kirsten Fermaglich, "'What's Uncle Sam's Last Name?' Jews and Name Changing in New York City During World War II," *Journal of American History* 102, no. 3 (December 2015): 740.

26. Jon Meacham, "Which Date Should Live in Infamy?" *New York Times*, December 10, 2016 (Hitler); "How to Tell Your Friends from the Japs," *Time*, December 22, 1941; Mark Brilliant, "Reimagining Racial Liberalism," in *Making the American Century: Essays on the Political Culture of Twentieth-Century America*, ed. Bruce J. Schulman (New York: Oxford University Press, 2014), 236–37.

27. Fermaglich, "'What's Uncle Sam's Last Name?,'" 719–45. Thanks to Daniel Immerwahr for the tip on *Captain America*.

28. Pippa Holloway, *Living in Infamy: Felony Disenfranchisement and the History of American Citizenship* (New York: Oxford University Press, 2014), xiv, 4; Lynn Hunt, *Inventing Human Rights: A History* (New York: Norton, 2007), 147; Marie Gottschalk, *Caught: The Prison State and the Lockdown of American Politics* (Princeton, NJ: Princeton University Press, 2015); Charles M. Blow, "Eye-for-an-Eye Incivility," *New York Times*, May 4, 2014.

29. *Congressional Record*, Appendix, Volume 91, Part 12, June 11–October 11, 1945 (Washington: U.S. Government Printing Office, 1945): A3980 (Vinson); Ken Coates and W. R. Morrison, "The American Rampant: Reflections on the Impact of United States Troops in Allied Countries During World War II," *Journal of World History* 2, no. 2 (Fall 1991): 207, table 1.

30. Ian Tyrrell and Jay Sexton, "Introduction," in *Empire's Twin: U.S. Anti-Imperialism from the Founding Era to the Age of Terrorism* (Ithaca, NY: Cornell University Press, 2015), 2 (Bryan); Joseph F. Kett, *Merit: The History of a Founding Ideal from the American Revolution to the Twenty-First Century* (Ithaca, NY: Cornell University Press, 2013), 3; Thomas Paine, *Common Sense* (Philadelphia: W. & T. Bradford, 1776), https://www.gutenberg.org/files/147/147-h/147-h.htm.

31. Tyrrell and Sexton, "Introduction," in *Empire's Twin*, 8.

32. Harry S. Truman, address before the Midcentury White House Conference on Children and Youth, December 5, 1950, *Public Papers of the Presidents*, http://www.presidency.ucsb.edu/ws/?pid=13677.

33. Drew Maciag, *Edmund Burke in America: The Contested Career of the Father of Modern Conservatism* (Ithaca, NY: Cornell University Press, 2013); Oleg Karkhordin, "From Priests to Pathfinders: The Fate of the Humanities and Social Sciences in Russia After World War II," *American Historical Review* 120, no. 4 (October 2015): 1284.

34. Harry S. Truman, special message to the Congress on Greece and Turkey, March 12, 1947, *Public Papers of the Presidents*, http://www.presidency.ucsb.edu/ws/index.php?pid=12846.

35. Woodrow Wilson, address to a joint session of Congress, April 2, 1917, *Public Papers of the Presidents*, http://www.presidency.ucsb.edu/ws/index.php?pid=65366; Frederick C. Luebke, *Bonds of Loyalty: German-Americans and World War I* (DeKalb: Northern Illinois University Press, 1974); Michaela Hönicke Moore, *Know Your Enemy: The American Debate on Nazism, 1933–1945* (New York: Cambridge University Press, 2010), 217–40; Franklin D. Roosevelt, radio address at a dinner of the Foreign Policy Association, New York, October 21, 1944, *Public Papers of the President*, http://www.presidency.ucsb.edu/ws/index.php?pid=16456.

36. Dean Rusk, "Report to the Nation on the Punta del Este Conference," radio and television address, February 2, 1962, in *The Winds of Freedom: Selections from the Speeches and Statements of Secretary of State Dean Rusk, January 1961–August 1962*, ed. Ernest K. Lindley (Boston: Beacon, 1963); U.S. Congress, Public Law 86-90, July 17, 1959, https://www.gpo.gov/fdsys/pkg/STATUTE-73/pdf/STATUTE-73-Pg212.pdf.

37. Vice President Richard Cheney, interview with *Meet the Press*, NBC, March 16, 2003, http://www.cheneywatch.org/speeches-and-interviews/cheney-interviews/interview-with-vice-president-dick-cheney-nbc-meet-the-press-transcript-for-march-16-2003; George Packer, *The Assassins' Gate: America in Iraq* (New York: Farrar, Straus and Giroux, 2005); Dexter Filkins, *The Forever War* (New York: Knopf, 2008).

38. Robert Gerwarth and Erez Manela, introduction to *Empires at War: 1911–1923* (Oxford: Oxford University Press, 2014), 15–16.

39. Mark Philip Bradley, *The World Reimagined: Americans and Human Rights in the Twentieth Century* (New York: Cambridge University Press, 2016), 15, 59.

40. Sara Fieldston, *Raising the World: Child Welfare in the Twentieth Century* (Cambridge, MA: Harvard University Press, 2015), 143; Susan L. Carruthers, *The Good Occupation: American Soldiers and the Hazards of Peace* (Cambridge, MA: Harvard University Press, 2016), 300–1.

41. Nick Cullather, *The Hungry World: America's Cold War Battle Against Poverty in Asia* (Cambridge, MA: Harvard University Press, 2010), 75; Robert L. Beisner, *Dean Acheson: A Life in the Cold War* (New York: Oxford University Press, 2006), 373; Michael E. Latham, *The Right Kind of Revolution: Modernization, Development, and U.S. Foreign Policy from the Cold War to the Present* (Ithaca, NY: Cornell University Press, 2011), 2–4.

42. Nick Cullather, "Development and Technopolitics," in *Explaining the History of American Foreign Relations*, 3rd ed., ed. Frank Costigliola and Michael J. Hogan (New York: Cambridge University Press, 2016), 108 (Bogart); Paul R. Pillar, *Why America Misunderstands the World: National Experience and Roots of Misperception* (New York: Columbia University Press, 2016), 42 (Bush).

43. Dwight D. Eisenhower, address to the Freedoms Foundation, New York, December 22, 1952, https://www.eisenhower.archives.gov/all_about_ike/quotes.html; Terry Eagleton, *Across the Pond: An Englishman's View of America* (New York: Norton, 2013), 45.

44. Jürgen Leonhardt, *Latin: Story of a World Language* (Cambridge, MA: Harvard University Press, 2016).

45. Minae Mizumura, *The Fall of Language in the Age of English*, trans. Mari Yoshihara and Juliet Winters Carpenter (New York: Columbia University Press, 2015), 126–32.

46. David W. Ellwood, *The Shock of America: Europe and the Challenge of the Century* (Oxford: Oxford University Press, 2012), 14 (Bismarck); Mizumura, *The Fall of Languages*, 60.

47. Mizumura, *The Fall of Language*, 41; Michael D. Gordin, *Scientific Babel: How Science Was Done Before and After Global English* (Chicago: University of Chicago Press, 2015).

48. Mizumura, *The Fall of Language*, 166; Education First, "The World's Largest Ranking of Countries by English Skills," http://www.ef.com/epi/; Jon Brand, "At Tour de France, Default Language Now Is English," *New York Times*, July 15, 2017.

49. Blower, *Becoming Americans in Paris*, 45–46; Esther Schor, *Bridge of Words: Esperanto and the Dream of a Universal Language* (New York: Metropolitan, 2016).

50. Mizumura, *The Fall of Language*, 60; Sudhir Hazareesingh, *How the French Think: An Affectionate Portrait of an Intellectual People* (New York: Basic, 2015), 181–85.

51. Oscar Wilde, *The Canterville Ghost* (repr., Boston: J. W. Luce, 1906); Eagleton, *Across the Pond*, 12–13.

52. Mary Louise Roberts, *What Soldiers Do: Sex and the American GI in World War II France* (Chicago: University of Chicago Press, 2013), 44.

53. *Elysium*, dir. Neill Blomkamp (TriStar Pictures, 2013).

54. Dennis E. Baron, *The English-Only Question: An Official Language for Americans?* (New Haven, CT: Yale University Press, 1990); James Crawford, ed., *Language Loyalties: A Source Book on the Official English Controversy* (Chicago: University of Chicago Press, 1992). That Nebraska legislator might have been influenced by William Blake's famous poem "Jerusalem" (1808), made into a popular Christian hymn and adopted as an informal anthem by the British. The poet asks, in reference to Jesus: "And did those feet in ancient time / Walk upon England's mountains green / And was the holy Lamb of God / On England's pleasant pastures seen!"

55. Filkins, *The Forever War*, 116.

56. Filkins, *The Forever War*, 116.

57. Walt Whitman, "Song of Myself," *Leaves of Grass* (Brooklyn: n.p., 1855).

58. Friedman, *Rethinking Anti-Americanism*, 35 (Twain); Coates and Morrison, "The American Rampant," 207, table 1.

3. Inbound: Immigrants from Internal Threat to Incorporation

1. A few other nations with much smaller populations had somewhat larger proportions of foreign-born residents, but their absolute numbers pale in comparison to those of the United States. Canada is an example, with roughly one-tenth of the U.S. population. There are more immigrants in the United States than there are total people in Canada (37 million in 2018).

2. Kathleen DuVal, "When We Opened Our Doors," *Wall Street Journal*, February 18–19, 2017; A. Roger Ekirch, *American Sanctuary: Mutiny, Martyrdom, and National Identity in the Age of Revolution* (New York: Pantheon, 2017).

3. Herman Melville, *Redburn: His First Voyage* (New York: Harper, 1849), chap. 33, "The Salt-Droghers, and German Emigrant Ships."

4. Peter H. Wood, *Black Majority: Negroes in Colonial South Carolina from 1670 Through the Stono Rebellion* (New York: Knopf, 1974).

5. Crosby, *Ecological Imperialism*, 300; Friedman, *Rethinking Anti-Americanism*, 45–46; Tara Zahra, *The Great Departure: Mass Migration from Europe and the Making of the Free World* (New York: Norton, 2016), 11–12.

6. Alan Taylor, *The Civil War of 1812: American Citizens, British Subjects, Irish Rebels, and Indian Allies* (New York: Knopf, 2010).

7. Daniel Kilbride, *Being American in Europe, 1750–1860* (Baltimore, MD: Johns Hopkins University Press, 2013), 75, 134–36; Viet Thanh Nguyen, *The Sympathizer* (New York: Grove, 2015), 246. Jonathan Freedland suggested about the United Kingdom that "monarchy and the aristocratic past are now perhaps the only aspects of the country that reliably attract global, and especially

American, interest." Freedland, "A Great Family Business," *New York Review of Books*, March 23, 2017, 16.

8. Jürgen Osterhammel and Niels P. Peterson, *Globalization: A Short History*, trans. Dona Geyer (Princeton, NJ: Princeton University Press, 2005), 25.

9. Frank Costigliola, *France and the United States: The Cold Alliance Since World War II* (New York: Twayne, 1992).

10. Max Paul Friedman, *Rethinking Anti-Americanism: The History of an Exceptional Concept in American Foreign Relations* (New York: Cambridge University Press, 2012), 80 (Twain); Dana Milbank, "Conservatives Find Their Inner Francophiles," *Lincoln Journal-Star*, January 14, 2015 (DeLay); Frédéric Bozo, "'We Don't Need You': France, the United States, and Iraq, 1991–2003," *Diplomatic History* 41, no. 1 (January 2017): 183–208.

11. Brian C. Etheridge, *Enemies to Allies: Cold War Germany and American Memory* (Lexington: University Press of Kentucky, 2016), 16.

12. Etheridge, *Enemies to Allies*, 21 (official); Peter Schrag, *Not Fit for Our Society: Nativism and Immigration* (Berkeley: University of California Press, 2010), 3 (Franklin).

13. Etheridge, *Enemies to Allies*, 23; Russell A. Kazal, *Becoming Old Stock: The Paradox of German-American Identity* (Princeton, NJ: Princeton University Press, 2004).

14. Etheridge, *Enemies to Allies*, 29–34.

15. Woodrow Wilson, "Address to a Joint Session of Congress Requesting a Declaration of War against Germany," April 2, 2017, *Public Papers of the Presidents*, http://www.presidency.ucsb.edu/ws/index.php?pid=65366; Frederick C. Luebke, *Bonds of Loyalty: German-Americans and World War I* (DeKalb: Northern Illinois University Press, 1974).

16. Michaela Hönicke Moore, *Know Your Enemy: The American Debate on Nazism, 1933–1945* (New York: Cambridge University Press, 2010), 8; John W. Dower, *War Without Mercy: Race and Power in the Pacific War* (New York: Pantheon, 1986).

17. Etheridge, *Enemies to Allies*, 44; Hönicke Moore, *Know Your Enemy*, 146, 214–40, 265 (*Pocket Guide*), 341 (quotation).

18. Susan L. Carruthers, *The Good Occupation: American Soldiers and the Hazards of Peace* (Cambridge, MA: Harvard University Press, 2016), 13–14 (quotations), 181, 309; Mary Louise Roberts, *What Soldiers Do: Sex and the American GI in World War II France* (Chicago: University of Chicago Press, 2013); Petra Goedde, *GIs and Germans: Culture, Gender, and Foreign Relations* (New Haven, CT: Yale University Press, 2002); Maria Höhn, *GIs and Fräuleins: The German-American Encounter in 1950s West Germany* (Chapel Hill: University of North Carolina Press, 2002); Susan Zeiger, *Entangling Alliances: Foreign War Brides and American Soldiers in the Twentieth Century* (New York: New York University Press, 2010).

19. "Italy in New York," *New York Times*, September 18, 1951, 30; Donna R. Gabaccia, *We Are What We Eat: Ethnic Food and the Making of Americans* (Cambridge, MA: Harvard University Press, 1998).

20. Thomas Bailey Aldrich, "Unguarded Gates" (1895), http://www.bartleby.com /248/689.html; Daniel Kanstroom, *Deportation Nation: Outsiders in American History* (Cambridge, MA: Harvard University Press, 2007); Roger Daniels, *Guarding the Golden Door: American Immigration Policy and Immigrants Since 1882* (New York: Hill and Wang, 2005).

21. Aristide R. Zolberg, *A Nation by Design: Immigration Policy in the Fashioning of America* (Cambridge, MA: Harvard University Press, 2006), 240–41; Christopher Capozzola, "Legacies for Citizenship: Pinpointing Americans During and After World War I," *Diplomatic History* 38, no. 4 (September 2014): 714; Emma Teng, *Eurasian: Mixed Identities in the United States, China, and Hong Kong, 1842–1943* (Berkeley: University of California Press, 2013), 56–72.

22. Gary Gerstle, *American Crucible: Race and Nation in the Twentieth Century* (Princeton, NJ: Princeton University Press, 2001)105 (Purnell); Zieger, *Entangling Alliances*, 51 (Creel); Mae N. Ngai, *Impossible Subjects: Illegal Aliens and the Making of Modern America* (Princeton, NJ: Princeton University Press, 2004), 30 (Walker); David E. Ruth, *Inventing the Public Enemy: The Gangster in American Culture, 1918–1934* (Chicago: University of Chicago Press, 1996), 11–15.

23. Gary Y. Okihiro, *Common Ground: Reimaging American History* (Princeton, NJ: Princeton University Press, 2001), 49–50; Dorothee Schneider, *Crossing Borders: Migration and Citizenship in the Twentieth-Century United States* (Cambridge, MA: Harvard University Press, 2011), 222–25.

24. Alison Frank Johnson, "'Our American Model': U.S.-Hapsburg Relations and European Race," *Passport: The Society for Historians of American Foreign Relations Review* 45, no. 1 (April 2014): 10–11.

25. Thomas Borstelmann, *The Cold War and the Color Line: American Race Relations in the Global Arena* (Cambridge, MA: Harvard University Press, 2001); Zeiger, *Entangling Alliances*; Carl J. Bon Tempo, *Americans at the Gate: The United States and Refugees During the Cold War* (Princeton, NJ: Princeton University Press, 2008), 1–9, 151, 180.

26. Robert L. Fleegler, *Ellis Island Nation: Immigration Policy and American Identity in the Twentieth Century* (Philadelphia: University of Pennsylvania Press, 2013), 176 (Rusk), 118–21; Margaret Sands Orchowski, *The Law That Changed the Face of America: The Immigration and Nationality Act of 1965* (Lanham, MD: Rowman & Littlefield, 2015). For an insightful reconsideration of the significance of the Hart-Celler Act, see Jesse Hoffnung-Garskof, "The Immigration Reform Act of 1965," in *The Familiar Made Strange: American Icons and Artifacts After the Transnational Turn*, ed. Brooke L. Blower and Mark Bradley (Ithaca, NY: Cornell University Press, 2015), 125–40.

27. U.S. Census Bureau, https://www.census.gov/newsroom/cspan/hispanic/2012
.06.22_cspan_hispanics_5.pdf, https://www.census.gov/newsroom/facts-for
-features/2016/cb16-ff16.html, https://www.census.gov/newsroom/cspan/1940
census/CSPAN_1940slides.pdf; Pew Research Center, http://www.pewsoci
altrends.org/asianamericans-graphics/; http://www.telegraph.co.uk/news/world
news/middleeast/12111108/Mapped-Which-country-has-the-most-immigra
nts.html.

28. Larry Siedentop, *Inventing the Individual: The Origins of Western Liberalism* (Cambridge, MA: Harvard University Press, 2014).

29. Stephen R. Prothero, *Religious Literacy: What Every American Needs to Know—and Doesn't* (New York: HarperSanFrancisco, 2007), 39; Wendy L. Wall, "Symbol of Unity, Symbol of Pluralism: The 'Interfaith Idea' in Wartime and Cold War America," in *Making the American Century: Essays on the Political Culture of Twentieth-Century America*, ed. Bruce J. Schulman (New York: Oxford University Press, 2014), 172–74; Fleegler, *Ellis Island Nation*, 137–60; Kevin M. Schultz, *Tri-Faith America: How Catholics and Jews Held Postwar America to Its Protestant Promise* (New York: Oxford University Press, 2011); Will Herberg, *Protestant-Catholic-Jew: An Essay in American Religious Sociology* (Garden City, NY: Doubleday, 1955).

30. Jon Gjerde, "The Burden of Their Song: Immigrant Encounters with the Republic," in *American Dreaming, Global Realities: Rethinking U.S. Immigration History*, ed. Donna R. Gabaccia and Vicki L. Ruiz (Urbana: University of Illinois Press, 2006), 13 (Morse); Richard D. Alba and Victor Nee, *Remaking the American Mainstream: Assimilation and Contemporary Immigration* (Cambridge, MA: Harvard University Press, 2003), xi–xii.

31. Patrick Allitt, *Religion in America Since 1945: A History* (New York: Columbia University Press, 2003). On the New Christian Right, see Molly Worthen, "The Theological Origins of the Christian Right," and Bethany Moreton, "Knute Gingrich, All American? White Evangelicals, U.S. Catholics, and the Religious Genealogy of Political Realignment," both in *Faithful Republic: Religion and Politics in Modern America*, ed. Andrew Preston, Bruce J. Schulman, and Julian E. Zelizer (Ithaca, NY: Cornell University Press, 2015), 101–16, 131–51.

32. Leonard Dinnerstein, *Antisemitism in America* (New York: Oxford University Press, 1994); David Nirenberg, *Anti-Judaism: The Western Tradition* (New York: Norton, 2013); Michelle Mart, *Eye on Israel: How America Came to View the Jewish State as an Ally* (Albany: State University of New York Press, 2006); Michelle Mart, "Tough Guys and American Cold War Policy: Images of Israel, 1948–1960," *Diplomatic History* 20, no. 3 (July 1996): 357–80; Gershom Gorenberg, *The Accidental Empire: Israel and the Birth of the Settlements, 1967–1977* (New York: Times Books, 2006), 48 (McPherson); Shaul Mitelpunkt, *Israel in the American Mind: The Cultural Politics of U.S.-Israeli Relations, 1958–1988* (New York: Cambridge University Press, 2018).

33. Camila Domonoske, "U.S. Soldier Honored Posthumously for Protecting Jewish POWs in 1945," National Public Radio, December 2, 2015. An echo of this incident came in 1986, when one of the first children in Illinois diagnosed with HIV (contracted from his biological mother), John Graziano, as an adopted second grader was welcomed by his school principal, Paul Nilsen. Nilsen refused to identify the child with HIV to other parents in the school when reports of the child's presence surfaced, and he instructed the second graders, if asked who had AIDS, to say simply, "We all have AIDS." Graziano lived just three more years. "For a Schoolboy with AIDS, a Principal Opened Doors—by Opening His Arms," National Public Radio, December 4, 2015.

34. Enid Nemy and William McDonald, "Bess Myerson, New Yorker of Beauty, Wit, Service, and Scandal, Dies at 90," *New York Times*, January 5, 2015; Peter Novick, *The Holocaust in American Life* (Boston: Houghton Mifflin, 1999), 41; Alba and Nee, *Remaking the American Mainstream*, 283.

35. Caitlin Carenen, *The Fervent Embrace: Liberal Protestants, Evangelicals, and Israel* (New York: New York University Press, 2012); Jeffrey Goldberg, "Is It Time for the Jews to Leave Europe?" *Atlantic*, April 2015; David Brooks, "How to Fight Anti-Semitism," *New York Times*, March 24, 2015.

36. Novick, *The Holocaust in American Life*, 32 (Cahan), 113.

37. Wall, "Symbol of Unity, Symbol of Pluralism," 172–74; K. Healan Gaston, "Waging the Conceptual Cold War: Secularism, Pluralism, and the Struggle for Religious Authenticity," paper presented at "Beyond the Culture Wars: Recasting Religion and Politics in the Twentieth Century," Washington University, St. Louis, Missouri, March 27–29, 2014; Patrick Henry, "'And I Don't Care What It Is': The Tradition-History of a Civil Religion Proof-Text," *Journal of the American Academy of Religion* 49, no. 1 (March 1981): 35–49 (first Eisenhower); Kevin Kruse, *One Nation Under God: How Corporate America Invented Christian America* (New York: Basic, 2015), xii (second Eisenhower).

38. 1856 Republican Party platform, https://web.archive.org/web/20070927195550 /http://www.assumption.edu/ahc/Kansas/Republican%20Platform1856 .html.

39. David Farber, *Taken Hostage: The Iran Hostage Crisis and America's First Encounter with Radical Islam* (Princeton, NJ: Princeton University Press, 2005).

40. Thomas Borstelmann, *The 1970s: A New Global History from Civil Rights to Economic Inequality* (Princeton, NJ: Princeton University Press, 2012), 247–70; Gilles Kepel, *The Revenge of God: The Resurgence of Islam, Christianity, and Judaism in the Modern World*, trans. Alan Braley (University Park: Pennsylvania State University Park, 1994).

41. Robin Wright, "The Adversary," *New Yorker*, May 26, 2014, 43; James A. Bill, *The Eagle and the Lion: The Tragedy of American-Iranian Relations* (New Haven, CT: Yale University Press, 1988).

42. Friedman, *Rethinking Anti-Americanism*, 1; Douglas Little, *Us Versus Them: The United States, Radical Islam, and the Rise of the Green Threat* (Chapel Hill: University of North Carolina Press, 2016); Juan Cole, *Engaging the Muslim World* (New York: Palgrave Macmillan, 2009).

43. Besheer Mohamed, "A New Estimate of the U.S. Muslim Population," January 6, 2016, Pew Research Center, http://www.pewresearch.org/fact-tank /2016/01/06/a-new-estimate-of-the-u-s-muslim-population/; Hani J. Bawardi, *The Making of Arab Americans: From Syrian Nationalism to U.S. Citizenship* (Austin: University of Texas Press, 2014), 13; Samuel G. Freedman, "North Dakota Mosque a Symbol of Muslims' Long Ties in America," *New York Times*, May 27, 2016.

44. Donald J. Trump, statement on preventing Muslim immigration, December 7, 2016, https://www.donaldjtrump.com/press-releases/donald-j.-trump-state ment-on-preventing-muslim-immigration; Ian Lovett, "Christians Lobby on Immigrant Policies," *Wall Street Journal*, January 16, 2018.

45. A recent trend in academic and political activist circles uses "Latinx" as a gender-inclusive alternative to "Latino/a."

46. Caitlin A. Fitz, "The Hemispheric Dimensions of Early U.S. Nationalism: The War of 1812, Its Aftermath, and Spanish American Independence," *Journal of American History* 102, no. 2 (September 2015): 357–59 (quotation), 376–77; Caitlin Fitz, *Our Sister Republics: The United States in an Age of Revolutions* (New York: Liveright, 2016).

47. Dan Fletcher, "Columbus Day," *Time*, October 12, 2009.

48. Tyche Hendricks, *The Wind Doesn't Need a Passport: Stories from the U.S.-Mexico Borderlands* (Berkeley: University of California Press, 2010), 17. As a native of the eastern parts of the United States who went off to college in California in the mid-1970s familiar with three other languages, I was intrigued and slightly mystified by the ubiquitous Spanish names for streets, towns, and features of the natural landscape.

49. Gary Y. Okihiro, *Common Ground: Reimaging American History* (Princeton, NJ: Princeton University Press, 2001), 51; Mae M. Ngai, *Impossible Subjects: Illegal Aliens and the Making of Modern America* (Princeton, NJ: Princeton University Press, 2004), 52–54; Peggy Pascoe, *What Comes Naturally: Miscegenation Law and the Making of Race in America* (New York: Oxford University Press, 2009).

50. Ngai, *Impossible Subjects*, 54 (quotation); Benjamin Heber Johnson, *Revolution in Texas: How a Forgotten Rebellion and Its Bloody Suppression Turned Mexicans Into Americans* (New Haven, CT: Yale University Press, 2003).

51. Neil Foley, "Partly Colored or Other White: Mexican Americans and Their Problem with the Color Line," in *American Dreaming, Global Realities: Rethinking U.S. Immigration History*, ed. Donna R. Gabaccia and Vicki L. Ruiz (Urbana: University of Illinois Press, 2006), 361.

52. Deborah Cohen, *Braceros: Migrant Citizens and Transnational Subjects in the Postwar United States and Mexico* (Chapel Hill: University of North Carolina Press, 2011), 115.

53. *A Day Without a Mexican*, dir. Sergio Arau (Altavista Films, 2004).

54. Cohen, *Braceros*, 116.

55. Cohen, *Braceros*, 127–29.

56. Joshua B. Freeman, *American Empire: The Rise of a Global Power, the Democratic Revolution at Home, 1945–2000* (New York: Viking, 2012), 135; Jenifer Van Vleck, *Empire of the Air: Aviation and the American Ascendancy* (Cambridge, MA: Harvard University Press, 2013), 214 (quotation).

57. Maria Cristina Garcia, *Havana USA: Cuban Exiles and Cuban Americans in South Florida, 1959–1994* (Berkeley: University of California Press, 1996).

58. Vargas Llosa, *Global Crossings*, 313; Jens Manuel Krogstad, "Key Facts About How the U.S. Hispanic Population Is Changing," FactTank: News in the Numbers, Pew Research Center, September 8, 2016, http://www.pewresearch .org/fact-tank/2016/09/08/key-facts-about-how-the-u-s-hispanic-popula tion-is-changing/; Miriam Jordan, "Asians to Represent Largest Foreign-Born Group in U.S. by 2055," *Wall Street Journal*, September 28, 2015; Hendricks, *The Wind Doesn't Need a Passport*, 66.

59. Alan M. Kraut, "Doing as Americans Do: The Post-Migration Negotiation of Identity in the United States," *Journal of American History* 101, no. 3 (December 2014): 708.

60. Gary Shteyngart, *Little Failure* (New York: Random House, 2014), quoted in Michiko Kakutani, "Welcome to America. Enjoy the Free Napkins and Straws," *New York Times*, January 7, 2014.

61. One of the best sources for this issue is Richard Alba and Nancy Foner, *Strangers No More: Immigration and the Challenges of Integration in North America and Western Europe* (Princeton, NJ: Princeton University Press, 2015). See also Russell A. Kazal, "Revisiting Assimilation: The Rise, Fall, and Reappraisal of a Concept in American Ethnic History," *American Historical Review* 100, no. 2 (April 1995): 437–71.

62. Vargas Llosa, *Global Crossings*, 127; Tony Judt with Timothy Snyder, *Thinking the Twentieth Century* (New York: Penguin, 2012), 46.

63. Miri Rubin, *The Middle Ages: A Very Short Introduction* (New York: Oxford University Press, 2014), 13; Gabaccia, *We Are What We Eat*, 54–55.

64. Gabaccia, *We Are What We Eat*, 150.

65. Vargas Llosa, *Global Crossings*, 4–5.

66. See Gerstle, *American Crucible*, on the historical struggle between these two kinds of nationalism.

67. Beth L. Bailey, *America's Army: Making the All-Volunteer Force* (Cambridge, MA: Harvard University Press, 2009).

68. Robert E. Bonner, *Colors and Blood: Flag Passions of the Confederate South* (Princeton, NJ: Princeton University Press, 2002).

69. Marisa Abrajano and Zoltan L. Hajnal, *White Backlash: Immigration, Race, and American Politics* (Princeton, NJ: Princeton University Press, 2015).

70. Zahra, *The Great Departure*, 8, 114 (quotation); Mark Wyman, *Round-Trip to America: The Immigrants Return to Europe, 1880–1930* (Ithaca, NY: Cornell University Press, 1993), 6, 9–10, 21.

71. Ruben Martìnez, *Crossing Over: A Mexican Family on the Migrant Trail* (New York: Metropolitan, 2001), 116.

72. Vargas Llosa, *Global Crossings*, 19, 32 (quotation); Alba and Foner, *Strangers No More*, 19.

73. Alba and Foner, *Strangers No More*, 72, 95 (quotation), 104.

74. Alba and Foner, *Strangers No More*, 200–1, 235.

75. Alba and Foner, *Strangers No More*, 2, 118–20.

76. Alba and Foner, *Strangers No More*, 118–19, 126–27, 132–33; Prema Kurien, "Becoming American by Becoming Hindu: Indian Americans Take Their Place at the Multicultural Table," in *Gatherings in Diaspora: Religious Communities and the New Immigration*, ed. R. Stephen Warner and Judith G. Wittner (Philadelphia: Temple University Press, 1998), 37–70; Uzma Quraishi, *Redefining the Immigrant South: Indian and Pakistani Immigration to Houston During the Cold War* (Chapel Hill: University of North Carolina Press, 2020).

77. On Trump's racism, see David Leonhardt, "Just Say It: Trump Is a Racist," *New York Times*, January 12, 2018; and David Leonhardt, "Details on the List of Trump's Racist Statements," *New York Times*, January 15, 2018.

78. Zahra, *The Great Departure*, 31–32.

4. Lurking: Communists and the Threat of Captivity

1. Bruce Levine et al., *Who Built America? Working People and the Nation's Economy, Politics, Culture, and Society*, vols. 1–2 (New York: Pantheon, 1989–1992).

2. Alexandr I. Solzhenitsyn, *The Gulag Archipelago, 1918–1956: An Experiment in Literary Investigation*, 2 vols., trans. Thomas P. Whitney (New York: Harper & Row, 1974–1975).

3. Stephen J. Whitfield provides an insightful overview of American anxieties about communist subversion in *The Culture of the Cold War*, 2nd ed. (Baltimore, MD: Johns Hopkins University Press, 1996).

4. Joshua Sanborn, "The Russian Empire," in *Empires at War, 1911–1923*, ed. Robert Gerwarth and Erez Manela (Oxford: Oxford University Press, 2014), 91.

5. Lloyd C. Gardner, *Safe for Democracy: Anglo-American Response to Revolution, 1913–1923* (New York: Oxford University Press, 1984).

6. N. Gordon Levin Jr., *Woodrow Wilson and World Politics: America's Response to War and Revolution* (New York: Oxford University Press, 1968); Anthony Read, *The World on Fire: 1919 and the Battle with Bolshevism* (New York: Norton, 2008); David S. Foglesong, *America's Secret War Against Bolshevism: U.S. Intervention in the Russian Civil War, 1917–1920* (Chapel Hill: University of North Carolina Press, 1995).

7. Nick Salvatore, *Eugene V. Debs: Citizen and Socialist* (Urbana: University of Illinois Press, 1982); Julia Mickenberg, "Suffragettes and Soviets: American Feminists and the Specter of Revolutionary Russia," *Journal of American History* 100, no. 4 (March 2014): 1021–51.

8. Sheila Fitzpatrick, *The Russian Revolution*, 2nd ed. (New York: Oxford University Press, 1994), 69.

9. Stephen Kotkin, *Magnetic Mountain: Stalinism as a Civilization* (Berkeley: University of California Press, 1995), 211 (Pravda), 357–60.

10. Gerhard L. Weinberg, *A World at Arms: A Global History of World War II* (Cambridge: Cambridge University Press, 1994).

11. Timothy Snyder, *Bloodlands: Europe Between Hitler and Stalin* (New York: Basic, 2010); Melvyn P. Leffler, "The American Conception of National Security and the Beginnings of the Cold War, 1945–48," *American Historical Review* 89, no. 2 (April 1984): 346–81; Melvyn P. Leffler, *A Preponderance of Power: National Security, the Truman Administration, and the Cold War* (Stanford, CA: Stanford University Press, 1992).

12. Richard M. Fried, *Nightmare in Red: The McCarthy Era in Perspective* (New York: Oxford University Press, 1990).

13. Ellen Schrecker, *Many Are the Crimes: McCarthyism in America* (Boston: Little, Brown, 1998).

14. Michael G. Kammen, *People of Paradox: An Inquiry Concerning the Origins of American Civilization* (New York: Knopf, 1972), 4; Robert Bothwell, *Your Country, My Country: A Unified History of the United States and Canada* (New York: Oxford University Press, 2015), 44.

15. Andrew Preston, "Monsters Everywhere: A Genealogy of National Security," *Diplomatic History* 38, no. 3 (June 2014): 477–500; Patrick J. Heardon, *Roosevelt Confronts Hitler: America's Entry Into World War II* (DeKalb: Northern Illinois University Press, 1987); John Fousek, *To Lead the Free World: American Nationalism and the Cultural Roots of the Cold War* (Chapel Hill: University of North Carolina Press, 2000).

16. During the Cold War, anti-Soviet rhetorical partisans used the term "totalitarian" as a political weapon to delegitimate communism in all its forms. This practice often dissuaded careful historians and other observers from using it.

With the Cold War now more than a quarter-century in the past, it seems reasonable to reappropriate a term that, while not perfect, does suggest the shared goal of full governmental control over the most intimate aspects of individual citizens' lives in the pursuit of remaking them into new and supposedly better people—a utopian project, whether of the Left or of the Right.

17. Robert O. Paxton, *The Anatomy of Fascism* (New York: Knopf, 2004); Archie Brown, *The Rise and Fall of Communism* (New York: Ecco, 2009).

18. Les K. Adler and Thomas G. Paterson, "Red Fascism: The Merger of Nazi Germany and Soviet Russia in the American Image of Totalitarianism, 1930's to 1950's," *American Historical Review* 75, no. 4 (April 1970): 1046–64; Susan L. Carruthers, *Cold War Captives: Imprisonment, Escape, and Brainwashing* (Berkeley: University of California Press, 2009), 12–13.

19. George F. Kennan, *Memoirs: 1925–1950* (1967; New York: Pantheon, 1983), 74, 551; Kennan, lecture 2 at Bad Nauheim, 1942, George F. Kennan Papers, Mudd Library, Princeton University, cited in n. 73 of David S. Foglesong, "Liberating Russia? American Thinking About the Russian Future and the Psychological Warfare of the Early Cold War, 1948–1953," unpublished manuscript, 1997 (in author's possession); David S. Foglesong, "Roots of 'Liberation': American Images of the Future of Russia in the Early Cold War, 1948–1953," *International History Review* 21 (March 1999): 57–79 (Stevens quotation at 73); Leslie C. Stevens, *Russian Assignment* (Boston: Little, Brown, 1953).

20. Richard Wright, *The Color Curtain: A Report on the Bandung Conference* (Cleveland: World, 1956), 133–36.

21. "The Kremlin," *Time*, November 12, 1956, 30–31; Frank Costigliola, "'Unceasing Pressure for Penetration': Gender, Pathology, and Emotion in George Kennan's Formation of the Cold War," *Journal of American History* 83, no. 4 (March 1997): 1309–39.

22. W. W. Rostow, *The Stages of Economic Growth: A Non-Communist Manifesto* (Cambridge: Cambridge University Press, 1960); Nils Gilman, *Mandarins of the Future: Modernization Theory in Cold War America* (Baltimore, MD: Johns Hopkins University Press, 2003); Michael E. Latham, *The Right Kind of Revolution: Modernization, Development, and U.S. Foreign Policy from the Cold War to the Present* (Ithaca, NY: Cornell University Press, 2011); David C. Engerman et al., eds., *Staging Growth: Modernization, Development, and the Global Cold War* (Amherst: University of Massachusetts Press, 2003).

23. Russell Porter, "Rusk Hints U.S. Aid to Revolt in China," *New York Times*, May 19, 1951; Lyndon B. Johnson, address at Johns Hopkins University, April 7, 1965, *Public Papers of the Presidents*, http://www.presidency.ucsb.edu/ws/?pid=26877.

24. NSC 68, "United States Objectives and Programs for National Security," April 7, 1950, https://history.state.gov/historicaldocuments/frus1950v01/d85.

25. Lawrence S. Kaplan, *"Entangling Alliances with None": American Foreign Policy in the Age of Jefferson* (Kent, OH: Kent State University Press, 1987), 112.

26. George Kennan, "Tasks Ahead in U.S. Foreign Policy," lecture at the National War College, Washington, D.C., December 18, 1952, box 18, Kennan Papers, Mudd Library; John Foster Dulles, "The Cost of Peace," *Department of State Bulletin*, June 18, 1956, 999–1000.

27. Murphy to Rockefeller, August 19, 1955, enclosing "Neutralism in the NEA Area," White House Office, Office of Special Assistant for National Security Affairs, NSC Staff Papers, 1948–1961, box 2, folder "#9 Bandung (1)," Dwight D. Eisenhower Library, Abilene, KS; CIA, "The Addis Ababa Conference and Its Aftermath," July 11, 1963, National Security Files, box 3, John F. Kennedy Library, Boston, Massachusetts.

28. Odd Arne Westad, *The Global Cold War: Third World Interventions and the Making of Our Times* (New York: Cambridge University Press, 2005).

29. Thomas G. Paterson, *On Every Front: The Making of the Cold War* (New York: Norton, 1979). For a recent overview, see Odd Arne Westad, *The Cold War: A World History* (New York: Basic, 2017).

30. Fitzpatrick, *The Russian Revolution*, 69. For unusual insight into the building of a new socialist society, see Kotkin, *Magnetic Mountain*, esp. 357–60.

31. Edward Crankshaw, "When Lenin Returned," *Atlantic*, October 1954; Catherine Merridale, *Lenin on the Train* (New York: Metropolitan, 2017). German disdain for Russians emerges in this diary entry of a German commander on the Eastern Front in early 1918, just before the Treaty of Brest-Litovsk halted the fighting: "The whole of Russia is no more than a vast heap of maggots—a squalid, swarming mass." Fitzpatrick, *The Russian Revolution*, 72.

32. Michael Schaller, *The United States and China in the Twentieth Century*, 2nd ed. (New York: Oxford University Press, 1990), 119.

33. Richard E. Welch, *Response to Revolution: The United States and the Cuban Revolution, 1959–1961* (Chapel Hill: University of North Carolina Press, 1985); Ted Widmer, "Ich Bin Ein Berliner," *New York Times*, June 25, 2013.

34. John Demos, *The Unredeemed Captive: A Family Story from Early America* (New York: Knopf, 1994); Jill Lepore, *The Name of War: King Philip's War and the Origins of American Identity* (New York: Knopf, 1998). On the lineage of "Reds" and subversives, see Richard Drinnon, *Facing West: The Metaphysics of Indian-Hating and Empire Building* (Minneapolis: University of Minnesota Press, 1980). On the important role of captivity in shaping the development of the British Empire, see Linda Colley, *Captives* (New York: Pantheon, 2002).

35. Douglas A. Blackmon, *Slavery by Another Name: The Re-enslavement of Black Americans from the Civil War to World War II* (New York: Doubleday, 2008); David M. Oshinsky, *"Worse Than Slavery": Parchman Farm and the Ordeal of Jim Crow Justice* (New York: Free Press, 1996). For a useful entry point into the

now vast literature on American race slavery, see Ira Berlin, *Generations of Captivity: A History of African-American Slaves* (Cambridge, MA: Harvard University Press, 2003).

36. Timothy B. Tyson, *The Blood of Emmett Till* (New York: Simon & Schuster, 2017), 185.

37. Carruthers, *Cold War Captives*, 14. Early entries into this literature on race and the Cold War were Mary L. Dudziak, *Cold War Civil Rights: Race and the Image of American Democracy* (Princeton, NJ: Princeton University Press, 2000); and Thomas Borstelmann, *The Cold War and the Color Line: American Race Relations in the Global Arena* (Cambridge, MA: Harvard University Press, 2001).

38. Peter H. Wood, "'I Did the Best I Could for My Day': The Study of Early Black History During the Second Reconstruction, 1960–1976," *William and Mary Quarterly* 35, no. 2 (April 1978): 185–225; Edward E. Baptist, *The Half Has Never Been Told: Slavery and the Making of American Capitalism* (New York: Basic, 2014).

39. Dwight D. Eisenhower, inaugural address, January 20, 1953, *Public Papers of the Presidents*, http://www.presidency.ucsb.edu/ws/index.php?pid=9600.

40. Dwight D. Eisenhower, "Proclamation 3303—Captive Nations Week, 1959," July 17, 1959, *Public Papers of the Presidents*, http://www.presidency.ucsb.edu/ws/?pid=107400; Irwin M. Wall, *France, the United States, and the Algerian War* (Berkeley: University of California Press, 2001); Caroline Elkins, *Imperial Reckoning: The Untold Story of Britain's Gulag in Kenya* (New York: Henry Holt, 2005).

41. Lizabeth Cohen, *A Consumers' Republic: The Politics of Mass Consumption in Postwar America* (New York: Knopf, 2003).

42. Anne O'Hare McCormick, "Abroad: The Grim Century of the Homeless Man," *New York Times*, August 6, 1952.

43. Matthew W. Dunne, *A Cold War State of Mind: Brainwashing and Postwar American Society* (Amherst: University of Massachusetts Press, 2013), 3–5, 13–18, 22–23, 68; Charles S. Young, *Name, Rank, and Serial Number: Exploiting Korean War POWs at Home and Abroad* (New York: Oxford University Press, 2014), 134; Carruthers, *Cold War Captives*, 174–216.

44. Bruce Cumings, *The Korean War: A History* (New York: Modern Library, 2010), 254n13.

45. Bruce Cumings, *The Origins of the Korean War*, 2 vols. (Princeton, NJ: Princeton University Press, 1981–1990).

46. Hanson W. Baldwin, "Captives Are Red Pawns: Foe Picks Up Advantage in Truce Talks in Expedient Release of Prisoner List," *New York Times*, December 21, 1951.

47. Young, *Name, Rank, and Serial Number*, 61; William Stueck, *Rethinking the Korean War: A New Diplomatic and Strategic History* (Princeton, NJ: Princeton University Press, 2002), chap. 6; Monica Kim, *The Interrogation Rooms of the Korean War: The Untold Story* (Princeton, NJ: Princeton University Press, 2019).

48. Brendan McNally, "The Korean War Prisoner Who Never Came Home," *New Yorker*, December 9, 2013.

49. Young, *Name, Rank, and Serial Number*, 40 (quotation), 86.

50. Young, *Name, Rank, and Serial Number*, 84, 114, 86. See also Tim Weiner, "Remembering Brainwashing," *New York Times*, July 6, 2008.

51. John F. Kennedy, Radio and Television Report to the American People on the Soviet Arms Buildup in Cuba, October 22, 1962, *Public Papers of the Presidents*, http://www.presidency.ucsb.edu/ws/index.php?pid=8986; Thomas G. Paterson, *Contesting Castro: The United States and the Triumph of the Cuban Revolution* (New York: Oxford University Press, 1994), 52.

52. Carruthers, *Cold War Captives*, 231.

53. Kenneth Osgood, *Total Cold War: Eisenhower's Secret Propaganda Battle at Home and Abroad* (Lawrence: University of Kansas Press, 2006), 288 (quotation); Stephen J. Whitfield, *The Culture of the Cold War* (Baltimore, MD: Johns Hopkins University Press, 1991), 127–52; Peter Biskind, *Seeing Is Believing: How Hollywood Taught Us to Stop Worrying and Love the Fifties* (New York: Pantheon, 1983).

54. American Psychological Association, "APA History," http://www.apa.org/about/apa/archives/apa-history.aspx; Jamie Cohen-Cole, *The Open Mind: Cold War Politics and the Sciences of Human Nature* (Chicago: University of Chicago Press, 2014).

55. Sara Fieldston, *Raising the World: Child Welfare in the American Century* (Cambridge, MA: Harvard University Press, 2015), 12–13, 110 (Truman). As a child of one of these midcentury developmental psychologists, I recall many family discussions of the importance of the self and a nurturing environment in which children could grow.

56. Robin D. G. Kelley, *Hammer and Hoe: Alabama Communists During the Great Depression* (Chapel Hill: University of North Carolina Press, 1990); Mark Solomon, *The Cry Was Unity: Communists and African Americans, 1917–1936* (Jackson: University Press of Mississippi, 1998).

57. Walter LaFeber, *The American Age: U.S. Foreign Policy at Home and Abroad, 1750 to the Present*, 2nd ed. (New York: Norton, 1994), 348; Christine A. White, *British and American Commercial Relations with Soviet Russia, 1918–1924* (Chapel Hill: University of North Carolina Press, 1992); Jane Mayer, *Dark Money: The Hidden History of the Billionaires Behind the Rise of the Radical Right* (New York: Doubleday, 2016), 28–31.

58. Frank Costigliola, *Roosevelt's Lost Alliances: How Personal Politics Helped Start the Cold War* (Princeton, NJ: Princeton University Press, 2012); Weinberg, *A World at Arms*.

59. Ronald Reagan, Remarks at the Annual Convention of the National Association of Evangelicals in Orlando, Florida, March 8, 1983, *Public Papers of the Presidents*, http://www.presidency.ucsb.edu/ws/index.php?pid=41023.

60. Lorraine M. Lees, *Keeping Tito Afloat: The United States, Yugoslavia, and the Cold War* (University Park: Pennsylvania State University Press, 1997); Ivan Laković and Dmitar Tasić, *The Tito-Stalin Split and Yugoslavia's Military Opening Toward the West, 1950–1954: In NATO's Backyard* (Lanham, MD: Lexington, 2016).

61. Lorenz M. Luthi, *The Sino-Soviet Split: Cold War in the Communist World* (Princeton, NJ: Princeton University Press, 2008); David A. Mayers, *Cracking the Monolith: U.S. Policy Against the Sino-Soviet Alliance, 1949–1955* (Baton Rouge: Louisiana State University Press, 1986); Ezra F. Vogel, *Deng Xiaoping and the Transformation of China* (Cambridge, MA: Harvard University Press, 2011).

62. John F. Kennedy, Commencement Address at American University in Washington, June 10, 1963, *Public Papers of the Presidents*, http://www.presidency.ucsb .edu/ws/index.php?pid=9266; Jenifer Van Vleck, *Empire of the Air: Aviation and the American Ascendancy* (Cambridge, MA: Harvard University Press, 2013), 267.

63. Todd Gitlin, *The Sixties: Years of Hope, Days of Rage* (New York: Bantam, 1987); Maurice Isserman and Michael Kazin, *America Divided: The Civil War of the 1960s* (New York: Oxford University Press, 2000). Skeptics also pointed to the parallel poisonous nuclear complexes built by the United States and the Soviet Union, finding them more similar than different. See the penetrating analysis in Kate Brown, *Plutopia: Nuclear Families, Atomic Cities, and the Great Soviet and American Plutonium Disasters* (New York: Oxford University Press, 2013).

64. David E. Sanger, "For Helms, His Home State Is Source of Foreign Policy," *New York Times*, April 2, 1996.

65. *The Americans*, dir. Joe Weisberg (FX, 2013).

66. Francis Spufford, *Red Plenty* (Minneapolis, MN: Graywolf, 2010), 21, 31.

67. During the Cold War, communist rulers at times implicitly acknowledged the motivating power of capitalist-style incentives. While denouncing Western materialism, Eastern European governments sought to lure home émigrés who had escaped to the West by promising material inducements such as apartments, cash bonuses, and pension benefits for years spent abroad. See Tara Zahra, *The Great Departure: Mass Migration from Eastern Europe and the Making of the Free World* (New York: Norton, 2016), 221.

5. Outbound: U.S. Expansion Into Foreign Lands

1. Among the best surveys of this history are Walter LaFeber, *The American Age: United States Foreign Policy at Home and Abroad: 1750 to the Present*, 2nd ed. (New York: Norton, 1994); and George C. Herring, *From Colony to Superpower: U.S. Foreign Relations Since 1776* (New York: Oxford University Press, 2008). For a penetrating brief critique, see William Appleman Williams, *Empire as a Way of*

Life: An Essay on the Causes and Character of America's Present Predicament, Along with a Few Thoughts About an Alternative (New York: Oxford University Press, 1980).

2. Edward Abbey, "The Second Rape of the West," in *The Journey Home: Some Words in Defense of the American West* (New York: Dutton, 1977), 183.

3. Eliot A. Cohen, *Conquered Into Liberty: Two Centuries of Battles Along the Great Warpath That Made the American Way of War* (New York: Free Press, 2011), 134.

4. Brooke L. Blower, "Thinking Across the Case Studies: Toward a Synthetic History of Americans Abroad," paper delivered at the annual meeting of the Organization of American Historians, Atlanta, Georgia, April 11, 2014; U.S. Department of State, Bureau of Consular Affairs, "CA by the Numbers," June 2016, https://web.archive.org/web/20160616233331/https://travel.state.gov/content/dam/travel/CA_By_the_Numbers.pdf. On U.S. governmental disinterest in citizens living abroad, other than for taxing purposes, see Brooke L. Blower, "Nation of Outposts: Forts, Factories, Bases, and the Making of American Power," *Diplomatic History* 41, no. 3 (June 2017): 439–59.

5. Blower, "Thinking Across the Case Studies"; Frank Costigliola and Michael J. Hogan, eds., *America in the World: The Historiography of American Foreign Relations Since 1941*, 2nd ed. (New York: Cambridge University Press, 2014).

6. Daniel Immerwahr, *How to Hide an Empire: A History of the Greater United States* (New York: Farrar, Straus & Giroux, 2019), 10 (emphasis in original). See also Daniel Immerwahr, "The Greater United States: Territory and Empire in U.S. History," *Diplomatic History* 40, no. 3 (June 2016): 373–91.

7. Thomas Bender, *A Nation Among Nations: America's Place in World History* (New York: Hill and Wang, 2006), 112.

8. Nicholas Guyatt, *Bind Us Apart: How Enlightened Americans Invented Racial Segregation* (New York: Basic, 2016), 211, 221–23.

9. James Ciment, *Another America: The Story of Liberia and the Former Slaves Who Ruled It* (New York: Hill and Wang, 2013), xix; John Stauffer, "You Can't Go Home Again," *Wall Street Journal*, December 21–22, 2013.

10. Madeleine G. Kalb, *The Congo Cables: The Cold War in Africa—from Eisenhower to Kennedy* (New York: Macmillan, 1982), 40 (Bunche); William Attwood, *The Reds and the Blacks: A Personal Adventure* (New York: Harper and Row, 1967), 188 (Malcolm X).

11. Blower, "Thinking Across the Case Studies"; David W. Ellwood, *The Shock of America: Europe and the Challenge of the Century* (Oxford: Oxford University Press, 2012), 33–34.

12. Todd Shepard, *The Invention of Decolonization: The Algerian War and the Remaking of France* (Ithaca, NY: Cornell University Press, 2006).

13. Gerald J. Bender, *Angola Under the Portuguese: The Myth and the Reality* (Berkeley: University of California Press, 1978).

14. Beth Bailey and David Farber, *The First Strange Place: The Alchemy of Race and Sex in World War II Hawai'i* (New York: Free Press, 1992).

15. Important early entries in this scholarship included Walter L. Williams, "United States Indian Policy and the Debate Over Philippine Annexation: Implications for the Origins of American Imperialism," *Journal of American History* 66, no. 4 (March 1980): 810–31; and Richard Drinnon, *Facing West: The Metaphysics of Indian-Hating and Empire Building* (Minneapolis: University of Minnesota Press, 1980). See also Brian Rouleau, *With Sails Whitening Every Sea: Mariners and the Making of an American Maritime Empire* (Ithaca, NY: Cornell University Press, 2014).

16. Bender, *A Nation Among Nations*, 231; David J. Silbey, *A War of Frontier and Empire: The Philippine-American War, 1899–1902* (New York: Hill and Wang, 2007).

17. Michael E. Latham, *The Right Kind of Revolution: Modernization, Development, and U.S. Foreign Policy from the Cold War to the Present* (Ithaca, NY: Cornell University Press, 2011), 13; Paul A. Kramer, *The Blood of Government: Race, Empire, the United States, and the Philippines* (Chapel Hill: University of North Carolina Press, 2006).

18. *Sixth Annual Report of the Philippine Commission*, 1905, part 2 (Washington: U.S. Government Printing Office, 1906), 210; U.S. Census Bureau, "Population of the 100 Largest Urban Places: 1900," https://www.census.gov/population/www /documentation/twps0027/tab13.txt.

19. *Sixth Annual Report of the Philippines Commission*, part 2, 211. For a sustained analysis of racial practices in U.S. enclaves abroad, see Jason M. Colby, *The Business of Empire: United Fruit, Race, and U.S. Expansion in Central America* (Ithaca, NY: Cornell University Press, 2011).

20. Paul A. Kramer, "Colonial Crossings: Prostitution, Disease, and the Boundaries of Empire During the Philippine-American War," in *Body and Nation: The Global Realm of U.S. Body Politics in the Twentieth Century*, ed. Emily S. Rosenberg and Shanon Fitzpatrick (Durham, NC: Duke University Press, 2014), 17–41.

21. Jill E. Martin, "'Neither Fish, Flesh, Fowl, nor Good Red Herring': The Citizenship Status of American Indians, 1830–1924," in *American Indians and U.S. Politics*, ed. John M. Meyer (Westport, CT: Praeger, 2002), 51–72.

22. Mary Beard, *SPQR: A History of Ancient Rome* (New York: Liveright, 2015), 527–29; Ronald P. Formisano, *Plutocracy in America: How Increasing Inequality Destroys the Middle Class and Exploits the Poor* (Baltimore, MD: Johns Hopkins University Press, 2015). For a penetrating comparison of modern America to ancient Rome, see Cullen Murphy, *Are We Rome? The Fall of an Empire and the Fate of America* (Boston: Houghton Mifflin, 2007).

23. Sarah Miller-Davenport, *Gateway State: Hawai'i and the Cultural Transformation of American Empire* (Princeton, NJ: Princeton University Press, 2019).

24. Ellen D. Wu, *The Color of Success: Asian Americans and the Origins of the Model Minority* (Princeton, NJ: Princeton University Press, 2014), 210–41.

25. Brooke L. Blower, *Becoming Americans in Paris: Transatlantic Politics and Culture Between the World Wars* (New York: Oxford University Press, 2011), 141–43.

26. Tyler Stovall, *Paris Noir: African Americans in the City of Light* (Boston: Houghton Mifflin, 1996); Blower, *Becoming Americans in Paris*, 137, 144; Victoria de Grazia, *Irresistible Empire: America's Advance Through Twentieth-Century Europe* (Cambridge, MA: Harvard University Press, 2005).

27. Mary Louise Roberts, *What Soldiers Do: Sex and the American GI in World War II France* (Chicago: University of Chicago Press, 2013), 39.

28. Roberts, *What Soldiers Do*, 2–3.

29. Roberts, *What Soldiers Do*, 10, 19–20, 115, 195, passim.

30. Iris Chang, *The Rape of Nanking: The Forgotten Holocaust of World War II* (New York: Basic, 1997); Timothy Snyder, *Bloodlands: Europe Between Hitler and Stalin* (New York: Basic, 2010); Norman M. Naimark, *The Russians in Germany: A History of the Soviet Zone of Occupation, 1945–1949* (Cambridge, MA: Harvard University Press, 1995).

31. Susan Zeiger, *Entangling Alliances: Foreign War Brides and American Soldiers in the Twentieth Century* (New York: New York University Press, 2010), 72; David Reynolds, *Rich Relations: The American "Occupation" of Britain, 1942–1945* (New York: Random House, 1995).

32. Zeiger, *Entangling Alliances*, 3, 73 (quotation), 100.

33. Donna Alvah, *Unofficial Ambassadors: American Military Families Overseas and the Cold War, 1946–1965* (New York: New York University Press, 2007), 47–48, 131–66.

34. Max Friedman, *Rethinking Anti-Americanism: The History of an Exceptional Concept in American Foreign Relations* (New York: Cambridge University Press, 2012), 94; Alvah, *Unofficial Ambassadors*, 59. See also Petra Goedde, *GIs and Germans: Culture, Gender, and Foreign Relations, 1945–1949* (New Haven, CT: Yale University Press, 2003); Maria Höhn, *GIs and Fräuleins: The German-American Encounter in 1950s West Germany* (Chapel Hill: University of North Carolina Press, 2002).

35. Alvah, *Unofficial Ambassadors*, 59.

36. Ji-Yeon Yuh, *Beyond the Shadow of Camptown: Korean Military Brides in America* (New York: New York University Press, 2002); Madeline Hsu, comments on "Race and the Cold War" roundtable, annual meeting of the Organization of American Historians, Atlanta, Georgia, April 11, 2014.

37. Rob Stein, "Data Find a Taller, Fatter America Since 1960," *Washington Post*, October 28, 2004. By 2017 the weight gain was almost thirty pounds since 1960. CDC National Center for Health Statistics, "Body Measurements," https://www.cdc.gov/nchs/fastats/body-measurements.htm. Another common blurring

of the concept of Asia in contemporary American life was the spread of "Asian fusion" restaurants by the 1990s.

38. Edward Said, *Orientalism* (New York: Pantheon, 1978).

39. Sarah M. A. Gualtieri, *Between Arab and White: Race and Ethnicity in the Early Syrian American Diaspora* (Berkeley: University of California Press, 2009), 1–5.

40. There is growing awareness of this in both subfields. An early initiative in this regard is Donna R. Gabaccia, *Foreign Relations: American Immigration in Global Perspective* (Princeton, NJ: Princeton University Press, 2012). See also Paul A. Kramer, "The Geopolitics of Mobility: Immigration Policy and American Global Power in the Long Twentieth Century," *American Historical Review* 123, no. 2 (April 2018): 393–438.

41. Charles C. Mann, *1491: New Revelations of the Americas Before Columbus* (New York: Knopf, 2005).

42. Gary Y. Okihiro, *Common Ground: Reimaging American History* (Princeton, NJ: Princeton University Press, 2001), 21.

43. Gordon H. Chang, *Fateful Ties: A History of America's Preoccupation with China* (Cambridge, MA: Harvard University Press, 2015), 23–25. See also Odd Arne Westad, *Restless Empire: China and the World Since 1750* (New York: Basic Books, 2012).

44. Chang, *Fateful Ties*, 25, 66–67.

45. Emma Teng, *Eurasian: Mixed Identities in the United States, China, and Hong Kong, 1842–1943* (Berkeley: University of California Press, 2013), 30–43; Chang, *Fateful Ties*, 25, 68.

46. Michael Schaller, *The United States and China: Into the Twenty-First Century*, 4th ed. (New York: Oxford University Press, 2015), chaps. 1–2; Warren I. Cohen, *America's Response to China: A History of Sino-American Relations*, 5th ed. (New York: Columbia University Press, 2010), chaps. 1–2.

47. Warren I. Cohen, *The Asian American Century* (Cambridge, MA: Harvard University Press, 2002), 59–63.

48. Time Cover Store, http://www.timecoverstore.com/category/chiang-kai-shek/.

49. Cohen, *The Asian American Century*, 58; Seth Jacobs, *America's Miracle Man in Vietnam: Ngo Dinh Diem, Religion, Race, and U.S. Intervention in Southeast Asia, 1950–1957* (Durham, NC: Duke University Press, 2004).

50. Rotem Kowner, *From White to Yellow: The Japanese in European Racial Thought, 1300–1735* (Montreal: McGill-Queen's University Press, 2014), 309–10.

51. Michael H. Fisher, *Migration: A World History* (New York: Oxford University Press, 2014), 72; Jürgen Osterhammel and Niels P. Peterson, *Globalization: A Short History*, trans. Dona Geyer (Princeton, NJ: Princeton University Press, 2005), 68.

52. Frederick R. Dickinson, "The Japanese Empire," in *Empires at War: 1911–1923*, ed. Robert Gerwarth and Erez Manela (Oxford: Oxford University Press,

2014), 198–200 (Stoddard); Chris Suh, "What Yun Ch'i-ho Knew: U.S.-Japan Relations and Imperial Race Making in Korea and the American South, 1904–1919," *Journal of American History* 104, no. 1 (June 2017): 79–80 (adviser, Jordan).

53. Dickinson, "The Japanese Empire," 203–5.

54. Naoko Shimazu, *Japan, Race, and Equality: The Racial Equality Proposal of 1919* (New York: Routledge, 1998): Walter LaFeber, *The Clash: A History of U.S.-Japan Relations* (New York: Norton, 1997), chaps. 4–7.

55. John W. Dower, *War Without Mercy: Race and Power in the Pacific War* (New York: Pantheon, 1986); Greg Robinson, *A Tragedy of Democracy: Japanese Confinement in North America* (New York: Columbia University Press, 2009); Roger Daniels, *The Japanese American Cases: The Rule of Law in Time of War* (Lawrence: University of Kansas Press, 2013); Roger Daniels, *Prisoners Without Trial: Japanese Americans in World War II* (New York: Hill and Wang, 2004); Gordon K. Hirabayashi, *A Principled Stand: The Story of* Hirabayashi v. United States (Seattle: University of Washington Press, 2013).

56. W. H. Anderson, "The Question of Japanese-Americans," *Los Angeles Times*, February 2, 1942; Daniels, *Prisoners Without Trial*, 64; Ellen D. Wu, *The Color of Success: Asian Americans and the Origins of the Model Minority* (Princeton, NJ: Princeton University Press, 2014), 74. For a careful evaluation of the relationship between U.S. citizens and residents of Japanese descent and the Japanese government in the 1930s and 1940s, see Robinson, *A Tragedy of Democracy*, chap. 1, esp. 39, 46, 57.

57. Studs Terkel, *"The Good War": An Oral History of World War II* (New York: Pantheon, 1984), 90.

58. Ken Coates and W. R. Morrison, "The American Rampant: Reflections on the Impact of United States Troops in Allied Countries During World War II," *Journal of World History* 2, no. 2 (Fall 1991): 206–7.

59. Wu, *The Color of Success*, 50–55.

60. James Michener, "Blunt Truth About Asia," *Life*, June 4, 1951, quoted in Nick Cullather, *The Hungry World: America's Cold War Battle Against Poverty in Asia* (Cambridge, MA: Harvard University Press, 2010), 2; Murphy, *Are We Rome?*, 50.

61. Scott Kurashige, *The Shifting Grounds of Race: Black and Japanese Americans in the Making of Multiethnic Los Angeles* (Princeton, NJ: Princeton University Press, 2008), 183; Meredith Oda, *The Gateway to the Pacific: Japanese Americans and the Remaking of San Francisco* (Chicago: University of Chicago Press, 2019).

62. Jon Halliday and Bruce Cumings, *Korea: The Unknown War* (New York: Pantheon, 1988).

63. T. Christopher Jespersen, *American Images of China, 1931–1949* (Stanford, CA: Stanford University Press, 1996); Charles S. Young, *Name, Rank, and Serial*

Number: Exploiting Korean War POWs at Home and Abroad (New York: Oxford University Press, 2014), 77 (quotation), 83.

64. Cindy I-Fen Cheng, *Citizens of Asian America: Democracy and Race During the Cold War* (New York: New York University Press, 2013), 4–5; Meredith Oyen, *The Diplomacy of Migration: Transnational Lives and the Making of U.S.-Chinese Relations in the Cold War* (Ithaca, NY: Cornell University Press, 2015); Wu, *The Color of Success*; Madeline Y. Hsu, *The Good Immigrants: How the Yellow Peril Became the Model Minority* (Princeton, NJ: Princeton University Press, 2015); Charlotte Brooks, *Between Mao and McCarthy: Chinese American Politics in the Cold War Years* (Chicago: University of Chicago Press, 2015).

65. Hsu, *The Good Immigrants*, 104–29; Madeline Y. Hsu, *Asian American History: A Very Short Introduction* (New York: Oxford University Press, 2017), 91–92; Mae Ngai, *Impossible Subjects: Illegal Aliens and the Making of Modern America* (Princeton, NJ: Princeton University Press, 2004), 341; Wu, *The Color of Success*, 94.

66. Robert D. McFadden, "Sammy Lee, First Asian-American Man to Earn Olympic Gold, Dies at 96," *New York Times*, December 3, 2016; Mary Ting Yi Lui, "Sammy Lee: Narratives of Asian American Masculinity and Race in Decolonizing Asia," in *Body and Nation*, ed. Rosenberg and Fitzpatrick, 209–29; Frank Litsky, "Victoria Manalo Draves, Olympic Champion Diver, Dies at 85," *New York Times*, April 29, 2010.

67. McFadden, "Sammy Lee" (quotation); Lui, "Sammy Lee"; Penny M. Von Eschen, *Satchmo Blows Up the World: Jazz Ambassadors Play the Cold War* (Cambridge, MA: Harvard University Press, 2004).

68. McFadden, "Sammy Lee" (quotation); Cheng, *Citizens of Asian America*, 83; Arnold R. Hirsch, *Making the Second Ghetto: Race and Housing in Chicago, 1940–1960* (New York: Cambridge University Press, 1983); Thomas J. Sugrue, *The Origins of the Urban Crisis: Race and Inequality in Postwar Detroit* (Princeton, NJ: Princeton University Press, 1996).

69. Wu, *The Color of Success*, 3, 159–60 (*Reader's Digest*); Demaree Bess, "California's Amazing Japanese," *Saturday Evening Post*, April 30, 1955, 38–39; Gladwin Hill, "Japanese in U.S. Gaining Equality," *New York Times*, August 12, 1956.

70. Thomas W. Zeiler, "Opening Doors in the World Economy," in *Global Interdependence: The World After 1945*, ed. Akira Iriye (Cambridge, MA: Harvard University Press, 2014), 316–17.

71. Michael H. Hunt and Steven I. Levine, *Arc of Empire: America's Wars in Asia from the Philippines to Vietnam* (Chapel Hill: University of North Carolina Press, 2012).

72. Daniel Golden, *The Price of Admission: How America's Ruling Class Buys Its Way Into Elite Colleges—and Who Gets Left Outside the Gates* (New York: Crown, 2006); Andrew Delbanco, *College: What It Was, Is, and Should Be* (Princeton, NJ: Princeton University Press, 2012); Dan A. Oren, *Joining the Club: A History of Jews and Yale*, 2nd ed. (New Haven, CT: Yale University Press, 2001).

73. Wu, *The Color of Success*, 209.

74. Cheng, *Citizens of Asian America*, 5, 88–92; Seth Mydans, "U.S. Officer Revisits His Past in Vietnam," *New York Times*, November 9, 2009.

75. Edward Wong, "Photo Turns U.S. Envoy Into a Lesson for Chinese," *New York Times*, August 17, 2011; Tracy Connor, "Chinese Government Media Calls Chinese Ambassador Racial Slur," NBC News, February 28, 2014, http://www .nbcnews.com/news/world/chinese-government-media-calls-u-s-ambassador -racial-slur-n41486; Murphy, *Are We Rome?*, 31; Sharon LaFraniere, "Chinese, but Not Their Leaders, Flock to U.S. Envoy," *New York Times*, November 12, 2011 (factory worker). Of China's 1.27 billion people in 2000, only 941 were naturalized citizens. Eric Liu, "The Chinese American Way," *Wall Street Journal*, August 30–31, 2014.

76. Migration Policy Institute, "Largest U.S. Immigration Groups Over Time, 1960–Present," https://www.migrationpolicy.org/programs/data-hub/charts /largest-immigrant-groups-over-time; Blower, "Thinking Across the Case Studies."

77. Marilyn Lake and Henry Reynolds, *Drawing the Global Colour Line: White Men's Countries and the International Challenge of Racial Equality* (New York: Cambridge University Press, 2008); Adam McKeown, *Melancholy Order: Asian Migration and the Globalization of Borders* (New York: Columbia University Press, 2008).

78. Daniel McDermon, "How Bruce Lee Exploded a Stereotype with a One-Inch Punch," *New York Times*, January 25, 2017.

79. Richard Halloran, *Sparky: Warrior, Peacemaker, Poet, Patriot* (Honolulu: Watermark, 2002).

6. Subversion: The Power of American Culture in a Global Era

1. Minae Mizumura, *The Fall of Language in the Age of English*, trans. Mari Yoshihara and Juliet Winters Carpenter (New York: Columbia University Press, 2015). An illustrative example is the current share of elite natural sciences journals that are published in English: more than 98 percent. Laura J. Snyder, "They Really Do Speak Another Language," *Wall Street Journal*, June 20–21, 2015. See also Michael D. Gordin, *Scientific Babel: How Science Was Done Before and After Global English* (Chicago: University of Chicago Press, 2015).

2. George W. Bush, address before a joint session of Congress, September 20, 2001, *Public Papers of the Presidents*, http://www.presidency.ucsb.edu/ws/index .php?pid=64731; Max Paul Friedman, *Rethinking Anti-Americanism: The History of an Exceptional Concept in American Foreign Relations* (New York: Cambridge

University Press, 2012); "AHR Forum: Historical Perspectives on Anti-Americanism," *American Historical Review* 111, 4 (October 2006): 1041–129.

3. "National Geographic–Roper 2002 Global Geographic Literacy Survey," November 2002, http://www.nationalgeographic.com/geosurvey2002/down load/RoperSurvey.pdf; Garry Trudeau, "Doonesbury," December 12, 2002, http://www.gocomics.com/doonesbury/2002/12/12.

4. Dexter Filkins, *The Forever War* (New York: Knopf, 2008), 115, 118.

5. Donna R. Gabaccia, *We Are What We Eat: Ethnic Food and the Making of Americans* (Cambridge, MA: Harvard University Press, 1998), 225–26.

6. Terry Anderson, "The New American Revolution: The Movement and Business," in *The 1960s: From Memory to History*, ed. David Farber (Chapel Hill: University of North Carolina Press, 1994), 175–205.

7. Alexandra Wolfe, "Jhumpa Lahiri," *Wall Street Journal*, September 21–22, 2013.

8. Mario Puzo, *The Fortunate Pilgrim* (1964; New York: Ballantine, 2004), 6–7; Richard Alba and Victor Nee, *Remaking the American Mainstream: Assimilation and Contemporary Immigration* (Cambridge, MA: Harvard University Press, 2003).

9. Christopher Dickey, "No End in Sight," *New York Review of Books*, July 12, 2015, 21; Emma Sky, *The Unraveling: High Hopes and Missed Opportunities in Iraq* (New York: PublicAffairs, 2015).

10. Friedman, *Rethinking Anti-Americanism*, 69–70.

11. See, for example, Vine Deloria Jr., *Custer Died for Your Sins: An Indian Manifesto* (New York: Macmillan, 1969).

12. Michael H. Fischer, *Migration: A World History* (New York: Oxford University Press, 2014), 92.

13. Hasan al-Banna, *Between Yesterday and Today*, https://islambasics.com/wp -content/uploads/Books/yesterday.pdf. Al-Banna founded the Muslim Brotherhood in 1928 and composed his various essays in the 1930s and 1940s before being imprisoned and executed by the Egyptian state in 1949. An English-language version is *Five Tracts of Hasan al-Banna (1906–1949)*, trans. Charles Wendell (Berkeley: University of California Press, 1978).

14. Robert Bothwell, *Your Country, My Country: A Unified History of the United States and Canada* (New York: Oxford University Press, 2015); John Herd Thompson and Stephen J. Randall, *Canada and the United States: Ambivalent Allies*, 4th ed. (Athens: University of Georgia Press, 2008).

15. Amy S. Greenberg, *A Wicked War: Polk, Clay, Lincoln, and the 1846 U.S. Invasion of Mexico* (New York: Knopf, 2012); Lars Schoultz, *Beneath the United States: A History of U.S. Policy Toward Latin America* (Cambridge, MA: Harvard University Press, 1998); Walter LaFeber, *Inevitable Revolutions: The United States in Central America* (New York: Norton, 1983); Jason M. Colby, *The Business of*

Empire: United Fruit, Race, and U.S. Expansion in Central America (Ithaca, NY: Cornell University Press, 2011).

16. Caitlin Fitz, *Our Sister Republics: The United States in an Age of American Revolutions* (New York: Liveright, 2016).

17. Michel Gobat, "The Invention of Latin America: A Transnational History of Anti-Imperialism, Democracy, and Race," *American Historical Review* 118, no. 5 (December 2013): 1345–75.

18. Friedman, *Rethinking Anti-Americanism*, 124.

19. Tyche Hendricks, *The Wind Doesn't Need a Passport: Stories from the U.S.-Mexico Borderlands* (Berkeley: University of California Press, 2010), 18; James Crawford, ed., *Language Loyalties: A Source Book on the Official English Controversy* (Chicago: University of Chicago Press, 1992).

20. Alan M. Kraut, *The Huddled Masses: The Immigrant in American Society, 1880–1921*, 2nd ed. (Hoboken, NJ: Wiley-Blackwell, 2001); Tara Zahra, *The Great Departure: Mass Migration from Eastern Europe and the Making of the Free World* (New York: Norton, 2016); Mark Wyman, *Round-Trip to America: The Immigrants Return to Europe, 1880–1930* (Ithaca, NY: Cornell University Press, 2013).

21. David W. Ellwood, *The Shock of America: Europe and the Challenge of the Century* (Oxford: Oxford University Press), 30–31.

22. Ellwood, *The Shock of America*, 25.

23. Victoria de Grazia, *Irresistible Empire: America's Advance Through Twentieth-Century Europe* (Cambridge, MA: Harvard University Press, 2005).

24. Friedman, *Rethinking Anti-Americanism*, 159, 229. For an extended analysis of the mixed European reaction to American popular culture after 1945, see Richard Pells, *Not Like Us: How Europeans Have Loved, Hated, and Transformed American Culture Since World War II* (New York: Basic, 1997).

25. Ben Judah, *Fragile Empire: How Russia Fell In and Out of Love with Vladimir Putin* (New Haven, CT: Yale University Press, 2013).

26. Roger Cohen, "Incurable American Excess," *New York Times*, August 7, 2015; James J. Sheehan, *Where Have All the Soldiers Gone? The Transformation of Modern Europe* (Boston: Houghton Mifflin, 2008); T. R. Reid, *The United States of Europe: The New Superpower and the End of American Supremacy* (New York: Penguin, 2004).

27. The best survey to date is Odd Arne Westad, *The Cold War: A World History* (New York: Basic, 2017). On the failure of Western observers to predict the demise of the USSR, see John Lewis Gaddis, *The United States and the End of the Cold War: Implications, Reconsiderations, Provocations* (New York: Oxford University Press, 1992).

28. Thomas G. Paterson, *Contesting Castro: The United States and the Triumph of the Cuban Revolution* (New York: Oxford University Press, 1994), 12; W. T. Stead, *The Americanization of the World* (New York: H. Markley, 1902).

29. Bruce Cumings, *The Korean War: A History* (New York: Modern Library, 2010), 14; Robert K. Brigham, *ARVN: Life and Death in the South Vietnamese Army* (Lawrence: University of Kansas Press, 2006); Nathan Hodge, "When U.S. Troops Battled Bolsheviks," *Wall Street Journal*, January 27–28, 2018; Kenton Clymer, "Culture and Diplomacy in Cold War Laos," *Diplomatic History* 37, no. 5 (November 2013): 1169.

30. See, for example, Thomas Fuller, "Capitalist Soul Rises as Ho Chi Minh City Sheds Its Past," *New York Times*, July 20, 2015; Odd Arne Westad, *The Global Cold War: Third World Interventions and the Making of Our Times* (New York: Cambridge University Press, 2005).

31. Douglas Little, *Us Versus Them: The United States, Radical Islam, and the Rise of the Green Threat* (Chapel Hill: University of North Carolina Press, 2016); Derek Chollet and James Goldgeier, *America Between the Wars: From 11/9 to 9/11—The Misunderstood Years Between the Fall of the Berlin Wall and the Start of the War on Terror* (New York: PublicAffairs, 2009).

32. Lawrence Wright, *The Looming Tower: Al-Qaeda and the Road to 9/11* (New York: Knopf, 2006), 210; Steve Coll, *Ghost Wars: The Secret History of the CIA, Afghanistan, and Bin Laden from the Soviet Invasion to September 10, 2001* (New York: Penguin, 2004).

33. Filkins, *The Forever War*, 152–53.

34. Susan L. Carruthers, "Produce More Joppolos," *Journal of American History* 100, no. 4 (March 2014): 1086–113; Susan L. Carruthers, *The Good Occupation: American Soldiers and the Hazards of Peace* (Cambridge, MA: Harvard University Press, 2016).

35. Filkins, *The Forever War*, 161 (sergeant); *Raiders of the Lost Ark*, dir. Steven Spielberg (Paramount, 1981); *Aladdin*, dir. Ron Clements and John Musker (Walt Disney, 1992); Cumings, *The Korean War*, 232 (professor).

36. Jeffrey Goldberg, "The Obama Doctrine," *Atlantic*, April 2016.

37. Wright, *The Looming Tower*, 16–24; Pankaj Mishra, *From the Ruins of Empire: The Intellectuals Who Remade Asia* (New York: Farrar, Straus and Giroux, 2012), 21; Juan Cole, *Engaging the Muslim World* (New York: Palgrave Macmillan, 2009).

38. David Leonhardt and Ian Prasad Philbrick, "Donald Trump's Racism: The Definitive List," *New York Times*, January 15, 2018; Josh Dawsey, "Trump Derides Protections for Immigrants from 'Shithole' Countries," *Washington Post*, January 12, 2018; Brian Naylor, "Homeland Security Secretary Says She 'Did Not Hear' Trump Use 'That' Vulgar Word," National Public Radio, *All Things Considered*, January 16, 2018; Kathleen Belew, *Bring the War Home: The White Power Movement and Paramilitary America* (Cambridge, MA: Harvard University Press, 2018).

39. Dan Barry and John Eligon, "A Rallying Cry or a Racial Taunt Invoking the President: 'Trump!,'" *New York Times*, December 17, 2017. Anti-Jewish

harassment and violence also surged during Trump's first year in office. Emily Sullivan, "Anti-Semitic Incidents See Largest Single-Year Increase on Record, Audit Finds," National Public Radio, February 27, 2018.

40. After all, roughly six million people who voted for Obama in 2012 (10 percent of his supporters) voted for Trump in 2016. Nate Cohn, "The Obama-Trump Voters Are Real. Here's What They Think," *New York Times*, August 15, 2017.

41. Dani Rodrik, "What Does a True Populism Look Like? It Looks Like the New Deal," *New York Times*, February 21, 2018.

42. Amy Chua, *Political Tribes: Group Instinct and the Fate of Nations* (New York: Penguin, 2018), 5–6.

43. Thomas B. Edsall, "College Men for Trump," *New York Times*, July 14, 2016.

44. John Sides, Michael Tesler, and Lynn Vavreck, *Identity Crisis: The 2016 Presidential Campaign and the Battle for the Meaning of America* (Princeton, NJ: Princeton University Press, 2018).

45. Timothy N. Thurber, *Republicans and Race: The GOP's Frayed Relationship with African Americans, 1945–1974* (Lawrence: University Press of Kansas, 2013); Marisa Abrajano and Zoltan L. Hajnal, *White Backlash: Immigration, Race, and American Politics* (Princeton, NJ: Princeton University Press, 2015); Rick Perlstein, *Nixonland: The Rise of a President and the Fracturing of America* (New York: Scribner, 2008).

46. Jeffery C. Mays, "CPAC Official Says Ex-Republican Chief Was Chosen Because He's 'a Black Guy,'" *New York Times*, February 25, 2018.

47. On the increase of white violence in the United States, see "This Week in Hate," a column reported regularly by the *New York Times* beginning in early 2017; the "Hate & Extremism" and "Hatewatch" reports of the Southern Poverty Law Center; and Eric Lichtblau, "U.S. Hate Crimes Surge 6%, Fueled by Attacks on Muslims," *New York Times*, November 14, 2016.

48. Michael D. Shear and Maggie Haberman, "Trump Defends Initial Remarks on Charlottesville; Again Blames 'Both Sides,'" *New York Times*, August 15, 2017; Glenn Thrush, "Congress Passes Measure Challenging Trump to Denounce Hate Groups," *New York Times*, September 12, 2017.

49. Joshua Green, *Devil's Bargain: Steve Bannon, Donald Trump, and the Storming of the Presidency* (New York: Penguin, 2017); George Hawley, *Making Sense of the Alt-Right* (New York: Columbia University Press, 2017).

50. Miriam Jordan, "Is America a 'Nation of Immigrants'? Immigration Agency Says No," *New York Times*, February 22, 2018.

51. Jonathan Blitzer, "So There Dept.: Resistance Genealogist," *New Yorker*, February 5, 2018, 16. Trump's parents-in-law, the Slovenian mother and father of First Lady Melania Trump, held green cards as legal residents of the United States in 2018, apparently another case of chain migration, in having been sponsored by their daughter. Kate Bennett and Tal Kopan, "Melania Trump's Parents'

Immigration Status Could Be Thanks to 'Chain Migration,'" CNN, February 22, 2018.

52. Sally McGrane, "The Ancestral German Home of the Trumps," *New Yorker*, April 29, 2016.

53. Steve Eder and Dave Philipps, "Donald Trump's Draft Deferments: Four for College, One for Bad Feet," *New York Times*, August 1, 2016; Stern 1997 interview with Trump, *Daily Mail* (UK), http://www.dailymail.co.uk/video/news/video-1266623/Trump-says-sex-Eighties-personal-Vietnam.html.

54. Ronan Farrow, "Donald Trump, a Playboy Model, and a System for Concealing Infidelity," *New Yorker*, February 16, 2018.

55. Thomas L. Friedman, "Out of Africa," *New York Times*, April 13, 2016; "Out of Africa, Part II," *New York Times*, April 20, 2016.

56. Thomas Borstelmann, "A Losing Campaign: The United States and 'White Nationalism' Since 1945," in *The Global History of White Nationalism: From Apartheid to Donald Trump*, ed. Daniel Geary, Camilla Schofield, and Jennie Sutton (Manchester: Manchester University Press, 2020); Jeff Yang, "Fresh on the Screen: How TV Is Redefining Whom We Think of as 'American,'" National Public Radio, November 9, 2015. For a summary of useful polling data, see Meagan Day and Bhaskar Sunkara, "Fighting Bannonism at Home and Abroad," *New York Times*, August 7, 2018.

57. Andrew J. Bacevich, *The New American Militarism: How Americans Are Seduced by War* (New York: Oxford University Press, 2005), 79 (Angstrom); Lynn Hunt, *Writing History in the Global Era* (New York: Norton, 2014), 44.

58. David Northrup, "Globalization and the Great Convergence: Rethinking World History in the Long Term," *Journal of World History* 16, no. 3 (September 2005): 249–67; Jürgen Osterhammel and Niels P. Petersson, *Globalization: A Short History* (Princeton, NJ: Princeton University Press, 2005).

59. Alison Bashford, *Global Population: History, Geopolitics, and Life on Earth* (New York: Columbia University Press, 2014), 6; Richard D. Alba and Nancy Foner, *Strangers No More: Immigration and the Challenges of Integration in North America and Western Europe* (Princeton, NJ: Princeton University Press, 2015), 23–25; Deborah Cohen, *Braceros: Migrant Citizens and Transnational Subjects in the Postwar United States and Mexico* (Chapel Hill: University of North Carolina Press, 2011).

60. Jenifer Van Vleck, *Empire of the Air: Aviation and the American Ascendancy* (Cambridge, MA: Harvard University Press, 2013), 4, 199, 220.

61. Van Vleck, *Empire of the Air*, 261–62.

62. Dana Frank, *Buy American: The Untold Story of Economic Nationalism* (Boston: Beacon, 1999).

63. A 2016 Associated Press poll concluded: "The vast majority of Americans say they prefer lower prices instead of paying a premium for items labeled 'Made in the USA,' even if it means those cheaper items were made abroad." "Americans

Prefer Low Prices to Items 'Made in the USA,'" *Omaha World-Herald*, April 15, 2016.

64. Catherine Rampell, "Ivy League Economist Ethnically Profiled, Interrogated for Doing Math on American Airlines Flight," *Washington Post*, May 7, 2016.

65. Brooke L. Blower, *Becoming Americans in Paris: Transatlantic Politics and Culture Between the World Wars* (New York: Oxford University Press, 2011), 7, 41.

66. Friedman, *Rethinking Anti-Americanism*, 104–5.

67. Donna Alvah, *Unofficial Ambassadors: American Military Families Overseas and the Cold War, 1946–1965* (New York: New York University Press, 2007), 128.

68. Paul Pillar, *Why America Misunderstands the World: National Experience and Roots of Misperception* (New York: Columbia University Press, 2016), 13–14.

69. Thomas Friedman, "Follow the Money," *New York Times*, April 1, 2014.

70. Pillar, *Why America Misunderstands the World*, 12–13.

71. Cullen Murphy, *Are We Rome? The Fall of an Empire and the Fate of America* (Boston: Houghton Mifflin, 2007), 203.

72. Jeff Yang, "Fresh on the Screen: How TV Is Redefining Whom We Think of as 'American,'" National Public Radio, November 9, 2015; Diana Kapp, "The Fishy Taste That Children Love," *Wall Street Journal*, September 10, 2015; Warren I. Cohen, *The Asian American Century* (Cambridge, MA: Harvard University Press, 2002), 88; David Karp, "Most of America's Fruit Is Now Imported. Is That a Bad Thing?" *New York Times*, March 13, 2018; Andrew C. McKevitt, *Consuming Japan: Popular Culture and the Globalizing of 1980s America* (Chapel Hill: University of North Carolina Press, 2017); Walter LaFeber, *Michael Jordan and the New Global Capitalism* (New York: Norton, 1999).

73. Francis Fukuyama, *The End of History and the Last Man* (New York: Free Press, 1992); Thomas Borstelmann, *The Cold War and the Color Line: American Race Relations in the Global Arena* (Cambridge, MA: Harvard University Press, 2001), 265; David Harvey, *A Brief History of Neoliberalism* (New York: Oxford University Press, 2005).

74. Thomas Jefferson to Roger C. Weightman, June 24, 1826, Library of Congress exhibit, https://www.loc.gov/exhibits/declara/rcwltr.html, cited in Ryan Irwin, "Some Parts Sooner, Some Later, and Finally All," *H-Diplo*, October 28, 2016, https://networks.h-net.org/node/28443/discussions/149735/h-diplo-state -field-essay-united-states-and-world-h-diplo-essay. On human rights, see Mark Philip Bradley, *The World Reimagined: Americans and Human Rights in the Twentieth Century* (New York: Cambridge University Press, 2016); Sarah B. Snyder, *Human Rights Activism and the End of the Cold War: A Transnational History of the Helsinki Network* (New York: Cambridge University Press, 2011).

75. Galatians 3:28 (English Standard Version); Larry Siedentop, *Inventing the Individual: The Origins of Western Liberalism* (Cambridge, MA: Harvard University Press, 2014), 51, 60.

76. Thomas Borstelmann, *The 1970s: A New Global History from Civil Rights to Economic Inequality* (Princeton, NJ: Princeton University Press, 2012), 122–74. In *The Complacent Class: The Self-Defeating Quest for the American Dream* (New York: St. Martin's, 2017), the economist Tyler Cowen argues that the United States may have now passed the peak of mobility in pursuit of economic opportunity, with younger Americans starting to become more complacent and less adventurous.

77. One of the earliest historians to explore this dynamic of "hip consumerism" was Thomas Frank, *The Conquest of Cool: Business Culture, Counterculture, and the Rise of Hip Consumerism* (Chicago: University of Chicago Press, 1997).

78. Stephen Kotkin, *Magnetic Mountain: Stalinism as a Civilization* (Berkeley: University of California Press, 1995), 39; Francis Spufford, *Red Plenty* (Minneapolis, MN: Greywolf, 2010), 30–31; Nicholas Kristof, "Welcome Back, Cuba!," *New York Times*, December 17, 2014.

79. National Academies of Sciences, Engineering, and Medicine, "Report Finds Immigrants Come to Resemble Native-Born Americans Over Time, but Integration Not Always Linked to Greater Well-Being for Immigrants," September 21, 2015, http://www8.nationalacademies.org/onpinews/newsitem.aspx?RecordID=21746.

80. National Academies of Sciences, Engineering, and Medicine, "Report Finds Immigrants Come to Resemble Native-Born Americans Over Time"; Robert L. Paarlberg, *The United States of Excess: Gluttony and the Dark Side of American Exceptionalism* (New York: Oxford University Press, 2015), 12, 20.

81. William Finnegan, "A Righteous Case," *New Yorker*, May 15, 2017, 37, 75; Alba and Foner, *Strangers No More*, 17, 204.

82. Walied Shater, "To Stop Radicalization, the French Need More Fraternité," *New York Times*, November 19, 2015.

83. Eric Liu, "Why I Just Can't Become Chinese," *Wall Street Journal*, August 29, 2014; Roger Cohen, "Can-Do Lee Kuan Yew," *New York Times*, March 23, 2015.

84. Valerie Hansen, *The Open Empire: A History of China to 1600*, 2nd ed. (New York: Norton, 2015); Catherine Ceniza Choy, *Global Families: A History of Asian International Adoption in America* (New York: New York University Press, 2013), 2; Nina Bernstein, "Hospitals Aren't Waiting for Verdict on Health Care Law," *New York Times*, June 11, 2012.

85. Susan Zeiger, *Entangling Alliances: Foreign War Brides and American Soldiers in the Twentieth Century* (New York: New York University Press, 2010), 14.

86. Viet Thanh Nguyen, *The Sympathizer* (New York: Grove, 2015), 166; Ellwood, *The Shock of America*, 114; Celestine Bohlen, "Moscow Journal; For the Rolling Stones' Fans, Satisfaction at Last," *New York Times*, August 12, 1998; "Rolling Stones Get Cuba Started Up," *Lincoln Journal Star*, March 26, 2016; William H. Marling, *How "American" Is Globalization?* (Baltimore, MD: Johns Hopkins University Press, 2006).

87. Aatish Taseer, "Why Do I Love Bollywood?" *New York Times*, August 24, 2016; Chris Buckley, "Chinese Youth Admire American Culture but Remain Wary of U.S. Policy," *New York Times*, September 28, 2015.

88. Maria Cheng (Associated Press), "Diets of People Worldwide Getting Worse," *Lincoln Journal Star*, February 19, 2015; Niraj Chokshi, "Overweight Asian-Americans Are Seen as More 'American,' Study Finds," *New York Times*, August 3, 2017; Greg Critser, *Fat Land: How Americans Became the Fattest People in the World* (Boston: Houghton Mifflin, 2003).

89. Robin Wright, "The Adversary," *New Yorker*, May 26, 2014, 40–41.

90. Robert D. Putnam, *Bowling Alone: The Collapse and Revival of American Community* (New York: Simon & Schuster, 2000); Janice Shaw Crouse, "The Loneliness of American Society," *American Spectator*, May 18, 2014; Paarlberg, *The United States of Excess*, 109–10; Borstelmann, *The 1970s*, 122–74; Christopher Lasch, *The Culture of Narcissism: American Life in an Age of Diminishing Expectations* (New York: Norton, 1978).

91. Judith Thurman, "A Loss for Words," *New Yorker*, March 30, 2015, 36; Frances FitzGerald, *Fire in the Lake: The Vietnamese and the Americans in Vietnam* (1972; New York: Vintage, 1973), 30. See also, for example, "Vietnam: Where Saying 'I Love You' Is Impossible," *BBC News*, August 29, 2013, https://www.bbc.com/news/world-asia-23501757; or "Introduction to Vietnamese Pronouns," https://yourvietnamese.com/vietnamese-phrases/learn-pronouns-in-vietnamese/.

92. For representative case studies, see de Grazia, *Irresistible Empire*; Reinhold Wagnleitner, *Coca-Colonization and the Cold War: The Cultural Mission of the United States in Austria After the Second World War* (Chapel Hill: University of North Carolina Press, 1994); John W. Dower, *Embracing Defeat: Japan in the Wake of World War II* (New York: Norton, 1999).

Conclusion: Not So Foreign After All

1. Jake Halpern, "A New Underground Railroad," *New Yorker*, March 13, 2017, 40.

2. Eric Foner, *Gateway to Freedom: The Hidden History of the Underground Railroad* (New York: Norton, 2015); John Hagan, *Northern Passage: American Vietnam War Resisters in Canada* (Cambridge, MA: Harvard University Press, 2001).

3. Adam Liptak, "Sotomayor Finds Her Voice Among the Justices," *New York Times*, May 6, 2014; Greg Robinson, *A Tragedy of Democracy: Japanese Confinement in North America* (New York: Columbia University Press, 2009). For a powerful argument about the not merely continuing but resurgent significance of race in American life, see Nils Gilman, "The Collapse of Racial Liberalism," *American Interest*, March 2, 2018.

4. Adam Serwer, "A Crime by Any Name," *Atlantic,* July 3, 2019; Janet Murguía, "The El Paso Shooting Is the Violence Latinos Have Been Dreading," *New York Times,* August 6, 2019.

5. Patrick Healy, "Politics and Philosophy Clash Where the Pope Urges an Embrace of Refugees," *New York Times,* September 27, 2015; Peter Baker and Jim Yardley, "Pope Francis, in Congress, Pleads for Unity on World's Woes," *New York Times,* September 24, 2015. The earliest First Ladies, like their husbands, had been born in what were then British colonies. The only other exception was Louisa Catherine Johnson, born in London to an American merchant father and an English mother, who married John Quincy Adams, the sixth U.S. president. Olivia B. Waxman, "Meet the Only First Lady Before Melania Trump Not to Have Been Born in the U.S.," *Time,* November 9, 2016.

6. George W. Bush, address before a joint session of the Congress, September 20, 2001, *Public Papers of the Presidents,* http://www.presidency.ucsb.edu/ws/index .php?pid=64731; Julie Bosman, "Iowans Question G.O.P. Talk on Illegal Immigration," *New York Times,* September 4, 2015: Colin Powell, "What American Citizenship Makes Possible," *Wall Street Journal,* July 27, 2016.

7. Tyler Dennett, *Americans in East Asia* (1922), quoted in Gordon H. Chang, *Fateful Ties: A History of America's Preoccupation with China* (Cambridge, MA: Harvard University Press, 2015), 64; Paul R. Pillar, *Why America Misunderstands the World: National Experience and Roots of Misperception* (New York: Columbia University Press, 2016), 81.

8. *Whiskey Tango Foxtrot,* dir. Glenn Ficarra and John Requa (Paramount, 2016); National Security Strategy of the United States of America, December 2017, 4, https://www.whitehouse.gov/wp-content/uploads/2017/12/NSS-Final-12-18 -2017-0905.pdf.

9. John Kenneth Galbraith, *The Affluent Society* (Boston: Houghton Mifflin, 1958); Rachel Carson, *Silent Spring* (Boston: Houghton Mifflin, 1962); J. R. McNeill, *Something New Under the Sun: An Environmental History of the Twentieth-Century World* (New York: Norton, 2000); J. R. McNeill and Peter Engelke, *The Great Acceleration: An Environmental History of the Anthropocene Since 1945* (Cambridge, MA: Harvard University Press, 2014); Rebecca Solnit, "The War of the World," *Harper's,* February 2015, 5–6.

10. David Leonhardt and Kevin Quealy, "The American Middle Class Is No Longer the World's Richest," *New York Times,* April 22, 2014; David P. Forsythe and Patrice C. McMahon, *American Exceptionalism Revisited: U.S. Foreign Policy, Human Rights, and World Order* (New York: Routledge, 2017), 20–21; Ronald P. Formisano, *Plutocracy in America: How Increasing Inequality Destroys the Middle Class and Exploits the Poor* (Baltimore, MD: Johns Hopkins University Press, 2015); "World Happiness Report 2018," http://www.worldhappin ess.report.

11. Emily Badger, "Immigrant Shock: Can California Predict the Nation's Future?" *New York Times*, February 1, 2017; Michelle Alexander, "We Are Not the Resistance," *New York Times*, September 21, 2008.

12. William A. Link, *Righteous Warrior: Jesse Helms and the Rise of Modern Conservatism* (New York: St. Martin's, 2008).

13. Victoria de Grazia, *Irresistible Empire: America's Advance Through Twentieth-Century Europe* (Cambridge, MA: Harvard University Press, 2005); Lizabeth Cohen, *A Consumers' Republic: The Politics of Mass Consumption in Postwar America* (New York: Knopf, 2003); Josiah Strong, *Our Country: Its Possible Future and Its Present Crisis* (New York: Baker & Taylor, 1885), 14.

14. Joseph A. Schumpeter, *Capitalism, Socialism, and Democracy* (New York: Harper, 1942), 83.

15. See, for example, Walter LaFeber, *The American Search for Opportunity, 1865–1913* (New York: Cambridge University Press, 1993).

Index

anticommunism, 17, 48, 107, 121–22, 167–68; anti-Soviet rhetorical partisans, 220n16; of Catholics, 72; Korean War and, 70; political repression of, 56; repression of, 99

anti-immigrant sentiment, 59, 68

anti-Japanese sentiment, 147

antimiscegenation statutes, 144

anti-Muslim discourse, 92

anti-Semitism, 40, 72–73, 74, 235n39

antislavery sentiment, 67

Apache, 161

Apollinaris, Sidonius, 87

Appalachian Mountains, 21

Arab Americans, 141

Arc of Empire (Michael Hunt and Steven Levine), 154

Argentina, 5, 80

Armstrong, Lance, 51

Articles of Confederation, 9

ARVN. *See* South Vietnamese Army of the Republic of Vietnam

Asia, xii, 5, 139, 140–41; Cold War and, 151; World War II and, 150

Asian Americans, 141–42, 148, 151–54, 157; obesity and, 189; World War II and, 149

Asian Tigers, 139

Asiatic Barred Zone, 10–11, 68, 69

Aslam, Iftekhar, 187

Atlantic Rim, 156

Auschwitz, 93

Australia, xi, 5, 55

Austro-Hungarian Empire, 69

authoritarianism, 111

baby boomers, 8

Bacon's Rebellion of 1676, 21

Baghdad University, 170

Baker, Josephine, 135

Baldwin, Hanson, 114

Ball, George, 165

Bannon, Steve, 174

Barbary Coast states, 24

Battle of the Bulge, 73

Beard, Mary, 133

Beloved (Toni Morrison), 10

Bender, Thomas, 6, 30

Berlin Wall, 96, 109, 168

Beveridge, Albert, 132

Bilek, Anton, 148

Bill of Rights, 20, 190

bin Laden, Osama, 171, 197

"birther" movement, 172

Black Hawk War of 1832, 161

Blackmon, Douglas, 110

black nationalism, 129

blood types, 16

Blower, Brooke, 38–39, 130

Bogart, Humphrey, 48

Boiardi, Hector, 88

Bolshevik Revolution, 103–4; capitalism, alternative to, 100; Germany and, 108–9; Japan and, 147; success of, 68; survival of, 99; U.S. and, 166; World War I and, 97–98

border controls, 68

Bracero program, 178

brainwashing, 4, 96, 113, 115–18

Brazil, 80

Breitbart News, 174

Brexit, 176

Britain. *See* England

British Loyalists, 21, 102, 128

British-sounding names, 42

Brooks, Charlotte, 151

Brooks, David, 74

Brown University, 60

Bruno, Giordano, 35

Bryan, William Jennings, 43

Buckingham Palace, 13

Buckley, Chris, 189

class exploitation, 95

Clay, Henry, 21

Clinton, Hillary, 172

Clymer, Kenton, 168

Coates, Ken, 149

Cohen, Deborah, 83

Cold War, xii, 3, 6, 7, 37, 56, 70, 111, 177, 196, 220n16; Asia and, 151; black-and-white struggle of, 112; communism, depictions of, 104; competition of, 108; dawn of, 43; end of, 45; logic of American exceptionalism and, 2; psychological warfare and, 118; quintessential challenge of, 4; start of, 105, 119

colonial era, 5, 30, 53, 125

colonialism, 22, 25, 57–58, 112; colonists, 32; Middle East and, 46; Portuguese, 130; racism and, 107, 182

Color Matching System, 15

Columbus, Christopher, 57, 59, 80–81, 142

Columbus Day, 81

Cominform. *See* Communist Information Bureau

Common Sense (Paine), 43

communism, xii, 4, 23, 44, 47, 77, 108, 115, 220n16; China and, 112, 151; Cold War depictions of, 104; collectivist challenge from, 118; in Eastern Europe, 105; fascism, opponent of, 103; indigenous communists, 105; influence of, 102; mainstream U.S. views of, 103; motivation of communists, 167; secular left of, 166; Third World and, 167; threat to U.S. of, 95. *See also* anticommunism; socialism

Communist Information Bureau (Cominform), 120

Communist Manifesto, The (Marx and Engels), 97

Communist Party of the United States of America (CPUSA), 119

concentration camps, 66, 112

conservatives, 33, 44, 172, 199

Constitution, 2, 20, 30, 35

consumer culture, 160

Continental Congress, 9, 127

Costigliola, Frank, 63

counterculture, 159

counterterrorism, 186

CPUSA. *See* Communist Party of the United States of America

Creel, George, 69

Crèvecoeur, J. Hector St. John de, 31

Cronkite, Walter, 117

Crosby, Alfred, 60

Cuba, 48, 105, 116, 130; after 1898, 131; nuclear missiles in, 117, 121; revolution in, 85, 109, 167

cultural relativism, 4

Cultural Revolution, 121

Czechoslovakia, 77

Damon, Matt, 53

Daniels, Roger, 148

Dauphin (ship), 24, 25

Day Without a Mexican, A (2004), 83

D-Day invasion, 39, 137, 138

Debs, Eugene V., 98

Declaration of Independence, 9, 20, 46, 58, 171

de Gaulle, Charles, 165

Dehn, Paul, 164

DeLay, Tom, 63

Democratic Party, 8, 27, 61, 173, 176

democratic socialism, 7

demographic changes, 67

Deng Xiaoping, 120–21

Dennett, Tyler, 196

despotism, 22, 26

détente, 121, 124

Detroit, 79

Diaz, Porfirio, 163

digital revolution, 179

disease, 5

diversity, 55, 136, 140, 198

Dower, John, 147

Downton Abbey (television series), 52

Draves, Vicki Manalo, 152

Dublin, ix

Dudziak, Mary, 17

Duke University, ix

Dulles, John Foster, 107, 111

Eagleton, Terry, 48, 52

Eastern Europe, 7, 45, 49, 62, 87, 111;
   communism in, 105; Jewish diaspora
   and, 127; migrants from, 67–69;
   officials from, 93; Red Army in, 100;
   USSR and, 43, 109, 120

Eastern Hemisphere, 57

East Germany, 109

Eastwood, Clint, 156, 157

economic self-interest, 27

Edmonds, Roddie, 73

Egypt, 171

Eisenhower, Dwight, 45, 48, 75, 153, 180

electoral politics, 95

elites, cultural insecurity among, 3

Elysium (2013), 53

end of history, 11

England, xi, 21, 101–2, 144, 150; churn
   of human movement shaping, 13;
   concentration camps ran by, 112;
   early Americans from, 19; high
   culture and, 12; immigration and, 61;
   settlers from, 2

Enlightenment, 183

Enter the Dragon (1973), 156

environmental damage, 197

Epic of America, The (James Truslow
   Adams), 38

Episcopal Church, 12

Episcopalians, 75

Ethiopia, 105

ethnolinguistic identities, 69

Europe, 33–34, 58–59, 164; immigration
   from, 62; immigration to, 92; Nazi
   aggressions in, 102; political
   discourse in, 48; Western European
   empires, 46. *See also* Eastern Europe

evangelical Protestants, 74

expropriation, 31

family reunification, 70

fascists, 40, 103

Faulkner, William, 17–18, 110

Feast of San Gennaro, 67

feminism, 98–99

Fieldston, Sara, 47, 118

Filkins, Dexter, 54–55, 159, 170

Fire in the Lake (FitzGerald), 191

First Gulf War, 78

First Nations peoples, 81

First Opium War of 1839–1842, 144

First Presbyterian Church, 33

First Red Scare, 99

Fist of Fury (1972), 156

Fitz, Caitlin, 80

FitzGerald, Frances, 191

Fitzgerald, F. Scott, 7

Flags of Our Fathers (2006), 157

Florida Straits, 125

Fong, Hiram, 135, 153

Ford, Harrison, 170

foreigners, xi, 1, 10, 31

foreign-language requirements, 54

foreignness, 10, 17, 189; nonwhiteness
   and, 19; U.S. and, 184

foreign policy, 95

Forest Nymph, The (Tyl), 60

human movement, 11, 13, 14
human nature, 2, 29
Hungary, 104, 111
Hunt, Michael, 154
Hunter, Edward, 113
Hussein, Saddam, 78, 159
Hutchinson, Anne, 60
hyperindividualism, 183
hyphenated identities, 91

Immerwahr, Daniel, 128
immigration, 212n1; anti-immigrant
    sentiment, 59, 68; controlling, 69;
    diversity brought by, 58; England
    and, 61; from Europe, 62; to Europe,
    92; Mexican, 83–84; of Muslims, 79,
    92; parents, immigrant, 86, 160;
    policy regarding, 67; positive
    influence of, 185; Puerto Rican, 85;
    receiving nations of, 55; reforms, 79,
    82, 85; restriction of, 173, 176; uptick
    in, 54; to U.S., 71, 174–76. *See also*
    Latin American immigration
imperialism, 43–44, 46, 48, 107, 122, 132;
    capitalism and, 108; peaking of, 177
incarceration camps, 194
Independence Hall, 30, 31
India, 150, 188
Indian-captivity narratives, 25
indigenous communists, 105
indigent English workers, 21
individual freedom, 2
individualism, xii, 113, 188, 191;
    concerns about preserving, 118;
    culture of, 31; gospel of, 37;
    hyperindividualism, 183; viruses
    of, 199
Indonesia, 76, 150
industrialization, 9, 37, 50, 96, 100, 105,
    146
Industrial Revolution, 177

in-groups, 8
Inouye, Daniel, 135, 153
intercultural contact, 5
intermarriage, 5
international crises, 55
International Date Line, 149
interracial marriage, 18
interwar years, 38
Invasion of the Body Snatchers (1956), 117
Iran, 48, 196; Islamic Republic of Iran,
    76; students from, 78
Iranian Revolution, 78
Iraq, 2, 94, 105, 169–70; civilians killed
    in, 55; English language and, 54;
    invasion of, 63, 159, 161, 166, 196;
    open-ended conflicts in, 182;
    preemptive war in, 4; torture at Abu
    Ghraib prison in, 89
Ireland, ix, 27
Islam, 26, 76; Sunni, 78; U.S. citizens
    knowing almost nothing about, 77.
    See also Muslims
Islamic Republic of Iran, 76
Islamism, 168–70, 173, 182
Islamophobic Americans, 173
isolationism, 128
Israel, 73, 74, 168, 171, 180
Italy, 33, 42, 66–67
Iturriaga, José, 163

James, LeBron, 18
James River, 125
Japan, xi, 7, 11, 42, 138, 144, 150; shoguns
    in, 146; World War I and, 147
Japanese Americans, 141–42, 148, 153, 155
Japanese internment camps, 41
Jason Bourne (fictional character), 117
Jefferson, Thomas, 22–23, 30, 62, 106,
    182–83, 187, 190
Jewish Americans, 41, 73–75, 83
Jews in America (Price), 86

Jim Crow, 17, 107, 110, 132
Joan of Arc, 71
John Paul II (pope), 77
Johnson, Alison Frank, 69
Johnson, Lyndon, 105
Johnson, Richard M., 21
Johnson, Samuel, 20
Johnson-Reed Immigration Act of 1924, 68, 147
Jordan, David Starr, 147
Judaism: antisemitism, 40, 72–73, 74, 235n39; Eastern European Jewish diaspora, 127; Jewish Americans, 41, 73–75, 83
Judeo-Christian tradition, 39–40, 72, 75
Jussim, Lee, 8

Kawuneeche ("Coyote") Valley, 7
Kellogg, Mary Louise, 143
Kennan, George, 103–4, 106
Kennedy, John, 12, 72, 109, 117, 121
Kenya, 112, 129
Kerry, John, 63, 190
Khomeini, Ruhollah (ayatollah), 76
Khrushchev, Nikita, 109, 123, 184
Kibei, 149
Kim Il-sung, 145
Kim Jong-un, 145
Kipling, Rudyard, 34
Kirby, Jack, 42
Knightly, Philip, 167
Know-Nothing Party, 64
Koch, Charles, 119
Koch, David, 119
Koch, Fred, 119
Koch Industries, 119
Korean War, 23, 70, 114, 139, 167
Kotkin, Stephen, 100
Kristof, Nick, 184
Kubrick, Stanley, 1–2
Kurashige, Scott, 150

labor union movement, 95
Labour Party, 43
Lahiri, Jhumpa, 160
languages, 49–53
Latin, 49
Latin America, 78, 80, 126, 158, 162–63
Latin American immigration, 53, 79–80; first-generation adults, 87; prevalence of, 90; World War II and, 85
Latinos, 83, 85
Le, H. B., 155
League of Nations Class C Mandates, 147
Lee, Bruce, 156
Lee, Sammy, 152–53
Lee, Stan, 42
left-wing organizers, 95
Lenin, Vladimir, 43, 44, 97, 98, 108, 167
Letters from an American Farmer (Crèvecoeur), 31
Letters from Iwo Jima (2006), 157
Levine, Steven, 154
liberal democracy, 11, 102
Liberia, 3, 127, 129
libertarianism, 183
liberty, 19, 166
Liberty Bell, 35
Life (magazine), 39, 150
Linnaeus, Carl, 146
Liu, Eric, 186–87
Llosa, Alvaro Vargas, 87
Locke, Gary, 155
Louisiana, 142
Louis XVI (king), 35
Loving v. Virginia, 139
Loyalists, 22
lynching, 18

Maasdam (ship), ix
Malcolm X, 129, 160
Mandarin, 49, 50

socialism, 46, 95, 97, 105, 109, 122, 124; allure of, 108; collectivist values of, 96; democratic, 7; dream of, 107; egalitarianism of, 98; faith in, 100; Third World and, 113

social science, 26

Solidarity, 77

Solnit, Rebecca, 197

Soong Mei-ling, 145

Southern Historical Association, 17–18

South Korea, 114

South Pacific (musical), 150

South Vietnam, 105

South Vietnamese Army of the Republic of Vietnam (ARVN), 167

Soviet Union (USSR), 71, 77, 111, 122–23, 166, 182, 183; agents of, 101; American communists visiting, 119; anticommunist struggle against, 17; anti-Soviet rhetorical partisans, 220n16; anxieties rising about, 138; competition with, 70, 118, 156; U.S. Congress and, 7; cultural identity of, 103–4; détente and, 121; Eastern Europe and, 43, 109, 120; establishment of, 97; faith in, 100; Germany and, 97, 99; influence of, 96; North Korea and, 105; nuclear missiles of, 117; People's Republic of China and, 120; respect for, 167; technical advances of, 51; threat of, 98; U.S. relations with, 46, 119; World War I and, 59; World War II and, 100. *See also* Bolshevik Revolution

spaghetti, 88

Spain, 24, 80

Spanish, 50

Spock, Benjamin, 118

Spufford, Francis, 123, 184

Stalin, Josef, 119, 120

State Department, 3

Stead, W. T., 167

Steele, Michael, 174

stereotypes, 11, 140

Stern, Howard, 175

Stevens, Leslie C., 104

Stiles, Ezra, 142

Strong, Josiah, 199

Students for a Democratic Society (SDS), 121

suffrage, 99

Sukarno, 104

Sumner, Charles, 43, 46

Sunni Islam, 78

Sun Yat-sen, 145

Supreme Court, 18, 69

Suzuki, Zenko, 157

Sympathizer, The (Nguyen), 61

Syria, 79, 105, 176, 195

Syrian Americans, 141

Taber, Robert, 167

Taguba, Antonio, 89

Taiwan, 115, 145

Talleyrand, Charles Maurice de, 34

Taseer, Aatish, 188

taxation, 27

Taylor, Alan, 5, 23

technological innovations, 55

Terkel, Studs, 148

terrorism, 26, 51, 79, 179, 186

Texas, 81

Thind (Supreme Court decision), 69

Third Reich, 112

Third World, 7, 46, 47, 48, 70, 106, 152; communism and, 167; justice and equality for, 96; leaders in, 168; nonaligned nations of, 104; resistance from, 110; socialism and, 113